DARK DREAMERS
CONVERSATIONS WITH THE MASTERS OF HORROR

Other Interview Collections by
Stanley Wiater
Coming Soon from Avon Books

DARK VISIONS:
CONVERSATIONS WITH THE MASTERS
OF THE HORROR FILM

Avon Books are available at special quantity discounts for bulk purchases for sales promotions, premiums, fund raising or educational use. Special books, or book excerpts, can also be created to fit specific needs.

For details write or telephone the office of the Director of Special Markets, Avon Books, Dept. FP, 105 Madison Avenue, New York, New York 10016, 212-481-5653.

DARK DREAMERS
CONVERSATIONS WITH THE MASTERS OF HORROR

by STANLEY WIATER

AVON BOOKS • NEW YORK

DARK DREAMERS is an original publication of Avon Books. This work has never before appeared in book form. Many of the interviews contained herein have appeared, in part, in fanzines.

AVON BOOKS
A division of
The Hearst Corporation
105 Madison Avenue
New York, New York 10016

Copyright © 1990 by Stanley Wiater
Front cover art by Peter Mueller
Published by arrangement with the author
Library of Congress Catalog Card Number: 90-93004
ISBN: 0-380-75990-X

All rights reserved, which includes the right to reproduce this book or portions thereof in any form whatsoever except as provided by the U.S. Copyright Law. For information address Helen Rees Literary Agency, 308 Commonwealth Avenue, Boston, Massachusetts 02116.

First Avon Books Trade Printing: October 1990

AVON TRADEMARK REG. U.S. PAT. OFF. AND IN OTHER COUNTRIES, MARCA REGISTRADA, HECHO EN U.S.A.

Printed in the U.S.A.

OPM 10 9 8 7 6 5 4 3 2 1

To Iris—
of whom nothing written, said, or sung is truly worthy

and

To Ray Bradbury—
in partial payment of a lifelong debt

and

To Dark Dreamers everywhere—
who have always known that to best enjoy the light,
one must first explore the heart and soul of the darkness

ACKNOWLEDGMENTS

This book took a decade to write, in a manner of speaking, so there's a whole unruly mob of people I must thank. I certainly couldn't have done it alone and lived to tell these tales.

For friendship and support from day one: James Aaron Cooke, G. Michael Dobbs, Stephen R. Bissette, Peter Laird, Jeannine Atkins, Kevin Eastman.

For editorial support along the way: Mimi Rigali, the Springfield *Morning Union*; Leah Sullivan, William Swislow, *Valley Advocate*; Bob Martin, David Everitt, Anthony Timpone, *Fangoria*; Robert A. Collins, *Fantasy Review*; T.E.D. Klein, Michael Blaine, Tappan King, *Rod Serling's Twilight Zone Magazine*; William Brohaugh, *Writer's Digest*; John Gilbert, *Fear*.

For very special services: Roger Anker, Philip Nutman, my sister Michele Wiater. And finally, all the good folks of "Necon," especially Mr. & Mrs. Bob Plante and Mr. & Mrs. Bob Booth.

 # Contents

A Conversation with the Interviewer
by Philip Nutman
1

CLIVE BARKER
9

ROBERT BLOCH
19

GARY BRANDNER
27

RAMSEY CAMPBELL
35

LES DANIELS
43

DENNIS ETCHISON
51

JOHN FARRIS
59

CHARLES L. GRANT
67

JAMES HERBERT
75

STEPHEN KING & PETER STRAUB
83

DEAN R. KOONTZ
101

JOE R. LANSDALE
111

CONTENTS

RICHARD LAYMON
119

GRAHAM MASTERTON
127

RICHARD MATHESON
135

ROBERT R. McCAMMON
145

DAVID MORRELL
155

ANNE RICE
163

JOHN SAUL
173

JOHN SKIPP & CRAIG SPECTOR
183

WHITLEY STRIEBER
193

CHET WILLIAMSON
201

J. N. WILLIAMSON
209

GAHAN WILSON
219

A Conversation with the Interviewer

by
Philip Nutman

All writing begins with a word.
That word grows into a sentence, a paragraph, a work of fiction or nonfiction.

This book actually began with a question—"Why is horror fiction so popular?"—and grew into a body of interviews that pose other questions. The answers come not from the author, Stanley Wiater, but from the twenty-six writers who comprise the cast of this volume.

To the public at large the authors appearing in the following pages may be instantly recognized as horror writers; Wiater, however, refers to them as *dark dreamers*. The reason is, in part, because the epithet *horror writer* is too limiting a label to pin on the talents featured here, but there are other reasons and those will be made clear by the authors themselves. And part of the explanation has to do with the timing of this book.

Horror fiction—or "dark fantasy" or "the fiction of fear" or "dark suspense"—has never been so successful, so prominent in our popular culture as it is at present. This is not just due to the creative strengths displayed by the writers or the increasing appetite of an ever-expanding audience; it's also due to people like Wiater.

As a journalist and critic with nearly twenty years of experience behind him, he's toiled long into the night to bring the value of horror in the mass media to a greater public awareness, to show there's life in the genre beyond Stephen King, to free the subject from its undeserved aura of bad taste and its unwarranted reputation as an indulgence for one's "guilty pleasures."

It wasn't a religious crusade, just a deeply heartfelt one, for Wiater, like everyone else in this book, is a devout fan at heart. Unlike most aficionados who pursue their interests in their off-hours, he has been fortunate to explore his lifelong passion as a working reporter. As a feature writer, columnist, and critic, he has contributed to every major genre publication (including *Fangoria, Rod Serling's Twilight Zone Magazine, Horrorstruck, Fear*) as well as to several mainstream periodicals and newspapers. But this considerable body of nonfiction work is only one side of the coin, for Stanley is also a writer who works in the fictional realms of dark dreams. His infrequent short stories have been published in magazines such as *Cavalier* and in the anthologies *Masques II* and *Masques III*—with more forthcoming. His interest in the comic book medium is indicated by the stories that have been adapted for such publications as *Shriek* and *Taboo*. In addition, his editorial eye is displayed in *Night Visions 7*, where he also ingeniously manages to interview the trio of writers—Richard Laymon, Chet Williamson, Gary Brandner—that he selected for this annual showcase anthology.

It really comes down to two reasons why Wiater was the right man to assemble this book: timing and experience. He's paid his dues on both counts; was there, pen and tape recorder at the ready, when the horror boom started in the mid-seventies, and is still here, well over a decade later. A seasoned veteran in the conflict between those in the literary establishment who misunderstand and revile the subject and those who have warmed to its most chilling nightmares.

In the course of the conflict, Stan Wiater has established a reputation, quite simply, as the top interviewer in the field. His definitive interviews have served as more than postcards from the edge; they've helped road-map the hellish territories these dark dreamers so willingly explore. In my role as a fellow freelance journalist, I met with him to learn how this present volume came together.

NUTMAN: I know you've been considering a book like this for a few years. What made you decide that now was the time to compile *Dark Dreamers*?
WIATER: Primarily because the horror genre has become so popular—and important—that the critics have finally had to take it seriously. And once a popular phenomenon is taken seriously, it's time for the journalists to step in and investigate. That's the approach, at least, I tried to take. Not as a critic or a scholar, but as a responsible journalist who

also happens to be a lifelong fan. And a working horror writer as well.
NUTMAN: Were there any surprises along the way? Any difficulties?
WIATER: Not really. Horror writers compose such a small percentage of the literary community that nearly everyone knows each other professionally, if not personally. And thanks to such organizations as the Horror Writers of America and the annual Necon and World Fantasy conventions, many of these writers are in fact good friends and colleagues. It made the interviews a lot easier for me to conduct, since we all speak the same language.
NUTMAN: Why do you think this particular group of writers was so candid with their opinions and revelations about themselves?
WIATER: Well, without sounding too pompous, it's because I'm also a dark dreamer. I've published short stories in the field for several years, and have other irons in the fire. The point is, even though my credentials are as a reporter, I'm not an outsider looking in. I'm right next to these dark dreamers, heart and soul. It's us against *them*, as far as I'm concerned. I like to think I know what makes these people tick as well as anybody.
NUTMAN: I noticed the volume was dedicated, in part, to Ray Bradbury. He's mentioned by several other writers, isn't he?
WIATER: Yes, with the obvious exceptions of Edgar Allan Poe and H. P. Lovecraft, Bradbury is the one major influence which comes up again and again. I'd say nearly half the people I interviewed have mentioned him at one point or another as a profound influence on their lives. As to why I partially dedicated the book to him, it's simply because he was the man who—when I discovered *R Is for Rocket* in 1965—made me realize I had no other choice in life than to become a writer.
NUTMAN: One of your favorite questions is "Are horror writers born or made?" That is, were they destined to write about horror, or did they do it because it's commercially popular. What's your reason?
WIATER: First, it's not fair to use one of my own questions against me [*laughs*]. Second, I guess I asked for it because I thought this format would get the reader past a flat, stereotyped introduction and more into the spirit of the book. Let me try for "twenty-five words or less." All I can say is that I was writing for horror "fanzines" in the sixties, sold my first national magazine article to *Fate* in 1970, and sold my first short story in 1980. I've been conducting interviews with writers and filmmakers since 1974, beginning with Ray Bradbury and the late George Pal. I've enjoyed every minute.
NUTMAN: Do you think it was your "destiny" to be a writer?

WIATER: Since I've never held a nine-to-five job in my life and been fired from every youthful part-time job because of the dreaded "bad attitude," I think that's as far as I'll go in saying that horror and fantasy have always been my destiny. But I've always wanted to be a writer, though up to this point I've made my mark—such as it is—mostly in nonfiction.

NUTMAN: As a fellow interviewer, I realize we all work in basically the same way, but everyone has his or her own approach to interviewing. What's yours?

WIATER: As you well know, it's nothing elaborate or mysterious. I try to read every major work of an author I'm going to interview. Study the published criticism. Then I prepare my questions, and have follow-up questions to go along with the first set. I try to meet at persons' homes whenever possible, to make them feel most comfortable, though many interviews by necessity were conducted in the various hotels and watering holes where the conventions take place. Needless to say, it helps if you truly love the genre and already know how to talk to a wide range of people. (I've had a few excursions into the chaos known as "talk radio.") Then I return home and rewrite all the responses so my simplistic questions sound brilliant [*laughs*]. Actually, it's standard journalistic courtesy for the subjects to be allowed to edit their own responses before an interview finally sees publication. I'm pleased to say very few saw the need to, since I've spoken to them so many times before.

NUTMAN: From my own experience, it would seem difficult to get a solid interview just from a single two-hour meeting.

WIATER: Well, as I said, the secret to that may be because of my repeatedly interviewing most of these authors over a ten-year span of time. In a few cases, I was the first to ever profile them for a national magazine such as *Fangoria* or *Rod Serling's Twilight Zone Magazine*. If you develop a good relationship with someone right from the start, they usually have no hesitation to allow you to delve into their creative lives time and time again. Without mentioning any by name, I can say there are several brand name writers whom I've interviewed more times than any other journalist, in or out of the field.

NUTMAN: Did you detect any overall theme emerging through the interviews? Did you have one in mind from the outset?

WIATER: I purposely wasn't really looking for a specific theme. You can see the authors aren't put into any artificial categories of "loud horror" and "quiet horror." Or "Old Pros" versus "Young Turks." I don't deny there may be some discussion of those topics occurring now and again—especially on the validity of violence in the arts. But I basically had only two broad themes in mind: First, how do you work as a writer? And second, what do you think the importance of writing horror is? I tried to keep my personal opinions as much out of the picture as possible, though I confess they sneak in from time to time.

NUTMAN: You've stated elsewhere that's why you prefer the Q&A format, as is done, say, in *Playboy* magazine.

WIATER: That's true. I may fully understand the cult of personality in our society, but I don't like to perpetuate it. Now I admire the hell out of somebody like Harlan Ellison, for example. I can listen to him all day tell the reader, "I, Harlan, did this with so and so. Then I, Harlan, did that with so and so." But I ain't Harlan [*laughs*]! Anyway, that's why I usually prefer the Question-and-Answer style of interview rather than the personality profile. As a reader, I'm more interested in what the subject has to say rather than letting everyone know how profound, witty, and intelligent Stan Wiater really is. (Hopefully, being on the other end of the microphone, I can get away with saying that in strictest confidence.)

NUTMAN: Right. What inspired you to become an interviewer?

WIATER: Not too surprisingly, it was *Playboy*. When I was a kid, my parents honestly thought that my interest in monster movies and monster magazines such as *Famous Monsters of Filmland* and the great *Castle of Frankenstein* was going to quote "warp my mind" unquote. The fact that it eventually did is besides the point [*laughs*]. But the point is, my folks foolishly made a deal with me when I was fifteen that if I gave up reading monster magazines, then I would be given a gift subscription to any other magazine. Guess which one I chose?

But it was strange—I could read *Playboy* openly in front of my parents, yet at the same time I literally had to continue sneaking in monster magazines underneath my shirt, and when I got in the house, hide *them* under the mattress. Which is a long way of saying I've been a disciple of the *Playboy* interview since 1968. I'll read just about any interview I come across, and of course I'm an avid watcher of Larry King. I love the way he takes his subjects seriously, but not himself so seriously. I watch the talk shows like some people do soap operas, I guess.

NUTMAN: In general, how would you describe this particular group of writers, many of whom you know personally?

WIATER: Nothing too unusual, really. They like to read a a lot—and I mean *a lot* —and they like to go to the movies. A lot. Startling, right? Actually, I think I can best sum it up by the fact that the World Fantasy

Convention—remember horror is often defined as part of the overall term *fantasy* —is usually held on Halloween. It's always humorous to see the hotel staff dressed up like witches and ghouls, while people who create nightmares for a living are walking among them wearing business suits and gowns! The way I look at it, every day is Halloween for the dark dreamers. They're really the nicest group of people you can imagine, all of whom I wouldn't mind meeting in a dark alley.

NUTMAN: You've mentioned that you often initially meet these writers at various conventions. Do you recall the first one?

WIATER: Vividly. For horror, it was in 1979, at the Fifth World Fantasy Convention in Providence, Rhode Island. At the time, I was stringing for a western Massachusetts newspaper and had convinced the editor it would make for a "cute" story to cover a group of horror writers who were meeting nearby, and then publish it as a Halloween feature. Imagine my shock—and pleasure—to find myself interviewing, in the matter of a few hours, Charles L. Grant, Ramsey Campbell, Stephen King, Peter Straub, and director George A. Romero! I guess you can say I've been more or less professionally obsessed with finding out the secret to their own "hearts of darkness" ever since.

NUTMAN: Did you get everything that you wanted out of *Dark Dreamers*? It was a massive project, needless to say.

WIATER: Time and circumstances permitting, I'd like to think so. But before anybody complains to the publisher for my not including a particular author, let me say up front that I *know* I didn't get every dark dreamer in the world between these covers. For several reasons, including the obvious—that I ran out of room before I ran out of names. Also, not everyone I approached wished to be formally recognized as a "master of horror." And not everyone, quite frankly, who writes in the genre is automatically worthy of this title. Beyond that, a few writers asked to be included instead in the forthcoming companion volume, *Dark Visions*. You also have to consider that such folks as Clive Barker and Chet Williamson were basically unknown only five or six years ago, so the next great talent may appear on the scene the day after this volume appears. I can't tell you now if there's going to be a *Dark Dreamers II*. But there *is* a rapidly growing list of qualified contenders, believe me.

NUTMAN: So you already have a companion volume in the works?

WIATER: Yes, it's called *Dark Visions: Conversations with the Masters of the Horror Film*. I'm currently interviewing the major screenwriters, directors, and actors in the genre. For some strange reason this has never been done before, at least not as a definitive book of interviews.

Hopefully the two volumes will say it all, at least as far as observing where the state of the art in horror is today.

NUTMAN: After that, what's next?

WIATER: Well, I have a few more anthologies that I'd like to edit, then who knows? If you spent your life to date observing, studying, and interviewing the world's greatest talents in horror, what would you do with all that knowledge?

NUTMAN: Start looking for a real job? Become a psychotherapist?

WIATER: Phil, I want to thank you for donating your payment for this interview to charity. Forget what I said about giving you a plug as my successor in the field, or that as a reporter you are both the British correspondent for *Fangoria* and yet somehow also the American correspondent for England's *Fear*.*

NUTMAN: And frequently confused as to where I should be at any given time.

WIATER: Absolutely! Now let's meet our first dark dreamer.

---

*Yes, my colleague Philip Nutman is both bicoastal and transatlantic. Consequently, there is much confusion as to where he resides and just how many projects he's working on, which include short stories, screenplays, and a novel-in-progress. He is a native of England, and his writings have appeared in numerous publications, including *Penthouse, Cable Guide, Premier, L'Eran Fantastique, Rod Serling's Twilight Zone Magazine*, and *Segno Cinema*. Needless to say, he's also a dark dreamer.

Clive Barker

Momentarily relaxing in his huge study, Clive Barker gives the decided impression that there must be a dozen people working for him—a small corporation which could be given the name Fantastiques, Inc. Given the size of this room—and his imagination—it's certainly possible. He currently resides in a beautifully kept Georgian house in the middle of London, his work area situated on the third floor. Even this far up, the hum of the city can still be heard, as the playwright-artist-writer-director specifically chose to live here so that he can, at any time, step back into the ordinary world of everyday hustle and bustle.

His office is basically one large room, filled with bookcases and filing cabinets. A sophisticated stereo system is in one corner, along with assorted special-effects props from his various movie projects. Piles of manuscripts, magazines, and comic books are also in evidence. Along the walls are photographs of movie crews and framed sketches of some of the monsters he has designed for those same movies, as well as illustrations from Milton's *Paradise Lost*. His desk is placed before a large window overlooking the busy street below. A few fossils are nearby, presumably making for unique paperweights. Scattered about on the floor are numerous sketches and drawings, which seem to have been placed there without any apparent rhyme or reason. Barker cheerfully admits that he is in the center of "complete chaos," yet seems quite content with his lot.

Born in Liverpool on October 5, 1952, Clive Barker has every reason to be content. Of nearly all the dark dreamers, he typifies the classic scenario of the overnight success, when in 1984 he exploded onto the horror scene with the first three volumes of the controversial, award-winning *Books of Blood*. Even before the publication of a second trio of volumes appeared, it was obvious that a major new talent had arrived. Following the six volumes of short fiction, Barker turned his sights on the novel and to date has published four: *The Damnation Game*, *Weaveworld*, *Cabal*, and *The Great and Secret Show*. If this wasn't enough to keep him busy, the reason of course for the movie material in his home is that Barker has also done the screenplays for *Underworld* and *Rawhead Rex*, as well as writing and directing the films *Hellraiser* and *Nightbreed*.

Even though he has become what the publishing industry refers to as a brand name in a scant half-dozen years, Barker fully realizes that a writer has to do better each time out if he is to keep his reputation and his readership satisfied. However, he seems in no danger of losing his critical status or his fans, owing to the very simple fact that he truly loves everything and anything that has to do with the bizarre, the unknown, and the fantastical.

WIATER: I can't help noticing that there doesn't seem to be a word processor or a typewriter lurking about. Just where might they be?
BARKER: Everything is handwritten. Always has been and, I suspect, always will be. I don't own a typewriter or a word processor.
WIATER: Then how does writing in longhand best serve the creative process?
BARKER: It frees me from thinking in the technical sense of writing. I don't think about putting in a new piece of paper or a new ribbon; I don't think about the machine's hum or any technical process at all. I enter the "dreamscape" I propose and describe it. When I'm doing my best work, it has the feeling of journalism. In my mind's eye, I'm seeing something very clearly, very strongly, and I'm simply communicating what I'm seeing in the most direct manner possible.

That describes the first draft. The second draft then becomes much more about the way the material is shaped on the page. It becomes a question of refining vocabulary, of refining syntax, and so on. So the hand is there, working away in this very simple manner, in the very first way we learn to put words down: a pen and a piece of paper. I started writing when I was four, and it's certainly served me well these past thirty-three years, so I see no specific reason to change it now [*laughs*]!

WIATER: Seeing the massive amount of artwork you have in every corner, not to mention the floor, it's obvious that drawing the fantastic is as important to you as writing about it. How so?

BARKER: The drawings all over the floor are, in many cases, drawings which directly relate to what's on the page. Midnight sketches, done feverishly, which then become a starting place for something in a chapter the following morning. A *lot* of that goes on. The creatures that I put on a page I try to imagine minutely, and will sometimes result in a drawing after I've done a first draft. Very often, I'll have sketches around anyway. So it's very much a part of my creative process. What I'm trying always to do is to create as much of the image as I possibly can on the page, and let it jump out at people.

WIATER: You mentioned your "dreamscape"; to what extent do you use your dreams and nightmares in your work?

BARKER: I keep a dream diary, though it's not just for dreams. It's one kind of internal reporting. But I also write down notes as you would when you feel particularly happy, or how you feel when you feel particularly bad after some loss or some sense of disappointment. I'm constantly making notes about my own mental processes as starting places for other projects. I'll just file those away, and I have boxes and boxes of notes filled with snatches of poetry and snatches of self-analysis, if you like. Which may or may not find their way into a piece of prose, many years down the line.

WIATER: Even if they don't, you could make some biographer very famous someday when it's discovered just who the "real" Clive Barker was after you've passed on.

BARKER: Oh, no—then I'll burn them [*laughs*]! It'll be in my will that they'll all get trashed. Absolutely!

WIATER: Do you make any conscious division between your dreams and what most people consider as nightmares?

BARKER: No. In truth, I don't think I've had a nightmare for years and years and years. I've had a few dreams which have left me uneasy in the negative sense, but there are also dreams of unease which are hugely inspiring. Inevitably, one dreams about the loss of something, such as a loved one, and I suppose that comes close to the nightmare. But I don't wake up terrified that my body is being ripped up by one of my own creatures.

I'm very aware of the relationship I have with my imagination, both consciously and unconsciously. I think that my prime obsession has been the honing and sophisticating and the employing of my imagination. It's obviously the chief tool of my craft. It's also a major place for self-explanation, the means by which I understand myself best.

WIATER: Considering some of the incredible characters and situations you've created, to what extent have you included—or purposely excluded—any degree of autobiography?

BARKER: Generally speaking, I think good horror fiction has been the fiction of the confessional. *Books of Blood* was very *much* about what was going on inside me at the time. I think that in order to convince readers that these extraordinary events are valid and real, you *have* to be writing from deep places in your psyche. You can't construct these things casually or in a detached fashion. They are passions that are rooted in your deepest feelings; in my case, they always have been.

WIATER: Some writers have told me that they write in this genre because they are able to creatively purge certain elements in their psyche. I get the sense you don't quite feel that way?

BARKER: No—the word I would use is *celebrating*. I don't *want* to get rid of any of this stuff [*laughs*]! It's existed in all the arts—you shouldn't just limit it to the written word. We should celebrate the sheer variation, the fecundity of the imaginative process. I don't think that Bosch, when he was painting his manuscripts, teeming with extraordinary visions and creatures and demoniacal scenes, was, in the strictest sense, purging. I think he was finding that material within himself and using his art to celebrate it.

WIATER: You're one of the few authors who readily falls into the cliche known as the overnight success. How does it affect your creative vision when you realize that virtually everything you produce has a ready—and obviously favorable—audience?

BARKER: Well, I'm always trying very hard to find a new hole to pop out of. New areas to work in. The four novels that I've written have been as different from each other as is possible within the realms of the *fantastique*. The novel that I'm working on now will again be a major departure; there are certainly large areas of fictional life that I want to investigate. That I haven't even begun to touch upon. What I *don't* want to do is repeat myself. I finished up on the *Books of Blood* feeling that I had discharged my duty to short horror fiction as best I could. I don't want to go back over old ground. I owe that to my audience, I owe that to myself, to my craft. My craft, as I said before, is my major way of explaining myself *to* myself.

I don't want to be repeating old adventures. I want to be finding new adventures. I hope that I do have an audience now that will follow me from one genre to another. I hope I'm not given a freedom in the negative sense of just being able to run around, doing whatever I like. But rather be given a latitude to investigate new ideas and know that the audience is going to say, "Well, Clive Barker's got his name on it—we'll give it a go." It allows me a sense of... addressing the adventure properly.

WIATER: You're aware of course of the term *splatterpunk*, coined tongue in cheek by David J. Schow in reference to what some consider the "new wave" in horror fiction. Do you feel you have to "go over the edge of the map" regarding territories that others have not previously dared to explore?

BARKER: Let's deal with the craft of storytelling. I think the whole purpose to telling a story is to take the audience on a journey which they otherwise wouldn't get to take. It's one of the reasons why I've never been deeply interested in what we'll loosely call "naturalistic fiction." Were I to write the male menopause novel—when I reach that age—I would presumably be addressing it to only those people who were actually having a male menopause. Which does not seem to me to be a hugely interesting process.

Let's go where only *imagination* can take us! Some of those places are going to be very dark and dangerous, and yes, they're going to be "over the edge of the map," if you like. They are going to be the places where we can confront the forbidden. Some of them are also going to be "dreamscapes" where we can feel reassured, and where we feel as though we have a glimpse of comprehension rather than of panic. I am as interested in those areas as I ever have been; I'm interested in ecstasy *and* terror.

I'm particularly interested in the place where one becomes the other. Those two extremes are the twin beacons out there, and I'm most excited when I actually find that I've reached one. Then I want to reach the other.

WIATER: Your work does show a definite willingness to explore the usually untried boundaries of sex and sensuality. "The Hellbound Heart," to name only one example, is essentially a romance between a woman and her formerly deceased lover.

BARKER: [*grins*] It's a major preoccupation of mine. I've always felt it's something that horror fiction—and let's use the more collective term *fantastique*—generally doesn't address as well as it should. Sex in horror fiction and movies doesn't tend to be the subject of the work as much as it is light relief between the darker goings-on. Or maybe you're just setting up the characters to be murdered in their beds, which again doesn't seem terribly interesting. But sex figures greatly in our sense of ourselves, and in our sense of how we physically appear in the world. Sex affects what our bodies do, how they change, how vulnerable they are. It affects our sense of personal ambition, and how much we want to achieve in terms of our sexual lives.

It certainly affects what our sense of nightmarish and scary is, because there are so many elements in the sexual process where we relinquish control. And loss of control, for most people most of the time, is a *very* scary notion. Sexual fever is essentially a place where reason is suspended. One of the things I love about art is you can employ reason and emotions simultaneously. The best fiction pricks the emotions: makes you laugh, cry. Be scared. And at the same time it stimulates the intellect.

WIATER: You also don't have any reservations to explore broad religious and metaphysical themes. Are you moving past what's potentially frightening about the unknown to attempting to explain what the "unknown" might possibly be?

BARKER: You know, writing about the unholy is one way to write about what's sacred. A major slice of me is preoccupied with the transcendental. I have a review here in England for *The Great and Secret Show* titled "The World Beyond: A User's Manual." And I thought, "Well, that's all right!" I like that! I like the idea that this is a fiction which does address, in a very straightforward way, what's going on beyond. In fact, if I wanted to use one phrase to describe the kind of fiction that I'm writing: "These are user's manuals for the world beyond," I wouldn't mind that at all!

WIATER: The idea of your novels being "manuals" goes back to the consideration that you consider yourself a special breed of journalist, one who happens to be reporting from—the beyond?

BARKER: Sure! One always has to look at art as having function. Art is not ever to be dismissed as escapism. I'm *hugely* preoccupied with the idea of claiming *fantastique* back from the critics and academics who would dismiss it as being escapist and useless.

It's very important to reiterate how significant and rich that tradition is, because those of us who are in the genre, the *fantastique* genre— and by that I mean horror fiction, and speculative fiction, high fantasy— that whole area of imaginative fiction, we are vulnerable to critical attitudes that will dismiss anything which is not "naturalistic" or "realistic." If we were writing in translation, if we were South American "magic realists," of course this wouldn't be a problem because they have such intellectual respect there. But that attitude doesn't take into account the rich and diverse work which is being done at the moment—and which has always been done—in this area.

WIATER: For someone who has never sampled your imagination before, which of your books would you first point out to them?

BARKER: A couple of the volumes of the *Books of Blood*.... I'd probably point to the one known as *In the Flesh*. I'd certainly point to *Weaveworld*. I'd point to *The Great and Secret Show*, simply because of its breadth of ambition.

WIATER: And yet, when speaking of the term *splatterpunk*, it's a phrase which is often used to describe your work, most specifically the *Books of Blood* (1984–1985). What's your view on that admittedly simplistic interpretation?

BARKER: I feel that though I made my reputation early on with some extremely visceral stories, such as "The Midnight Meat Train" and "Rawhead Rex," those represent a very small part of my output. They were wonderful to write, and I'm very fond of them as stories, but I've always felt that my real contribution would be pulling together various elements from the whole tradition of fantastical literature. I am interested in the visceral and in Grand Guignol, certainly. But I am also interested in the transcendental and the allegorical, and the fiction of fairy tales. Pulling those elements together and making a single fictional form of them; synthesizing elements from many varied sources is my ambition, and maybe in a novel I've achieved that best so far in *Weaveworld*.

WIATER: Since you've become so successful in such a relatively short amount of time, do you ever consider going back and rewriting some of your earlier work, in the sense that you now have all the time you want to make it "perfect"?

BARKER: In all honesty, no. The danger with that answer is that it sounds arrogant, it sounds like I know it's all perfect, and I don't believe that for a moment! But I do believe you have to get on with it. I don't look over my shoulder and think, "God, if I only had three more months for that book!" or whatever. You have to allow your imagination the freedom to make whatever statement it needs to make at a given time, and then move on to something else. There's scarcely enough time to write the books, never mind regret them!

WIATER: You dedicated the first volume of the *Books of Blood* to your parents. What influence did they have on your earliest, formative years as a writer and artist?

BARKER: My mother gave me *Peter Pan* and a few other fantasies such as *Wind in the Willows* when I was a kid, but they were benign volumes. It was only through my own pursuits that I came upon the darker stuff, like Poe. But I am not, nor have I ever been, the sort of person who thought that dark fantasy—horror fiction—would be my sole preoccupation. In the fullness of my career—supposing I continue to work another thirty or forty years—I think it will be perceived to be an element of my work, but by no means the dominant element.

WIATER: But did your parents ever recognize that their son was, in simple point of fact, a potentially "gifted child"?

BARKER: My parents always knew I was imaginative. I think they always *worried* about that. I don't believe they ever put pen and paper into my hands and said, "Get on with it," or, "Write whatever your imagination directs you." Far from it! I think they had the conventional belief of making sure that I somehow found a purpose in life which would pay the mortgage and allow me to be a sane and productive member of society. So they let me get on with my interests, but they certainly didn't encourage them.

WIATER: Do you ever feel that you and your fellow dark dreamers have ever done ill to society by bringing out into the light the unspeakable truths many people would rather keep secreted away?

BARKER: No, I don't. Our culture has been enriched throughout history by dark dreamers. Reenvisioning, reforming, reformulating images and ideas that have been part of the oral—and later the written—tradition in our culture since its instigation.

It's certainly the case that there have been voices raised against us, and what has been put on the screen, in the last twenty years. But if you actually look back, in the way that *Psycho* was reviewed in 1960, or the way the Hammer films were reviewed in the late 1950s, or the Universal horror films of the 1930s, you'll see the same vocabulary. Disgust. Accusing the filmmakers *and* the audience of depravity. I think that has to be the way of it.

If we were writing safe fiction, we wouldn't be interested in this process. But we're *not* writing safe fiction, at our best. We're writing a fiction which *is* confrontational. Which *is* dangerous. If *fantastique* fiction were indeed as "escapist" and "negligible" as many of the critics believe, one wonders why there are some critics who will raise their voices in disgust at it. If it's so harmless, why even bother to condemn it?

WIATER: At this point in your career, you're in the unusual position of being both a popular writer and a successful filmmaker. Are you ever concerned that, after you've passed beyond this vale of tears, you may be best remembered by those who have seen one of your movies rather than read one of your books?

BARKER: My great hero is Jean Cocteau. Cocteau made movies, wrote books, wrote plays, drew drawings.... The fact is, what's remembered about Cocteau is a *vision*. And the vision was expressed through a whole variety of media. What is extraordinary about the man was the consistency of his vision. Now, let's not even talk about when I've left this vale of tears, let's talk about the next five years. I mean... Let's assume people don't say "Clive who?" in five years! Let's assume the movies are still being made, the books have been translated into fourteen languages around the world, in millions of copies, and are required reading for high school students... really [*laughs*]! This is very important to me. This is important to me because books are still an immensely elaborate and elegant way to share your imagination with other people.

Books—the word on the printed page—carry an *immense* power to influence and will, in turn, generate other media events. Edgar Allan Poe, although he wrote a relatively small amount of material, has been transferred into movies, comic books, cartoons, and musicals, plays, television, and so on. You've got to look at that collective influence, and that is enormous.

Robert Bloch

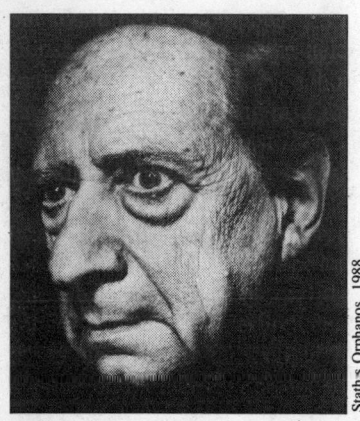

A proper introduction to Robert Bloch would actually take a book-length work. (In fact, there are *two* book-length studies of him available, both written by critic Randall D. Larson. *Robert Bloch* deals extensively with his writings; *The Complete Robert Bloch* is a 126-page illustrated bibliography exhaustively detailing Bloch's multi-media success in print, film, television, and radio over the past fifty years.)

Born on April 5, 1917, in Chicago, Bloch made his first magazine sales to the now-legendary pulp *Weird Tales* while still an adolescent. He was for a time a correspondent of no less than one of the all-time masters of the macabre, H. P. Lovecraft. (Bloch and Lovecraft even wrote stories in which they each created unspeakable dire fates for fictionalized versions of one another.) Bloch, however, came into his own as one of the first writers to explore the field of psychological horror and dark suspense in the 1940s and 1950s with such classic novels as *The Scarf* and *The Kidnapper* and *The Will to Kill,* the central philosophy of this form of horror being that the worst monsters are not from beyond the grave or another dimension, but from whatever lurks within our own minds.

He is of course now best known for a novel called *Psycho* (1959), later made into the motion picture by director Alfred Hitchcock. Beyond the immediate recognition that particular title has given him, Bloch has penned no less than fifty books and more than four hundred short stories. He has written for such classic television series as "Alfred Hitchcock Presents" and "Thriller." He has also done several screenplays, most notably a series of anthology films produced in England—*Asylum, Torture Garden, The House That Dripped Blood*—which he adapted from his own short stories.

Bloch is truly one of the legends of the genre, whose work has had an enormous influence on an entire generation of writers. As evidence, try to find an anthology of horror classics that doesn't list him in its table of contents. In spite of having been a professional writer for more than half a century, he shows no signs of slowing down. Every year heralds the publication of a new novel or short story collection, and every year his earlier work is being brought back into print by publishers who realize that much of what is considered "contemporary" was already done by him decades ago.

In spite of the grimness naturally associated with his work, Bloch in person is possessed of a very wry sense of humor, one which is used to calm visitors to his office, where he willingly will prove he still "has the heart of a little boy."

Robert will even let you pick it up and hold it.

WIATER: Considering that you've scripted your share of movies, what do you think of the recent trend in openly sadistic splatter films?
BLOCH: I don't care for this particular trend because I feel it does a disservice to the field. It's very much analogous to the use of four-letter words in contemporary fiction. These things are now buzzwords; they've lost their impact. They're a substantive device for actual thought, and the same thing is true in a horror film visually. Anyone can eviscerate—or seem to eviscerate—on camera. It doesn't call for any skill or any imagination. You just might as well go to a slaughterhouse and pick out a few animals and carve them up screaming and squealing—on camera—and the audience that is there for the sadistic effects will be just as pleased! The blood is spurting, the screams are coming—if that's what they want, they can have it. But this has nothing to do with the art or even the craft of the presentation of the fantastic, or the genuine horror film.
WIATER: Then what are your thoughts on the new wave in fiction, usually termed—though half in jest—as *splatterpunk*? Where every clinical detail of the violence is described so that the supposedly jaded reader has no other choice but to face it head-on?

BLOCH: To me, splatterpunk is merely a new label for the mixture as before. I don't believe it is a writer's mission to cater to the tastes—or lack of taste—of the supposedly jaded reader. I don't believe writers of horror fiction are engaged in a contest to see who can most nauseate these jaded readers, or present the most graphically disgusting descriptions. The Romans started with simple chariot races and ended up trying to devise extreme and atrocious methods of torture and mass murder. I don't regard this as an improvement.

WIATER: Yet critic Sam Moskowitz once described you as one of the first to "tell it like it is" in your psychological horror stories. In terms of realism, just how explicit do you allow yourself to be for the sake of the story?

BLOCH: I try to do what Hitchcock did in his films. I will suggest, and in effect cut away—as he would do with a camera, but in this case verbally—and let the rest be imagined by the audience and/or the reader. I think it's much more effective than to just do a graphic, detailed description, which is the equivalent of showing graphic violence on the screen. That's always been my technique.

WIATER: It's an easy parallel to state that, while crime and violence in our society is escalating, the popularity of horror has also never been greater. Is this popularity of the genre a cause or effect of the already existing troubles in our society?

BLOCH: I think it is symptomatic of a social disease—not a venereal disease, but a sociological disease—but we are talking now about the so-called horror films: the R-rated films, the X-rated films, the splatter films, the snuff pictures, that sort of thing. As I've said, I think these films don't make any sort of meaningful contribution whatsoever to society. But they *do* pander to the sadists. I've enjoyed very few films lately, to be perfectly blunt about it. There are many script assignments I would turn down because I wanted no part of this particular trend. To me the ideal film in this genre is *Diabolique*.

I used to get some very strange looks when twenty years ago I would talk about the really great silent films, particularly silent comedies. Buster Keaton, Harold Lloyd, and a few others. And people would say, "Ah, I saw them—they're no good!" Most of these people didn't even know the *names* of the comedians. Since that time, there's been this enormous interest in retrospectives. And not only have these films been shown, but they've been shown properly. Not in little eight-millimeter grainy prints. But in thirty-five millimeter, on a wide screen, with an organ accompanist. Those films bring the house down! They're just as good today—that comedy is timeless. And it's genuine.

It doesn't consist of a lot of car-smashings and vulgarities, and noise, and screaming matches. These are just genuine, well-structured comedies which build—just the way a horror-suspense film should build—to get a reaction from the audience. Now, that's the analogy I make. I think the good horror films—the old ones, when shown properly—are just as effective as they were originally. Even though, as in the case of the comedy films, the visual elements have been ripped off and excerpted and just plain outright stolen by some of the brilliant young "geniuses" now directing. And for an audience who never saw the originals, they think this is just fine, fresh, and original or new. But it isn't.

WIATER: Have others in effect "stolen" from your films or novels?

BLOCH: I've been told that there must be at least forty variations on *Psycho*. And people who are not familiar with the original film—or the novel—find this all very innovative. But I think everything, to a certain degree, is developed from a writer's readings and association with other work. It's just a matter of degree there as to whether it constitutes a point of departure or inspiration, or just plain plagiarism.

WIATER: Many writers believe in the age-old theory of catharsis: that to exorcise our darker nature through the arts, we can then better cope with them in life. Do you still hold to that belief?

BLOCH: Yes, but again we have to make that distinction of what I consider to be horror and what the exploitation filmmakers consider to be horror. In the types which exhibit a certain restraint, I think there is this catharsis that does come from within, because it's built up from within. It isn't shoved in one's face, a blood pie instead of a custard pie, the way it's done in so many of these other films. In that case, you're not achieving catharsis—you're merely catering to voyeurism. Sadistic voyeurism. But the basic premise I always try to stress is that it isn't so much what's shown, but the *attitude* toward it.

If the evil is condoned, or is presented in an amoral fashion by those who would recoil in disgust from the use of the word *evil* and then they walk away from it, I think it's quite a different story. But if the attitude is there, and you take a moral position, then I think it's a positive and constructive thing. But the antihero, the man or woman whose most atrocious activities are condoned because he or she is "avenging" something, establishes a very dangerous premise. And it ultimately leads to the Ku Klux Klan, the Inquisition, you name it.

WIATER: But in terms of so-called moral responsibility, isn't it always the artist who is ultimately blamed when someone commits a horrendous crime? One in which the criminal claims he was "inspired" by the novel or the film, otherwise he might not have committed that crime?

BLOCH: I merely refer them to the work in question. If they can find in any of my writings a weirdo with whom it would be pleasant to identify, then I would stand condemned. But I don't believe for example that anybody who has either read *Psycho* or seen the film is inspired to dress up in drag, grab a butcher knife, and head for the nearest shower stall! Because Norman Bates is *not* presented as a happy human being, or a fulfilled human being. There are no rewards for the Norman Bateses of this world in my work. And I don't think there ever will be. There are times when such a person goes unpunished, in the legal sense of the term, but we always know that he or she is a most unhappy person, and much more miserable than any one of the victims.

That's my position, and always has been, and I guess always will be. I believe that there's more genuine morality in that approach than there is in any number of pieces of fiction—whether in print or in film—where the antihero is presented as being justified simply because he's handsome and macho, and allowed to get away with these things.

WIATER: Do you consider that part of the legacy of your work that you always instilled a moral viewpoint into your characters?

BLOCH: Oh, actually I'm only trying to please an audience, or a certain segment of an audience. I don't think I'm writing for posterity, or that there's any particular survival value in what I do. So I don't approach it in that pretentious a fashion; it's just a personal viewpoint. I don't sit down and try to write a moral homily, but I do believe every writer should have an attitude.

When you just present something without a point of view, you're copping out. As a writer, as a creative individual, you just might as well do a documentary! You've contributed nothing; what you are doing is a fictional report of an atrocity that's meaningless unless you take a position. That position is certainly taken by the press in its reporting. We've yet to see the headlines that say, "Horray! Twelve More Crimes Committed Today!" or, "Wow! What an Axe Murder!" It's a subtle distinction, but it's there.

WIATER: Then what do you think are the beneficial aspects of horror fiction to society? Are there any?

BLOCH: Like many things in life, it can offer benefits to some people if taken in moderation. Catharsis, in any form, follows the same dictum.

WIATER: Do you feel that horror writers are "born," not made? Or can any competent writer learn the techniques to scare a reader?

BLOCH: I think horror writers evolve from undergoing trauma in childhood and draw upon their own fears in their adult careers. A competent writer can, by definition, usually fake almost any style in any genre,

but the results are patently imitation unless there's an emotional involvement. As for scaring the reader, it obviously depends on just who the reader happens to be. Most eight-year-old kids tend to scare somewhat easier than, let us say for an example, Stephen King. In fact, I'd venture that most eight-year-old kids scare even more easily than *I* do.
WIATER: Then what warnings would you give someone who feels it's their destiny to become a writer?
BLOCH: My first warning would be to stop believing in "destiny." My second warning would be to opt for a less demanding profession. Writing is a lonely occupation, exposing one to constant rejection, criticism, and (if one is successful) to jealousy and the malice of the envious. It is, in addition, quite arduous, and it takes its toll in stress. There are also accompanying perils to consider. If you don't watch out, you can end up giving interviews.
WIATER: One of the trademarks of your style is the way you so successfully meld humor with the horror. Why do you repeatedly use humor in the most macabre and grisly situations?
BLOCH: Humor and horror both invoke a reaction by means of shock and/or surprise. Both make effective use of the same element—the unexpected. I use either in order to startle the reader; I find this helps keep him awake.
WIATER: What do you consider your most important novel and short story?
BLOCH: Important to whom, and in what way? Financially, to me, I suppose *Psycho* would fit the description, since it has had so long a shelf life. In terms of personal effect, my short story "The Movie People" reassured me that I could deal with romance and sentiment without relying on rue or grue. Psychologically, my most important effort would be my recently completed autobiography. I prepared for writing it all my life! As to what others might consider important—if anything—you'll have to ask them.
WIATER: *Psycho* is *so* identified with you that almost every time you're identified in print it's as "Robert (*Psycho*) Bloch." To what extent has that one novel helped—or hurt—your career?
BLOCH: Its effect on my career is obvious. It helped give me a label, a means of quick identification. At the same time, it has probably hindered my efforts to move into other areas of writing; readers (and editors, and producers) expect and/or insist on the type of story with which they associate me. Lately—in my novels *Lori* and *Psycho House* —I've injected more humor and more sociological commentary, without diminishing the shock and suspense. It will be interesting to see how

this works: Thus far the reaction to *Lori* has been enthusiastic, and I'd imagine that *Psycho House* pleased old Norman's fans as well.

When the original *Psycho* was first published, I'd already had a professional writing career which extended back almost twenty-five years. On that basis it seems logical to assume I'd probably have continued as a professional writer without any problem: I'd also been invited to do television work a good six months before the film ever appeared, so that too would very likely have been part of my subsequent career. But *Psycho* did fix my image, for better or worse. For years afterward, many young ladies refused to take showers with me.

WIATER: Speaking of image, what compels you to write for so long about the dark side of humanity? Why are you so fascinated with exposing, in a sense, all the ugly things to be found when you turn over that proverbial rock?

BLOCH: Again we are concerned with semantics. The way this is worded, it's a loaded question. Nothing "compels" me to write about the dark side of humanity, nor am I so "fascinated" by exposing the ugly things found under rocks, proverbial or otherwise.

I do not write as I do out of any compulsion, but because experience has demonstrated that this is the most successful way for me to earn a living from my work. Efforts to write humor or "straight" mysteries have never afforded me a livelihood, whereas dealing with what you term "the dark side of humanity" seems to find a readership and meet with greater favor. I am not as much fascinated with the exposure of ugly things as I am interested and curious about their sources and causations. So, apparently, are the readers—and, for that matter, the psychotherapists, the theologians, the penologists, and those biologists involved in the study of genetics. I am, truth to tell, far less fascinated than many average individuals today, judging by their patronage of splatter films which I do not see, violent comic books which I do not read, or attendance at prizefights, hockey, and football games and other aggressive-activity spectacles which I avoid.

Writing about vampires doesn't make me a bloodsucker; writing about homicidal maniacs doesn't mean I'm a maniacal murderer myself. Intellectual curiosity is a far cry from obsession.

WIATER: You're undeniably prolific; have you ever encountered a dry spell in your career?

BLOCH: No, I've never had a dry period, and I trust I won't. I've been doing it for fifty-five years, and I'll do it another fifty-five years, God willing.

WIATER: What's your daily routine like?

BLOCH: I sit down at the manual typewriter every weekday morning at nine and get up again at one P.M. After lunch there are corrections to make, plus notes for the following day's work. By then the mail arrives, and that takes care of whatever's left of the day, in most instances. I've given up anthropomancy. Temporarily.

During the past sixteen months I've substituted a secretary and a word processor for the typewriter, but the routine is the same in dictation as in putting words directly into manuscript. I loathe all machines and subjected myself to the processor only to catch up with the backlog of work—turning out *Psycho House*, then the novel collaboration with Andre Norton, plus the autobiography. Now I'll toss out the processor (which the secretary brought in) and look for a quill pen.

WIATER: After a substantial career as a dark dreamer, what gives you the most satisfaction? Or are you rarely ever satisfied?

BLOCH: My satisfaction depends on the satisfaction of the reader. Not *all* readers. I do not yearn for the admiration of the yahoo audience, nor do I court it. On a personal level, I am more satisfied with my recent efforts because I think they'll be more satisfying to my readers. Both of them.

WIATER: Based on your experiences, have you developed a ready-to-deliver, twenty-five words or less "Statement on Horror and Its Future"?

BLOCH: Hmm. Now that's a toughie. I've never tried to arrive at a definition of it. You know, in science fiction there's that famous quote from Damon Knight, who, as a critic, says, "Science Fiction is where I happen to be pointing at the moment." But, unfortunately I think, through the years that if I had to point my finger at where horror is at the moment, I would point at the audience.

Gary Brandner

Although Gary Brandner may not be as major a box office draw as Stephen King or Clive Barker, it's safe to say Hollywood has done a better-than-average job of bringing several of his novels to the silver screen. His very first horror novel, *The Howling*, was made into a very successful film by director Joe Dante in 1981. Unfortunately, Brandner's second novel in the series, *The Howling II*, was turned into a far-less-successful film in 1986, starring Christopher Lee and Sybil Danning. Then the movie sequels began to take on a life of their own. The third novel in the series was also released as a motion picture in 1987, with an original screenplay and direction by Philippe Mora. Having little to do with the source novel, this completely Australian production was cheapened further with the new title *The Marsupials: Howling III*. (Mora was the director responsible for the terrible first sequel, which also had the equally ridiculous title *Howling II, or Your Sister Is a Werewolf.*)

If this weren't enough to keep an original paperback novel's title alive, a *Howling IV* was produced in 1988, and a *Howling V* has also been announced—even though Brandner has no intention to spawn any further novels in the now apparently endless movie series.

Also, 1988 saw the release of yet another movie from which Brandner adapted his own novel—*Cameron's Closet*, starring

Tab Hunter and directed by the young horror specialist Armand Mastroianni. And in the spring of 1989, a two-part miniseries, *From the Dead of Night* starring Lindsay Wagner, was adapted from his novel *Walkers*. To date, Brandner has published twenty-four novels, sixty-four short stories, and four screenplays. (Including, he reluctantly admits, the first draft script for *Howling II*.) His other novels in the genre include *Hellborn, Quintana Roo, The Brain Eaters, Carrion,* and *Floater*. His most recent is *Doomstalker*. Like many of his novels, it focuses heavily on demons, monsters, and diabolical supernatural forces from beyond the grave.

Totally unpretentious about his career, Brandner freely admits that he writes in the genre partially because one of the financial dividends is that the horror novels are frequently optioned by Hollywood. A native of Sault Sainte Marie, Michigan, the always-smiling Brandner now lives in southern California, close to the motion picture industry. He takes his recent success in stride, realizing that more people are aware of his name from the cinematic adaptations—both good and bad—of his work than from the novels themselves. And like his colleague Robert (*Psycho*) Bloch, he is resigned to having the name Gary (*The Howling*) Brandner for the rest of his career.

WIATER: There's currently no less than a half-a-dozen movies out which are based directly or indirectly on your novels. Why do you think Hollywood has taken such a liking to you?
BRANDNER: Well, being out here helps. It's certainly helped me in getting the screenplay work. But I've always written visually, and producers are not going to wade through a lot of interior dialogue unless it is somebody like John Updike. But I write visually—I write in scenes, so that makes it fairly easy to realize my books on screen.
WAITER: Have you ever considered writing an original screenplay? Or are you more content to do an adaptation of one of your novels so as to try and remain faithful to the source?
BRANDNER: That's about it. I'm a *book* writer. People have talked to me about originals a few times, but that's rough, in the sense you have to go about pitching your ideas, and taking lunches with producers [*laughs*] . . . ! It doesn't pay as much, but for me writing the book is much more rewarding artistically. For the obscene money, I'll do an adaptation of one of my books anytime.
WIATER: You had such luck with Hollywood, I'm tempted to ask if

you write your novels with the movie version already in mind?
BRANDNER: No, I don't. I set out to write a good *book*. And if it turns out later to make a good movie, that's so much the better. I want to do a book that satisfies the reader first.
WIATER: How involved were you with the film version of *The Howling*, directed by Joe Dante?
BRANDNER: I had zero involvement with it—I just sold the film rights. I liked the movie, though it was considerably changed from my book! The producers kept my basic idea of an entire community of werewolves, and they kept one of my favorite scenes: the werewolf-sex scene [*laughs*]. And they changed all the names, because director Joe Dante had this cute idea where he wanted to name everyone after old horror film directors.
WIATER: How did *Howling II* come about—as a movie first or a novel?
BRANDNER: That was requested by my publisher, because *The Howling* sold well. So they asked me if I would do a sequel, though I hadn't originally intended to do one. Then for *The Howling III* my British publisher originally put out a contract for that, and my American publisher picked it up. So they were both written due to the publishers' requests.
WIATER: Then how in the world did you become involved with the screenplay for *Howling II, or Your Sister Is a Werewolf*, which has to be one of the worst horror films ever made?
BRANDNER: Oh, I have to groan as I answer this! I was involved in it because my contract stated that to get the film rights I also had to do the first-draft screenplay. And I wanted to do it, because being kind of Hollywood-naive at the time, I thought it would be exciting to write my own movie. So I did. [*long, melodramatic pause*] I . . . I suppose you've seen it . . . ?
WIATER: That movie will live forever in infamy because of the shot in which Sybil Danning takes off her shirt again and again and again while the end-credits roll.
BRANDNER: That was their best shot, so they repeated it! Oh, well. All I can say is what I wrote ain't what's up there on the screen! But I can tell you some of the reasons why the screenplay was so badly screwed up. First, I wrote a pretty straight movie version of my book for the producers. And they said, "Gee, this is nice, Gary, but we just got a bunch of money from some Spanish people, and they'd like a large percentage of the film to be shot in Spain." Of course the story took place in Los Angeles and Mexico, but I said, "Okay, I can do that." So I moved everything to Spain for some reason or another. And then

they said, "Oh, one more thing: Fernando Rey is a good buddy of the producer, and he'd like a part written for Rey." And I had no Fernando Rey character, but again I said, "Okay—what the hell? I'll write Fernando Rey in." So I did.

I gave them another draft. And they said, "Gosh, Gary, this is nice, too, but you know what? The Spanish money just dropped out, and we're going to film in Yugoslavia." I had a book commitment by that time, so it was goodbye for me. They brought in another screenwriter, rewrote the script, took the production to Yugoslavia, ran out of money, spent about twelve dollars on special effects—filmed it mostly in the dark so nobody would notice—and that's the last I know about that one.

WAITER: Which brings us up to *Howling III*. This version, even though it has little to do with your novel, was once again directed by Philippe Mora?

BRANDNER: Unfortunately, the same guy who botched up *Howling II*! I had nothing to do with that one. The contract stated that everybody in the production, crew, actors, and so forth, had to be Australian. I really didn't mind, because at that time I didn't want to do a screenplay on that anyhow! It doesn't sound *anything* like my novel. The main character in the novel is a young boy, and in this one it seems to be a young girl. Beyond the sex change, I daresay there's a whole lot of other changes involved. At least I get the credit "Based on the novel by . . ."

WIATER: All things considered, it must be nice to keep selling just the *title* of a book and continue to get paid for it.

BRANDNER: Well, Brian Garfield has been doing that since he wrote *Death Wish*. And look at Bob Bloch and the *Psycho* films. There's no feeling of artistic accomplishment, but what the heck, by then you're just doing it for the money anyway, I suppose.

WIATER: So it doesn't appear to bother you that the movie sequels appear to be getting progressively worse? Because weren't they originally responsible for allowing you to work as a screenwriter?

BRANDNER: Yes, when the first one came out, it gave me an identifiable credit in the industry—although my connection with the movie was minimal. As for the sequels, it's kind of embarrassing. I *don't* run the videotapes for my friends! But I don't know—I'm a commercial writer, and I got well paid for the rights to them. And actually, in *Howling IV*, the producers went back and did a version that was actually closer to the original book than any of the others. If they had only spent a little money, they might have made a fair movie. I can't worry too much about it. It keeps my name up there, and besides, not enough people see these sequels to make me wear a bag over my head.

WIATER: Were you more involved with the film *Cameron's Closet*, based on your novel of the same name?

BRANDNER: Yes, I was pretty involved with this one, doing the screenplay and working with the director, Armand Mastroianni, who was a lot more personable guy than Joe Dante.

WIATER: You visited the set while in production?

BRANDNER: Well, I didn't go on the set, because again I had a book contract I was busy on. Often the writer is just not welcome on the set, though they invited me often. They even said I could have a walk-on part if I wanted to. But I was into the next book by then, and I was too immersed in that to go back to *Cameron's Closet*. But there were considerable changes in the shooting script after my final draft was done—there always are.

WIATER: You seem to take it pretty well, since no matter what your input, you can never be sure what the final results of the film adaptation are going to be.

BRANDNER: I'll tell you, Stan, that's the only way to look at it. The nice thing about it is you get paid a whole lot of money for movie involvement. And they *do* pay well. I hear writers crying all the time about, "They did this to my book, they did that to my book...." Now that's fair, because changes are made. But nobody puts you in a hammerlock and says, "You gotta sell your book to Hollywood or we're going to kill you!" These producers are making a movie, and a movie is *not* a book. They try to do what they think will be successful, and if it isn't, then you can go out and get drunk, cry, raise hell with the other writers. But in the long run, you *did* sell it, so just mellow out and take it!

WIATER: You wrote successfully in other genres before turning to this one. How seriously do you take horror?

BRANDNER: I take it pretty seriously. I don't mind being called a horror writer. Dean Koontz, I know, has his problems with being known as one. And I like to *read* horror—always have. I can't possibly enjoy writing something I don't enjoy reading, otherwise I would be a very rich and famous writer of romances by now! I enjoy it when I scare somebody with what I've written.

WIATER: When you're in the midst of a story, do you have to be actually frightened by what you're writing to make it truly successful?

BRANDNER: Yes, it works best if I can scare myself. When I was writing *Cameron's Closet*, I used the closet right across from my office room here as a model. And I kept looking over there when I was writing the scarier parts, and would hear these strange noises from in there! And if I can do *that* to myself, then I figure the writing is going well.

WIATER: Do you have any belief in the occult or the supernatural, or is it all purely academic research to you?

BRANDNER: I'd have to say it's mostly research, though when I'm really involved in a story, then I really *believe* in the subject while I'm writing. If I'm writing about werewolves, then I believe at the time in werewolves. I would have to say I can't absolutely deny the possibility of anything.

WIATER: I'm aware that you use a word processor, and work at it daily, from nine to five. Do you print out drafts and edit them as you go along?

BRANDNER: I do it all in the word processor, but it still winds up as three drafts. I do the first draft as fast as I can—I don't slow down so that I can put everything in. Then I clean it up somewhat and correct any errors in the second draft, and then the third draft is where I really polish it up. I don't print it out until I'm ready to mail it.

WIATER: Of your novels, are there any in particular that you would recommend to somebody reading you for the first time?

BRANDNER: Let's see. *Floater*, which I think is my best book to date. *Carrion* is a personal favorite of mine. And probably *The Howling III*. I think it was the best-written book of that entire series. It was not a direct sequel to the others, but only alluded to them before going off on a story of its own.

WIATER: Let me get you into the ongoing debate as to which is more effective in horror fiction—to be subtle and "quiet" or explicit and "loud" in tone. What's your approach to creating truly frightening scenes?

BRANDNER: I would have to say I'm somewhere in the middle. I like a good, generous helping of gore. I know about Charlie Grant's feelings on the subject; but I do like my horror a little more scary outwardly than he does. I think horror should be *horror*! so give me some gore [*laughs*]! I'm not sure if you're familiar with Richard Laymon? He's a good friend. He recently wrote a response to Grant in one of the small-press publications. And he's a bit gorier than *I* am. So I tend to lean more toward his side than Grant's.

WIATER: You're known for your powerful portrayals of demons and supernatural creatures. For example, the dogs in your recent novella *Damntown* are as memorable as any of the human characters. Do you recall why you made them an underlying theme of fear?

BRANDNER: At the time I was working on the first draft in 1981, I was living in a kind of seedy Los Angeles neighborhood. And there was this pack of loose dogs running around, terrorizing people. If I had somebody over to my apartment, I would have to walk them back to their car with a stick in my hand. They were on the mind at the time I started to write the story, so I wrote them into it. I personally am very fond of dogs, but this pack of apparently abandoned dogs was simply *mean*.

WIATER: What do you think of the people who say there's no redeeming value or message in horror, no matter what the medium?

BRANDNER: Oh, I have no sympathy at all for that kind of people [*groans*]! It's censorship that they're finally talking about, and I'm absolutely opposed to that. I think they're just a bunch of silly wimps.

WIATER: Then what do you think *is* the point of writing horror fiction, as there will always be those who can't see any entertainment value in what you're trying to do?

BRANDNER: First of all, scaring people *is* entertaining them. Fear is a powerful, visceral, and perversely *fun* kind of emotion. Especially if you know you can get out of the frightening situation just by closing the book or walking out of the theater. But those people who worry about "redeeming social values," well, they're just not my kind of people anyway. I don't care what they think.

WIATER: Critics also like to claim that the current popularity of horror is just a cycle—that it's eventually going to wane and fade away, then come back again in another temporary surge.

BRANDNER: I've been asked that question before. I think the core of good horror writers will always be there, and those who aren't any good will drop out. There's been a lot of bad horror novels on the market since it became really popular, but those writers don't last who can't do it well. I'm sure horror will maintain its popularity.

I write horror because, careerwise, this is what readers want from me. But from book to book I try to expand the boundaries so that, by keeping the core of horror there, I can go a little bit farther. Get closer to the mainstream, by expanding the definition of what "Horror" is. So being introduced as a horror writer just tickles me to death!

Ramsey Campbell

A simple question to ask: Just who is Ramsey Campbell?

For starters, *Publishers Weekly* has called Ramsey Campbell "a horror writer's horror writer." At age eighteen, his first collection of stories, *The Inhabitant of the Lake and Less Welcome Tenants*, was published by August Derleth's legendary Arkham House. Born in Liverpool on January 4, 1946, Campbell has these spare lines of biography currently placed by his American hardcover publisher in each of his books: "Ramsey Campbell has won more awards for his horror fiction than any other living writer. He lives in England." Along with the British Fantasy Award, many of these awards are the Howards (named after H. P. Lovecraft, who just happens to be the author Campbell was pastiching in his initial collection), awarded at the annual World Fantasy Convention.

Among the many books that Campbell has seen published over the past twenty years are the novels *The Doll Who Ate His Mother, The Parasite, Incarnate, Obsession, The Hungry Moon*, and his most recent, *Ancient Images*. Short story collections include 1973's ground-breaking *Demons by Daylight*, as well as *The Height of the Scream, Dark Companions*, and *Cold Print*. (The last a reprinting of many of the Cthulhu Mythos stories originally published in the long-out-of-print *The Inhabitant of the Lake*.) His anthologies include *The Gruesome*

Book, which Campbell specifically intended for younger readers, in that some of the stories are the very same ones that terrified *him* as a child.

Besides his numerous award-winning short stories, Campbell is perhaps best known for a short novel with the innocuous title *The Face That Must Die*. Originally published as a heavily edited paperback original in England in 1979, the book remained unpublished in the United States primarily owing to the fact that its subject matter was so unrelentingly grim and downbeat that none of the major publishers believed it had any possible chance for commercial success. Specialty publisher Scream/Press then brought out a limited hardcover edition in 1983, restoring the deleted text and including an incredibly revealing autobiographical essay by Campbell. One critic termed it "probably the most disturbing piece of non-fiction that I have ever read. If there was such a thing as a Petri dish for the breeding of horror writers, then his childhood would be the model."

Yet in spite of having—by most accepted standards—an undeniably warped childhood, one will always find Ramsey Campbell to be as cheerful and normal as any of the other dark dreamers.

Of course.

WIATER: Sex is something which is seemingly rarely discussed in horror fiction. Yet one of your recent collections has a deceptive title, when you really think about it.
CAMPBELL: Scream/Press first published a volume of all my erotic-horror stories. And its title—which I don't take any responsibility for!—is *Scared Stiff* [*laughs*]. I shouldn't say it's *all* my erotic-horror short stories; it's actually a group of stories that have been published in England but were never published in America. Now you could technically regard "Again" as an erotic-horror story, I suppose, but that's more of a horror story on an erotic *theme*. The erotica is much stronger in these stories; it's more central. And two of the stories in it have never been published before, anywhere.
WIATER: As you're well aware, there are numerous Stephen King imitators out there in the marketplace. Yet in spite of your prominence in the field, there doesn't seem to be any obvious Ramsey Campbell imitators. How do you feel about that?
CAMPBELL: Fine! Fine! I don't want any competition with myself—

why are you asking me such a question [*laughs*]! No, I suppose there aren't any *direct* imitations, though I think there are folk who have taken bits and pieces. Now, I hope he's not going to come after me when he reads this, but I thought Doug Winter's "Masks" in Charlie Grant's *Midnight* anthology read very oddly like a collaboration between me and Stephen King! There are elements in it where I thought that *I* would have done it that way, at any rate. I think there was some influence during the period of *Demons by Daylight*, though I suspect a lot of writers said, "Well, why isn't he writing the way he was in *The Inhabitant of the Lake*?" I do occasionally think that people feel a little bit cheated because the next book is not quite like the one I wrote before. As far as I'm concerned, the whole business of writing is a process of trying to do things you didn't do last time! Of trying to get *right* what you didn't do last time. I've been progressing in various directions of late. I mean, *Obsession* probably didn't read very much like the stories in *Demons by Daylight* at all!

WIATER: So true. With *Obsession*, if it had been written under a pseudonym, it might have not been readily recognized as being one of your novels. Yet 1983's *The Night of the Claw* was not only immediately recognizable as your work, it was also published under the most obvious pseudonym imaginable: "Jay Ramsey." Why?

CAMPBELL: Macmillan had bought several books—*The Parasite, The Nameless, Dark Companions*—so it seemed reasonable to give them some breathing space. As it happened, Macmillan didn't publish my other books as quickly as I'd anticipated, and I could have published *Incarnate* as well at the time without putting *Claw* out under a pseudonym. It was simply that.

WIATER: You made your initial reputation as a writer of short stories, yet now work primarily as a novelist. Is it any easier to write successful horror novels than it is short stories?

CAMPBELL: It's certainly easier writing novels *now* than it was when I first started; I'd rather write a novel than a short story these days. I suppose *The Nameless* was the point of transition when I got it together. Since then, I've gotten control of the technique of writing a novel. Now I don't tend to have a preconceived plot, whereas before, even with a short story, I would have a pretty clear idea of its structure and point of view. But I was a bit afraid of finding myself halfway through a novel and discovering I didn't know where the hell I was going next! Of course, that does happen, but I now find it interesting simply to find out where the novel is going. I mean, novels actually *do* go on their own momentum, and really build their own structures. I think if you can take that risk of not conceiving everything in advance, the novel actually becomes very organic, and I find that very satisfying. Short stories are something I do in-between novels now.

WIATER: When we first met several years ago, you were writing everything out in longhand. Any chance you've purchased your first word processor since then?

CAMPBELL: I've been using one from *The Influence* onward. But I always write in longhand first—I write on the right-hand side of a notebook, you see. I leave the left side blank so I can revise there. The main revision is then done on the keyboard. I actually *do* get into an entirely different frame of mind when I'm typing fiction. Anyway, with immense delight I then start hacking out great chunks of the book, throwing away days of work, which is one of the great pleasures of writing [*laughs*]!

We live in a very big house now, and I have a room that faces the dawn, with a view across the river to Liverpool. So I go up there at about seven A.M. with a large pot of tea which wakes me up, and I get on with it, basically. It goes on to about noon, even later sometimes. I do that seven days a week with any work of fiction until it's finished.

WIATER: Your work is highly respected in the States. But is the critical reaction to horror fiction any different in your native country?

CAMPBELL: No, not on the whole. But in a larger sense, horror fiction doesn't get much criticism; that is, it doesn't get much *notice* at all in England. Largely because—as is the case with most genres—you're actually competing with the worst in the field. You're all sort of stuck together there on the bookstore shelf. I'm inclined to favor the American method, where it's usually just there amidst the rest of the fiction. In England, you tend in the larger stores to find a "Horror" shelf. Which means you have a Clive Barker, and Straub, and King, and Robert Aickman, alongside *Slugs* and *Crabs* and *Pus*. And they're all competing with each other in terms of packaging as well, to some extent. Unfortunately, book distribution in England is largely in the hands of only two distributors, and if you don't get them, you don't get anywhere!

WIATER: I've heard of bookstores in England being raided from time to time, with horror literature being pulled along with the so-called pornographic material. Did you ever have censorship problems with your own work?

CAMPBELL: Well, *The Face That Must Die* certainly had problems at the outset. People said it was too grim, and too relentless. Eventually Star Books published it, but in a truncated version. I think publishers were particularly disconcerted with the way the book came on at the outset—it hits the reader at once instead of guiding him in a little bit.

So I perhaps wouldn't do it quite that way now. On the other hand, I don't think if I were to make the characters more palatable that that would in any way improve the book. I think it's least successful when it's trying to be a conventional thriller. And to make the victims more sympathetic . . . it's probably not in any way relevant to what the book is about. But now that people are reading it, I'll stand by how I did it in the first place.

WIATER: Recently I reread some of your work and was surprised how in several instances it has been revised. That's certainly uncommon, isn't it?

CAMPBELL: Well, John Brunner's done it, and Robert Silverberg has, hasn't he? But usually my revisions are very minor, just matters of style—a sentence will later look kind of clumsy to me, and I'll try and tighten it up a bit. Several of the stories in *Dark Companions* were lightly revised. The story "The Companion," for instance, comes on a bit too strong at the start, and it's overwritten in the first few opening pages, so I did try and tone that down a little bit. With *The Face That Must Die* I took out one chapter from the protagonist's point of view, but that was my decision. Star Books also took out several paragraphs that were nearly all from the viewpoint of Horridge. They tended to be these strange convoluted puns that he made to himself, that I really felt were part of the character. So I put them back in when the restored version came out. With the American paperbacks of *The Doll Who Ate His Mother*, *The Nameless*, and *The Parasite*, it was a case of writing alternative chapters because I didn't think the chapters in the original versions really quite worked. It was simply a question of trying to improve them.

WIATER: What advice would you give to someone who is a devout fan of the genre and thinks he may have it in him or her to write it as well? Are they in a sense "born" to write horror?

CAMPBELL: Well, if you read it, you presumably *have* got a feeling for the genre, and to that extent you probably are born to it. So if you have a sensitivity toward the field—put it this way, you don't have to have had a childhood like mine to write horror fiction! Clive Barker had a perfectly normal childhood—so he tells me. Well, you can believe *him* if you like!

WIATER: You've just brought up the point about the importance one's childhood plays in terms of being "born to write horror." Without making too much of the cliche, the introduction to the restored *The Face That Must Die* revealed a most disquieting skeleton in your closet, didn't it?

CAMPBELL: Hmm... there must be a few others like myself, though they may all be just like Clive Barker. I suspect M. R. James was a pretty normal guy.... On the other hand, people like Robert Aickman had a very strange childhood.

WIATER: From past interviews, I recall that you had more or less concocted a typical writer's childhood for those who asked you the terribly clichéd, "Did you have a warped childhood?" as the reason for becoming a horror writer. Why did you finally tell the world, "Yes, I genuinely did have a warped childhood?"

CAMPBELL: For a variety of reasons. Perhaps the obvious one is that I was able to talk about it at last once my mother died. It was also to put the novel into a kind of context because a lot of people had said, "How could you *write* such a book?" Initially it was meant only for the hard-core fan, because the introduction was first published in a small-press book, and I didn't consider at the time that my American paperback publisher, Tor Books, would ever do this terrific paperback edition. I mean, to see it in places like Ralph's Supermarket—my God! So a lot of people are going to be in for a strange experience when they take this home and think it's another slasher novel, I tell you!

Seriously, I wrote it because I was about to talk about my childhood at last, really. It was the most difficult thing I ever wrote, but I think it was worth writing.

WIATER: In terms of twenty/twenty hindsight, that introduction certainly sheds a whole new light on much of the purposely oblique, always shifting "shadows" that are a trademark of your writing.

CAMPBELL: Yes, to that extent, I thought it was the legitimate thing to do—to give people that insight. If I didn't do it, nobody *else* was going to do it, so there you go.

WIATER: But critics have always referred to you as an exceedingly "grim" writer, haven't they? In a much reprinted blurb, your friend and colleague Peter Straub has stated that "The world Ramsey Campbell takes for granted is the world of our darkest nightmares."

CAMPBELL: [*in a monster's voice*] Aggh! You should meet me as a human being! But it's strange, isn't it? I suppose I'm able to go into the darkness inside my head, going into those corners where these things are always creeping out. [*pauses*] It's funny; I suppose you're right...! But a lot of my grimness is simply as a sort of social commentary—in *The Nameless*, for example, if you take out all the mention of noise pollution, and how terrible it is to live in the city, you actually take out a large support of the plot.

WIATER: It's obvious that the style of fiction you're known for is not usually attempted by the writers of such novels as *Crabs* and *Slugs* and *Pus*. Of course, a great deal of your work could be classified by what Charles L. Grant terms *quiet horror*; it's low-key, suggestive, and understated. Is that something you consciously prefer?

CAMPBELL: I think that quiet horror—subtlety—is a great thing, though I think it can coexist with other styles. It certainly shows up in my work. I think what Charlie is up to is more that classic principle of showing just enough in order to suggest a great deal more. It's common to Lovecraft, to Machen, to Aickman, and a whole lot of good people in this field. I mean, there are two completely different kinds of horror: first, the "technicolor" kind of horror, and the other is the sort of grainy black-and-white kind. Like those old Val Lewton films, which Charlie takes as his ideal. Mine too! Lewton's films were quite wonderful and have never been equaled.

WIATER: Does that mean you occasionally censor your own work, to keep it from becoming too overtly gruesome?

CAMPBELL: No, no! I certainly don't say, "This is too gruesome." I don't often say, "This isn't gruesome enough!" because I usually hit it first time around, as far as I'm concerned. I'm much more likely to think to myself, "Oh, that's hideous! My God! Let's put *that* in!" I get very delighted when I create something that's pretty terrible.

WIATER: When you're working as an anthologist, what critical standards do you go by?

CAMPBELL: Only that it should *disturb* me in some way—that's what I like to find. Or somehow astonish me.

WIATER: Are there any writers who can still scare you?

CAMPBELL: Oh, yes! Robert Aickman, for a start. Things that he wrote have stayed with me for days; he is the writer in the field who I most reread. I'm always learning something new the next time around. But Stephen King, of course—I'll always remember that scene in Room 217 in *The Shining*. And Straub. Or Fritz Leiber, who often still instills that sense of awe in me. I suppose I look for that more than anything else in a writer. On the other hand, I quite like gory horror movies, but on an entirely different level of course. There it's more for the particular magic of the cinema—"My God, how did they get that spike through his head! Was it a cheap extra or something? [*laughs*]"

WIATER: You're one of the few authors who has ever been specifically asked to put together an anthology of "stories that scared me."

CAMPBELL: Well, my title was *Stories That Scared Me*. But they've put *Fine Frights* above that. My ambition for the book was that, for any given reader, fifty percent of the contents are going to be unfamiliar,

so it should still prove interesting. I mean, there's a hitherto unpublished story in there by David Case that was so bleak nobody else would touch it! And there's a another story in there which I read, thirty years ago at least, called "Child's Play," and which I think is possibly the most horrifying story I ever read, but which is now totally obscure to the general public.
WIATER: To use that old metaphor: How deep is the well from which you've been drawing for your work? Do you think you've got a long way to go before you run out of fabulous ideas?
CAMPBELL: Well—pretty good ideas, anyway! I certainly feel, though, when I gasp my last gasp there's going to be notebooks full of ideas that maybe somebody else will want to write. The one problem I don't have as a writer is a paucity of ideas.
WIATER: Finally, I'd like to have your reaction to the blurb from *Publishers Weekly* which terms you "a horror writer's horror writer."
CAMPBELL: Fine! Fine! But not only a horror writer's horror writer, but hopefully a *reader's* horror writer as well.... But, really, I don't know what that means! *I* didn't write it, I didn't write it [*laughs*]! But to be serious, when I was writing *Demons by Daylight*, I really did have an enormous sort of vulnerable sense that I was doing something that nobody else has done before. Whether this is true I'm not at all certain, but I certainly thought I was going out on a limb, that "God, nobody's going to like this!" Because I was picking up fiction by others and saying to myself, "This isn't how you do it—but maybe I'm getting it wrong because these guys are doing it a different way."

When I completed the book and packaged it up for August Derleth, I actually thought that he wasn't going to like it, that he was going to send the manuscript straight back, that it was terrible, that he wasn't going to want to touch it! So to have people say, "We think that you got it right," is just what I needed, basically. What can I say? It appears I must be doing something right.

Les Daniels

Courtesy Les Daniels

If there is anything more unfortunate than an overrated author, it is a talented writer who, so far, has been overlooked. While far from being unknown, Les Daniels has not yet gained wide recognition from the general public despite his steadfast group of fans. Never a prolific author, he has however received his share of critical acclaim, from *Playboy* to *The New York Times*. Simply stated, Daniels knows as much *about* the history of horror in film and literature as he does how to write both fiction and nonfiction *within* it.

Born in 1943, Daniels grew up in Redding, Connecticut. Partly due to his interest in the works of H. P. Lovecraft, he attended Brown University in Providence, Rhode Island. (His master's thesis was on *Frankenstein*.) He has remained in Providence ever since, residing in an unassuming house only a few hundred yards away from the more famous Shunned House in the story of the same name by Lovecraft.

Despite a lifelong interest in horror and the macabre, Daniels's first published book was *Comix: A History of Comic Books in America*. Published in 1971, it was the first book to seriously examine the impact of E. C. Comics and other horror comics in this definitive history of the art form. (Daniels was recently contracted to do the authorized history of Marvel Comics.)

In 1975, his most acclaimed and influential work appeared,

the pioneering study *Living in Fear: A History of Horror in the Mass Media*. *Kirkus Reviews* described it as "A serious, thorough, and amusing survey of Western horror literature. Daniels' familiarity with horror is staggering...." Although sorely in need of a revised edition, it remains to this day the definitive examination on this subject. As a sort of follow-up history of horror in short story form, Daniels then edited a companion volume entitled *Dying of Fright: Masterpieces of the Macabre*. This intensely researched book is considered one of the important anthologies of horror ever compiled, with Daniels supplying copious biographical and bibliographical notes before each entry.

On the other hand, Les Daniels is becoming best known for his continuing series of novels featuring Don Sebastian—vampire. Four have been published since 1978: *The Black Castle, The Silver Skull, Citizen Vampire,* and *Yellow Fog;* a fifth, *No Blood Spilled,* is forthcoming. In each tale, Don Sebastian enters a different period of history, and all too often finds the bloodletting of "normal" men far more terrifying and insane than his own. Daniels is also beginning to write terrific short stories—when Don Sebastian leaves him alone.

WIATER: Since you're such a recognized expert on horror, can you recall your initial exposure to it? It must have been something memorable, to change your life forever.
DANIELS: The earliest influence that I can think of was a book that I had when I was four or five years old, called *Georgie the Ghost*. It was a children's book about a ghost in a haunted house. And it's really not like Casper the Friendly Ghost; it was different, in that he was having a good time being a ghost! It didn't frighten me. There were so *many* influences. I'm old enough to have caught the end of the radio era, in terms of dramatic shows: "The Shadow, "Inner Sanctum," "Suspense." I still collect old radio shows on tape and record because they were an influence on me.

But I also read horror comics, of course, as most kids did during the fifties. And I was very impressed by the E. C. Comics—*Tales from the Crypt, Vault of Horror, The Haunt of Fear*. Everybody says they were influenced by them now, so that it's a cliche—which is why I started with *Georgie the Ghost!*—but I feel I can justify my claim to having been a sincere devotee since I wrote my first book on comics, and included the first E. C. horror reprint in color in about fifteen years.

So my credentials are intact and I can say I read the E. C.s without blushing. Strangely enough, my father—who always gave me a moderately hard time about the fact that I was morbidly interested in all this—used to introduce me to a lot of books in the field. My mother gave me a copy of Lovecraft's *The Outsider* as a high school graduation gift. I don't know how to explain this, even now.

WIATER: You were the first person to actually try to write an entire history of horror in the mass media. Even before the genre's current popularity, this seems like an insane project to take on single-handedly.

DANIELS: It was even more insane than *Comix*, in that it was intended to deal with all fiction, all films, a lot of plays, radio, television. Comics. Rock 'n' roll. *Anything* where there was a strong horror element. Of course I didn't cover every single thing, but it was pretty solid from the dawn of time to the mid-seventies when it came out! It took much too long to write—I had reams of papers and notes all over the place, I was reading constantly, I was trying to catch again all the old movies that I could, and generally driving myself insane. I finally decided to cut it off at *The Exorcist*, because that seemed like a landmark film— there's always a temptation to say, "Wait a minute, something else has just come!" and start writing again. So the book ended at a point just before the current horror boom.

WIATER: Any chance of updating it to the present?

DANIELS: Not really. I mean, you're doing it with these interviews [*laughs*]! So many other people have written so much about the field since, the idea of me doing it wouldn't be unique anymore. I probably won't do it.

WIATER: Completist collectors of Les Daniels might want to know something about your most "obscure" title, *Thirteen Tales of Terror* (1977).

DANIELS: It's a book of mine that even my most rabid fans are least familiar with. Scribner's had been doing a series of paperback anthologies for high schools on the premise that since they had difficulty in getting students to read, they might have better luck if they gave them something they were interested in. So they asked me to edit an anthology of horror stories to be used as a textbook. I did it in conjunction with my sister, who was an education professor at Tufts at the time.

She did a workbook which also has my name on it, which *must* be my most obscure work. With questions like, "What does it mean when the creature bores into Ralph's head?" It was all very strange. I enjoyed doing this—there was no reason not to—but I was marking time, too. Because the only things I know about are comics and horror

[*laughs*]...! I think I was trying to build up the strength to write my first novel, which I began working on while doing *Thirteen Tales of Terror*.
WIATER: That, of course, was *The Black Castle*, a historical vampire story. Where did it have its origins?
DANIELS: It came to me in 1965 or 1966, when I was still in graduate school. I was reading a lot of gothic novels at the time and I wanted to write my master's thesis on horror fiction in general—a version of what eventually appeared as *Living in Fear*. This was too massive a project and was squeezed down into writing on Mary Shelley's *Frankenstein*. But I was absorbed by the gothics. I especially liked *The Monk* by Matthew Gregory Lewis, which was lurid and tasteless—and right up my alley.

I'm embarrassed to say some of these things, but I wouldn't lie to you: I had a dream about two characters who essentially were a monk and a vampire. I guess I've always been more interested in the bad guys than the good guys. Instead of the usual good versus evil conflict, I thought it would be more interesting to have two fairly rotten people jockeying for position. Using it as a way to try to decide which sort of evil was actually more of a menace; usually the vampire is set up as a boogeyman character, and this is the source of all of our problems. Whereas I feel that even if there were such creatures—or whatever sort of aberrant social behavior we have such as Jack the Ripper or Charles Manson—as awful as they may be, they really don't cause as much trouble as the socially acceptable, institutionalized forms of cruelty, evil, and intolerance.
WIATER: So you always saw Don Sebastian, a bloodsucking creature of the undead, as inevitably the "lesser of two evils"?
DANIELS: I had the idea, even back then, that the vampire—without being whitewashed in any way—could be the hero by being a sort of antiestablishment character. But I didn't have the strength or the intelligence to write the book at the time. Then, when I decided I would have to write a novel if I wanted to keep writing, that resurfaced as the book that came out as *The Black Castle*. But the first novel was meant to stand on its own. I had no intention of writing another one with this character. But immediately thereafter, I again had the problem of *What am I going to do*?
WIATER: So you decided to satisfy your fans by continuing the nocturnal adventures of Don Sebastian. One noticeable aspect of your work is that practically all of your characters exist in varying degrees of gray—or black.
DANIELS: Who are the good guys and who are the bad? This goes back

to some of the horror fiction I read as a kid, which is different from much of what you get today. But this is what I wanted to do, partly for the philosophical reason of examining the nature of evil. And thinking, which *is* evil? Is it a supposedly supernatural force? Or just the way people behave?

WIATER: You're one of the few dark dreamers who is apparently more comfortable creating historical horror novels, with no obvious hero. That is certainly going against the tide of most of those working in the genre today, don't you think?

DANIELS: I find that almost all the books which have been coming out for the last few years are written with a very deliberate hero and/or heroine in mind. People I usually think of as "Betty and Bob," who are the wonderful folks who live in the suburbs, and are a cute couple, and have a kid. And something *bad* is going to happen to them! And the book is usually about how Betty and Bob managed to overcome "it." Sometimes only Betty manages to overcome "it." Sometimes only Bob . . . But I find that much less interesting to me—I want to get in and deal with the parts that are frightening. Having these sort of TV-style "nice folks" taking up the bulk of the book, and for me to be expected to really worry about them . . . !

WIATER: Yet your work has always been highly acclaimed, even if you've yet to achieve best-seller status. Especially within the "hardcore" horror community of serious readers and fans.

DANIELS: Maybe they're all polite, but from other writers I've had an awfully good response. Perhaps because of the lack of "Betty and Bob" material, or my variations on traditional approaches, my work appeals more to other writers—or to people who are specially interested in the field, as opposed to the general public. Because in some sense my novels are less accessible as they're not very warmhearted or they're set in the past—which may be confusing to some average readers who don't remember anything that happened before 1988!

WIATER: In spite of the gruesome scenes described in your novels, your style is generally considered both highly literate and, dare I say, tastefully rendered.

DANIELS: I don't know how I do that. My policy is "Nothing succeeds like excess." There is *nothing* one shouldn't be allowed to do in fiction. But in practice, it's worked out in strange ways. I often think I'm writing something that's outrageous and offensive because I'm dwelling on it at such length. It may take me an hour to write a paragraph that someone else will read in seven seconds. I *like* lurid, flamboyant, melodramatic horror. It's great fun. Maybe in the screenplays I've written that haven't been produced, what I was doing would have been considered excessive. Not because it was really any different, but people reading books sometimes just glibly pass over things that, if they actually saw them, would be too outrageous. But I'm in favor of outlandishness and bad taste. I haven't had too much trouble with publishers, though.

But it's funny—in terms of taste and what you should be allowed to do. I find that the one thing above all else which distinguishes the modern horror novel from what went before—in virtually every recent novel I've read—is that whenever a character is terrified, he or she immediately proceeds to wet his or her pants. And this seems to be the big "breakthrough" that modern horror has achieved. I'm thinking seriously of writing a novel about a small town, isolated, where you can tell that something has gone terribly wrong . . . because everyone is walking around with wet pants.

WIATER: In spite of that unlikely scenario, you take the craft of horror fiction extremely seriously.

DANIELS: [*pauses*] I'm writing out of the Poe–Lovecraft tradition in the sense of being someone who's not necessarily expecting to make huge amounts of money, or is writing for huge amounts of money. But writing because this is either what I want to do, or am "doomed" to do. I don't think I'm on a bandwagon. I started working in this field before the big breakthrough of the seventies came, and I imagine I'll be here even if it dies down.

WIATER: Your own creation notwithstanding, there are also vampire series from several other talented authors, including Anne Rice and Chelsea Quinn Yarbro. Why is there such a continued fascination with this theme, no matter what the approach?

DANIELS: The theory in the past, when these stories were popular in the Victorian era and afterward, was that there were a lot of sexual symbolism and sexual metaphors of people creeping into each other's rooms and doing things to one another. Although there's still some of that, vampires now relate more directly to the immortality concept. The idea that people have of maintaining their bodies forever, which is now part of our public consciousness in weird, desperate ways such as diets and exercise. People assume if they do these things, they will somehow cheat death. I think the appeal of vampires today has something to do with that idea.

My vampire characters *do* pay a price to be vampires. And part of that price is that they are predators. I suppose that's a more traditional approach. I'm ambivalent as to whether they're "admirable" or not—they always have a cruel and inhuman streak in addition to the advantages they obviously possess. The one advantage that interests me the most is not just extending their current life, but the idea that, by being a vampire, they have acquired mystical knowledge about the meaning of life and death, and the beyond, and the secrets of the universe. That's very attractive to me, though it's still sort of a Faustian theme the way my vampires are paying for this. They are suffering, and they are causing suffering, in order to maintain their existence.

WIATER: Do you truly believe that people are basically evil, rather than good?

DANIELS: I do have a tendency to believe that in the abstract. It's strange, because I generally *like* people, when I'm dealing with my own life. But as a philosophical concept, looking at the parade of history so to speak, it's not very encouraging.

WIATER: You're clearly not what some people would consider a prolific author, though that word is an undeniably relative term. My question is, do you enjoy writing, or prefer having written?

DANIELS: I never have reached a point where I get up the next morning and say, "Oh, boy, time to write!" [*laughs*] I really have to drag myself over to the typewriter; the pressure to do well intimidates me in getting there.

WIATER: Can you describe a typical workday?

DANIELS: A "typical workday" is mostly conducted at night. I live on an odd schedule, which I guess other horror writers have done—Sheridan Le Fanu and Lovecraft—but I'm not really doing it to imitate them or be affected. I usually spend the day doing research, going to the library, and reading. By midnight, except on occasions when something colorful comes up, there usually isn't much for me to do, and there's fewer distractions, so that's a good time for me to get started. I sometimes go on even to dawn. It helps for me to know that I have a project, and that somebody is waiting for me to finish it. I'm not one of those writers who has twenty books in a drawer that I wrote for the fun of it, hoping that someday maybe somebody would want them.

WIATER: Is there anything besides the skill of creating frightening situations which clearly sets horror writers apart from everyone else? In other words, can you as a professional writer of fear be "happy" in the usual sense of the word?

DANIELS: I think so. I mean, I write more or less instinctively—I try to write books that I would read if I hadn't written them. I don't have any list of rules or anything of that kind. I'm really happy in the sense that I'm doing approximately what I wanted to do in my youth: I *am* writing horror novels and stories, and they *are* being published. I'm at least flirting with the film industry. This is, in a way, a dream come true. I wouldn't be at all hurt if I became fabulously successful at it, which I haven't yet. But I'm still having a good time.

WIATER: In other words, you'll continue to actively explore the genre, no matter what.

DANIELS: Whatever is wrong that makes me this way—I have a fairly solid commitment to it [*laughs*]. In *Living in Fear*, I think I called it partially a "left-handed religious impulse"; that there is some fascination with mortality and death which is a major issue—unless either by being deeply religious or an atheist one knows precisely what is going to happen after death—that is a topic worthy of concern. I don't claim to be giving any pat answers, but there is a fascination that makes me want to speculate on it. This is part of what keeps me going.

And just to realize it's possible to "knock somebody's socks off" with stories about this subject inspires me. I don't know if it's the kind of inspiration that most people would be glad to have, but I assume a certain number of people who are reading this interview will relate to what I'm saying.

WIATER: But does this "impulse" indicate any personal beliefs in the supernatural or the occult?

DANIELS: I don't know if there really is a supernatural, but I just *love* to toy with it. As I said earlier, you also get opportunities to deal with moral questions of "What is Good and Evil?" as well as "What is death?" I don't think I'm dealing with these in the manner of a great philosopher or religious leader—or anything even close to that. But in my own way these subjects interest me and I deal with them as best I can, and try to be entertaining.

I find that I entertain myself: At three o'clock in the morning, I'm pounding away on the typewriter and having a hell of a time. So I keep doing it.

Dennis Etchison

Anne Knudsen, L.A. Herald Examiner

Although primarily known for his award-winning tales of dark fantasy, Dennis Etchison has had more than his share of "horror stories" as a professional writer. Until a few years ago, the man *Publishers Weekly* termed capable of "the state of the art in modern horror" was perhaps the best-kept secret in the field. The difficulties he's had in getting his career to its present state of widespread acceptance would have broken a lesser talent. Examples: His first collection of short stories, *The Night of the Eye*, never went beyond the cover proof; the publisher, Powell Books, went bankrupt as the book was going to press. When his novelization of John Carpenter's 1980 film *The Fog* was published in England, his name was misspelled as Etchinson. (He went on to write three other novelizations as "Jack Martin.") Then his first serious attempt at a novel, *The Shudder*, was shelved after more than two years of rewriting and editing for its intended publisher.

Regardless, Etchison has spent the last twenty-five years steadily carving out an enviable reputation with his short fiction, finding regular acceptance in such notable anthologies as *Whispers* and *The Year's Best Horror Stories*. (And winning numerous awards—the very first with an essay at age twelve.) Finally, with the publication in 1982 of his critically acclaimed collection *The Dark Country*, Etchison had undeniably arrived. Since *The Dark Country*, two more collections—*Red Dreams* and *The Blood Kiss*—have appeared in hardcover from Scream/Press. (Yet another is forthcoming in France.) His first novel—one not a novelization or written under a pseudonym—entitled *Darkside* was published in 1986 by Berkley Books. He has also edited five anthologies, including *Cutting Edge* and the three-volume *Masters of Darkness*. More short stories, in various anthologies, are also forthcoming.

Etchison, who was born in Stockton, California, on March 30, 1943, is also constantly at work as a screenwriter on several film projects. He is a writer who is perhaps best known in some circles for the motion picture work he has done, but which no one, beyond a few Hollywood producers, has ever been privileged to see. Indeed, his feature adaptation of Stephen King's novella *The Mist* was eventually released, not as a movie, but as a dramatized audiotape. Anyone meeting with him will find a cautious yet eloquent conversationalist, with the look and manner of a born survivor. In spite of a soft-spoken manner, Etchison appears to be born to do a job that few others would willingly choose to do.

WIATER: Knowing of your past frustrations in Hollywood, why are you still writing scripts? We understand you were even a staff writer for "The Hitchhiker" cable television series for a time, though none of your own stories was ever adapted.
ETCHISON: My greatest interest since the age of ten has been to direct movies. Writing has always been of considerably less interest to me—though I take it very, very seriously. And it seems the best way to have a shot at directing is through screenwriting. I *love* movies, which is one of the reasons why I remain a resident of Los Angeles. Incidentally, even though I found myself in the horror field sort of by accident, I just want to state that although in the past I may have given the impression that I don't really consider myself a "horror writer," that my interests "are much greater than that" and all the rest of it, I'm profoundly grateful to the field for having offered me a platform I couldn't find elsewhere. I'm deeply indebted to it.
WIATER: Fair enough. Even so, is that primarily why you became involved with novelizations for *The Fog*, *Halloween II*, *Halloween III* for John Carpenter, and *Videodrome* for David Cronenberg—because you so admire their work?
ETCHISON: That's right; I turned down a lot of other offers. I was very

pleased when John Carpenter asked me to do one because I very much wanted to meet him and work with him. In most cases, novelizers don't work with the filmmakers; in many cases they don't even *see* the film— they're only working from an early script. I worked on that novelization while viewing dailies and various versions of the edited picture in postproduction. The same thing happened with *Halloween II* and *Halloween III*. Then the opportunity to do *Videodrome* had a powerful appeal. I think Cronenberg's as intelligent as anyone working in the film industry today, either in or out of the genre. I was able to go to Toronto and view the film in various stages, and talk to him at length about it. It was a delightful opportunity, but basically I don't see myself doing any more novelizations. I did the very best I could with them, and in many ways they're more than "just" novelizations—at least in my mind.

WIATER: Early in your career, you were beginning to establish yourself as a science fiction writer, as indicated by your appearances in *The Magazine of Fantasy & Science Fiction, Fantastic, Orbit*, and so forth. Now you're best known as a horror writer. Whatever happened to those early science fiction stories?

ETCHISON: Those stories appear throughout the three collections I've published to date. They're "soft" science fiction rather than "hard" or high-tech, but they are science fiction stories. I simply found that the market had changed as time went on. My writing remained the same in its premises, but I was forced to seek new outlets. I think my writing is all of a piece—it's just the markets seem to change. I discuss this in detail in my introduction to *Cutting Edge*. I basically never set out to be a science fiction writer or any other kind of a writer. I just considered myself a writer. But because I grew up on science fiction and loved it so much, I did write a number of science fiction stories. I still do— only no one seems to notice! But I also wrote "mainstream" stories and "weird/dark" stories. It just so happened that the markets in the science fiction field changed, and at the same time the renaissance in the horror and dark-fantasy field happened. And so I found myself received much more warmly there. But these are really marketing definitions; I don't think they truly describe the nature of my work. The problem is with critical and commercial *boundaries*, not with quality or content.

WIATER: True enough; so what do you feel is so special about the anthologies you've edited?

ETCHISON: In *Masters of Darkness*, I asked authors to pick personal favorites of theirs in the area of dark fantasy, and to write an afterword to each story. What was particularly interesting to me was what happened when I asked for contributions from writers who are more closely associated with science fiction than they are horror. Because, as I stated in the introduction, it seems to me that no serious writer's work can fall easily into one camp or another. Many of the writers—such as Joe Haldeman or Damon Knight or George R. R. Martin or Jack Dann—are most commonly thought of as science fiction writers. Whereas they have all written a number of very dark and disturbing stories which very easily could have been published in the horror field. I'm not concerned with furthering the genrification of literature—I'm much rather break down the barriers between the genres. That's the way *my* career has always been—I've never considered myself a member of just one camp. This philosophy applies to *Cutting Edge* as well, because I don't see any advantage now to continuing these barriers. I want to encourage a new openness and lack of prejudice with the reader.

I've also edited an anthology for Lord John Press, which is probably the most distinguished specialty press in America, outside of the genre. It publishes signed, limited editions of authors like John Updike and John Cheever, Joyce Carol Oates—the major names in American letters. And they've never done anything connected with the genre. The anthology, called *Lord John Ten*, is not in the genre either; it's the tenth anniversary of the press, and includes those major literary names like Updike, but also new stories by Whitley Strieber and Jack Dann. It's an eclectic collection that spans mainstream literature as well as some of the finest representatives of our field.

WIATER: Tell me a little about your earliest influences as a child.

ETCHISON: When I was ten I read "An Occurrence at Owl Creek Bridge" by Ambrose Bierce. *That* had a powerful effect on me. When I was eleven, I began reading Ray Bradbury, which produced an incomparable, life-changing result. And Bradbury led me into reading Richard Matheson, Charles Beaumont, A. E. Van Vogt, and a number of wonderful science fiction writers. Of course those were the 1950s, when science fiction was happening; it was a growing field. . . .

WIATER: I understand that you were once a student under the late, great Charles Beaumont.

ETCHISON: Well, being such a great fan of Beaumont, I was struck to see his name in the UCLA Extension catalog in 1963 as the teacher of a workshop for science fiction. I immediately signed up for the course, and spent ten weeks—one night a week—listening to him teach. It was a wonderful experience. I spoke to him after each class, and he would always say, "Some of us are going out for a drink, why don't you join us?" And I had an old car, old clothes, and no money, and I was young and embarrassed, so I turned him down. I didn't realize he was ill then, and within a year after that he was desperately sick, and died four years later of a complicated form of Alzheimer's disease. But he was a great influence on me, especially in the way he brought many writers whom I admired—including Bradbury and Matheson—to speak at the workshop.

Twenty years later, I had opportunity to teach at UCLA Extension myself, and I began with a science fiction, horror, and fantasy workshop. Which in my mind was a continuation of Beaumont's class, and was my way of paying Beaumont back for the class he had taught in 1963. I'm still teaching that class today, and bringing many of those same writers in again to speak, as well as his son Chris—who is now a successful television writer and producer—Richard Christian Matheson, and other representatives of a new generation. In fact, a few years ago I put together a conference entitled "Masters of Darkness," in which several major horror writers appeared.

WIATER: Considering some of the horror stories you've experienced in real life in terms of the publishing and film business, just what *has* kept you going as a writer?

ETCHISON: For one thing, the realization that some of that "bad luck" may have been brought about, unconsciously, by me. It's easy to blame others when you have had luck, but when you stop and analyze what's happened to you, you may realize that it was just as much your fault as the rest of the world's. So that only makes you resolve to not make those mistakes again, and to try a little harder. J. G. Ballard has spoken of life as a search for psychological closure, and Philip K. Dick suggested that we may be unconsciously seeking a kind of stasis or dead end, a corner into which we've painted ourselves and from which there is finally no escape.

This is the most chilling concept I have ever encountered—that our best efforts at growth, self-help, health, and progress may in fact be designed, albeit unconsciously, to achieve quite the opposite: to bring about our own entrapment and defeat. In other words, that what we think we are doing and what we are *actually* doing may be diametrically opposed; that the human animal may be programed for self-defeat on a level that is not accessible to consciousness or mutable by will. Not just that the unconscious may throw up barriers and obstacles, out of some deep-seated conviction that we do not deserve to win, but that the unconscious may ultimately *refuse to allow* our success because it is preprogramed toward a different goal or purpose that we may never know and might not be able to comprehend. I pray to God that this is not true, but you never know.

Also, people who are in the arts like to pontificate that we're doing it out of some deep spiritual commitment... *and we are!!* But we are also doing it because, after a while, it's the only thing left that we can do in the world professionally! I never knew it was going to be as hard as it's turned out to be, but after a certain number of years have passed—and you're still working at your profession—you realize that you had better finish what you started and continue onward. The truth of the matter is: What else is left for you? Also, I love the arts. I really feel *committed* to them, almost in a spiritual sense.

There's a line which Ray Bradbury has quoted over the years: "There are two honorable professions in the world: doctors, because they heal the body, and artists, because they heal the soul." I just love doing this and, if the truth be told, I wouldn't have it any other way.

WIATER: But you've been a published writer since you were in your teens, and only now is the general reading public being made aware of your talents.

ETCHISON: Well, writers are different from other people in one respect: The rewards for our labors are not seen for a long time. Sometimes many years. So we end up learning to operate on faith. "The principle of deferred gratification." Everyone else who has a job receives a paycheck at a regular time; if you're an actor you receive the applause immediately after the performance. A writer will wait months, at the very least, before he receives any kind of feedback. So you learn early on as a writer to go by this principle—of not expecting much in the way of feedback or gratification. So you become toughened and learn to operate solely out of faith. In that sense, it *is* a spiritual profession.

WIATER: But you have no regrets, overall, for the sacrifices you've made to get this far?

ETCHISON: I have plenty of regrets! But it just... *is*. You know? Why wonder if I would ever do it all over again? I never knew what I was doing as I was *doing* it. I was following a path that presented itself to me, and I didn't understand where it was leading me, and I *still* don't understand where it is leading me. But this is *reality*. Whether you like it or not, here we are. You'd damn well better embrace your lot or commit suicide.

There's no other choice.

WIATER: I've heard that you've actually *dreamed* the writing of entire short stories.

ETCHISON: Yes, that's happened several times, and I'd like to know how many other writers have had this experience. If they have, it might be a very good idea for an anthology. Much of my work contains images or details that come from dreams. I even had the peculiar experience of dreaming the typewritten manuscript in two or three cases—I saw the entire story already written out in my dream! Examples include "Time Killer" and "The Night of the Eye," which I saw typed out for me in my dream in manuscript form. I find that fascinating. In fact, I must tell you that my novel *Darkside* originated with a dream I had one night a few years ago in which I dreamed of a Stephen King novel that doesn't really exist; it's never been written. But I dreamed I was involved in a certain kind of suburban paranoia. And I thought to myself as I was dreaming, "If I could just get this all down, it would be a great novel!" As it turned out, it had little to do with that unwritten King novel, though the aspects of a new family in a well-to-do suburban setting being menaced by teenagers comes directly from that dream [*laughs*]. God only knows where this all comes from! Maybe Plato was right. Or Phil Dick, who toyed with the idea that time is running backward and that all this has happened before.

WIATER: Considering you're a past winner of the World Fantasy Award and the British Fantasy Award, what do you think sets your work apart from others working in horror or so-called dark fantasy?

ETCHISON: That's really something for the critics to decide. But at least my readers know that *I'm not kidding*. That I'm serious. As long as you're only trying to fulfill what you perceive are the needs of the marketplace, you're not going to be anything but a hack—even if it's a high-order hack. Those writers who are true artists speak as honestly as possible about their deepest and most passionate concerns. Those who learn the technical skills to do that vividly then are considered exciting and important artists.

I often write about the "unreal," but I'm trying to write about it as *realistically* as possible. That seems to me to be different from what some other writers are doing, who are trying to write about that which is real, but write about it unrealistically. I don't know if there's really a distinction, but I am attempting to write realistically about the unreal. For what it's worth, I'd call myself a Romantic Realist, a term I've coined, if that means anything to you.

WIATER: It's been noted that your work deals predominantly with one's psychological—rather than supernatural—fears and loathings. Can you give us an example of a story directly inspired by a real-life incident?

ETCHISON: Oh, yes! "The Chill" was written after I saw a pair of tennis shoes sitting on the sidewalk, a policeman directing traffic, and a crowd gathering around. I then noticed that there was a huge dent in this car parked at the curb, and then I saw there was a canvas thrown over a body in the gutter. Then somebody told me that a man had jumped off the top of the building—had hit the street so hard that it knocked him out of his tennis shoes—and then the body had bounced on top of the car. The fact that that building was adjacent to a health food store, where I was headed to have lunch, was particularly provocative. The juxtaposition of life and death in that one building . . . ! But just as many stories come out of my dreams, or an experience of looking out a window at something.

It's all part of my memory. Usually I see the entire story flash in front of me in the space of a few seconds. I never know when it's going to happen. But I've trained myself to recognize and hold onto those moments. It may take years to explore that "flash" and nail it to the page in its most perfect form. In a larger sense, we may all be spending our entire lives writing only one story, the finest story we know: one with ourselves as hero rather than victim or archenemy. As D. W. Griffith said, "What you get is a living, what you give is a life." It's up to each of us to try and make it worth reading—or living.

WIATER: You've certainly had your share of highs and lows over the years, though it seems you're at last receiving your due share of success. As a writing instructor, what advice do you give to beginning writers?

ETCHISON: It just seems to me that you don't ever make a conscious decision to be an artist. You either wake up one day and realize that's what you are or you don't. If that's the case, then nothing can stop you from doing it. And if you're not that kind, then no amount of external rules or enforced discipline is going to force you to it. The motivation is internal, and the rewards are personal.

I would also say, *Never give up*. A lot of my students put a story away after only two or three rejections. I once had a story rejected seventy-two times; it took me six and a half years to sell it. But I *did*. It's like going to a party where there are sixty people. You can't expect to please all of them. But if you can just meet the right one, then you can forget the fifty-nine others you never connected with.

John Farris

Courtesy John Farris

Widely recognized as one of the major talents in both horror and dark suspense, John Farris still remains something of a mystery man. Since 1956, his twenty-seven books have twenty million copies in print worldwide, even though he has granted few interviews over the years to promote that work. He is perhaps best known for his 1976 novel, *The Fury*, which was made into a successful motion picture two years later by director Brian De Palma. Some of its success no doubt was due to the fact that Farris adapted his own novel to the screen. Lesser known to the general public is that he also wrote the original screenplay for—and directed—an earlier independent feature, *Dear Dead Delilah* in 1972. (Yet another novel, *When Michael Calls*, became a motion picture for television in 1969. Farris, however, had no direct involvement with that project.)

If it seems that this best-selling novelist has more than a passing interest in filmmaking, you're right. For with the exception of two books, Farris has written screenplays for—or has options on—such popular titles as *Sharp Practice, Shatter, The Uninvited, Nightfall*, and *Son of the Endless Night*. In fact, nearly all of his horror novels and thrillers remain in print. Like Robert Bloch and Richard Matheson, Farris is recognized as an important influence on an entire generation of writers, including his friend Stephen King. Of him, King has said, "In the years of my late adolescence and early adulthood, I did more than just admire his work—I adopted his career as both a goal to be reached and an example to be emulated."

In a career which began in the 1950s with mystery paperback originals, Farris has gone on to be ranked with the very best the genre has to offer with such memorable works as *The Captors, All Heads Turn When the Hunt Goes By* and *Minotaur*. His first collection of short fiction, *Scare Tactics*, was published in 1988 and was later expanded for its paperback edition. His most recent novel, *The Axman Cometh*, in fact began as a short story for that collection.

Born in Missouri, the author-poet-screenwriter-director currently makes his home in Georgia. When I spoke to him, he was simultaneously involved in more projects than most writers would dare to tackle in a lifetime. These include independently producing and directing feature film versions of *Nightfall* and *Shatter*.

And of course writing new novels.

WIATER: You've been writing horror and suspense novels since the 1960s. Have you ever lost interest in exploring the dark side of the human condition?
FARRIS: I'm very interested in what turns on the spigot for the dark side that is in all of us, and starts it flowing. A lot of people go through life without ever experiencing that in themselves; yet others get into situations which cause radical changes in personality. There's apparently an endless supply of situations—as reported in the media. I would be hard-pressed to write anything that would equal the stuff that shows up on television these days. Or to imagine it, really.

I don't know whether it's due to the miracle of modern communication or if there's simply more aberrations cropping up, but some of the things that go on.... Not too far from where I live, a guy abducted a six-year-old girl from her bedroom at two-thirty in the morning, took her into the woods, and raped her. The parents hadn't locked the back door. Fortunately, she's going to live. The rapist was visiting in the neighborhood and had a history of small crimes, but what he did to this little girl was a big move up for him at age thirty-one. Where does this sort of middling evil come from, and why? There are few total psychotics in the world, those who should be committed for what they are capable of doing or what they have done, such as Ted Bundy or the "Hillside Strangler." Although such people are rarities, this side of human nature is what fascinates me.

WIATER: If you weren't doing horror, what sort of writing do you think you would be involved with?

FARRIS: I would probably be a comedy writer.

WIATER: Seriously?

FARRIS: There's a humorous side to the horrible, too. But horror is difficult to do, and so is humor. Few writers do well in either genre. I'm not an expert on other people's horror because frankly I don't read a lot of it. I can't speak for other horror writers, and I don't know if I'm morbid by nature. I don't think so. I *am* deeply cynical. I'm always appalled by human nature yet fascinated by the contradictions, the perversity of people. Most of us are perverse. You just need to sit back and be tolerant or amused by it all.

WIATER: If you couldn't sit back and be "amused" by the madness all around us, do you think it could drive someone over the edge, contemplating such grisly topics day after day?

FARRIS: If I were going to go crazy, I would have done it by now. But it can get depressing. The novel I just finished, *The Axman Cometh*, which is about an axe murderer, obviously has some depressing aspects. At one point in the book I couldn't proceed. I knew what was coming, I had planned it, it was central to the book—but when I came to it, I just didn't want to do it! I liked the people I needed to get rid of. I had spent a lot of time with these characters, and for the first time since I started writing, I simply could not do something that I had to do. I got to feeling very morbid about this, and I was not fun to be around. Like an actor getting deeply into a role; you can imagine Laurence Olivier playing Richard III and how much fun he must have been around the house after the show.

WIATER: Most of your present fans may not be aware how you began your career with mystery and mainstream novels. Yet you've made your greatest reputation with dark suspense and the fantastic. Why stay in this genre when obviously you're capable of publishing any sort of story you please?

FARRIS: To return to the term *dark suspense*, the abnormal psyche is an endless source of material, of interesting stories. I dislike writing the same book over and over again. I prize humor in writing, concentrated plots, rich characters, good versus evil; I like a happy ending. I like stories I can use as a vehicle to show off; I mean that in a good sense, to show off what I can do. And I can do a hell of a lot. This type of fiction gives me the opportunity to take chances.

WIATER: Which of your own novels would you recommend to someone sampling your work for the first time?

FARRIS: That's difficult to answer because every book I write I try to make as different as I can from the one before. Also, I think I cover a pretty wide range, from straight suspense like *Sharp Practice* to out-and-out horror like *Son of the Endless Night*. But my favorite book is *All Heads Turn When the Hunt Goes By*. It's funny how that became my favorite book because I hated every page of it as I wrote it! It was one of the most difficult books I've ever written. But it stands up pretty well as a horror novel; I mean, there's nothing else I've seen or heard that's remotely like it. I had a rough time writing it for a lot of reasons I can't explain. I will say that I ground the last three chapters out the night before I got married, and the publishers were also setting the book up in type as I was going along writing it! And right up until the last night I didn't know how it would end. I don't mind being in suspense as I go along, but somewhere even *I* like to know where it's going to end [*laughs*]! But two years later, I went back and reread it, and I thought, "I wouldn't change a thing."

WIATER: When you sit down to write, are you concerned with censoring your own imagination, or are you only concerned that your publishers may later wish to tone down your work?

FARRIS: Yes, I've had a lot of fights with publishers over the years. There's a scene which is becoming famous in *Son of the Endless Night* in which a cop flushes himself down the toilet. I had a lot of trouble over that one.

WIATER: I can't imagine why [*laughs*] . . . !

FARRIS: Well, they didn't see the humor in it. Actually, I'm easily bored, and I don't do outlines. And when I purposely set out to write a long horror novel such as *Son of the Endless Night*, I'm aware that a lot of the readers will already be familiar with *The Exorcist*, which is an exceptional book. So I had to figure out—both consciously and unconsciously—what is it about the nature of Evil that really makes it *horrifying*? You start with the basics—putting people in a perfectly ordinary situation and then giving it a twist. Easier said than done!

WIATER: Just as *The Exorcist* was reportedly based on a genuine case, it would seem that your novel was based on the so-called Demon Murder case which occurred in Connecticut a few years ago.

FARRIS: Oh, yes, it's very much based on it. But the judge wouldn't allow the case to be heard. That's what set me thinking—what if a judge, for whatever reason, allowed a case of murder by demonic possession to be heard. So it was the inspiration for the novel. Actually, the first murder is closer to the Yale Murder, which took place in Scarsdale [New York], in which a kid beat his girlfriend to death with

a hammer. It's sort of an amalgam of the two incidents.
WIATER: Do you have any personal fears that you attempt to transmit or transform into your fiction?
FARRIS: My personal fears wouldn't really make for interesting fiction. I think it goes deeper than that, from people like Stephen King and Peter Straub and me to everybody else in the field right down to the first-time novelist; they're not doing this to just make a buck. They're really working on something that is intimately involving in their psyche—and this is going on twenty-nine or thirty books for me—and *I'm* still trying to work it out, whatever "it" is. I don't know if I'm any closer to the end or not.

I write a great deal of poetry. And I find that I can say something concisely in a poem that, for me, is a more concrete way of getting down on paper to whatever it is that's in the deepest-most part of your psyche. There are things that I would never put down in a novel that I can put into a poem—and hope nobody ever reads it.
WIATER: Considering the number of novels you've written dealing with occult and supernatural themes, has this in any way influenced your own personal beliefs in the paranormal?
FARRIS: That covers a lot of territory. But if you're asking do I believe in the possibility of evil spirits being influenced by good spirits from another plane, the answer is: probably. I would say I think it's a cinch, though I've never encountered any evil spirits personally. But I do believe everyone has some psychic ability to one degree or another. Through the ages, this has been a common theme in literature as well. There's too much, shall we say, emotional evidence to be ignored.
WIATER: Since you intend to independently make two, and perhaps even up to four, motion pictures based on your novels, it'll be some time then before we see any more new novels?
FARRIS: No, even that's not full-time work. I'll still do a book a year. I spend about three hours a day writing; my concentration is such that I can produce a book in about three or four months.
WIATER: So you're not intending to sacrifice one career for another?
FARRIS: I need to do both. If I were just making films—well, I need to do the writing. That's basic with me. Yet nothing but writing drives me crazy—and three hours a day is not enough to keep me occupied. So this a nice mix, if I can do it.
WIATER: Some people may be surprised at how rationally you approach this very personal and emotional profession. What advice do you have for someone considering following in your path?
FARRIS: Writing is a *job*. It is plain hard work. Anyone who's gone to

college and written terms papers knows what I mean. Just think of doing it every day, five days a week. Or three days one week and four another—whatever schedule suits you. Just as long as you do have a schedule, and even if you have a job on the side—which most people must have when they're beginning to write seriously.

I run every morning before I go to work. I hate running [*laughs*]. But I do it because it's beneficial, and I know other good things are going to come because of it. When you start out cold, saying to yourself, "I can't do this today," the first couple of laps are murder. Then you get yourself into a groove, and find that the experience becomes pretty mechanical, if not enjoyable. It's that way when you sit down to write something as long and difficult as a novel. Doesn't matter whether you can do it better in the morning or better at night, you have to establish a regular time to write. It may be a paragraph or a page, who knows? But if you stay with it the pages pile up, and you'll write a book. I know that as much as I don't like to sit down some mornings and look at that word processor, still the pages will happen. (I'm all for word processors; writing is a damn chore no matter what, and anything you can find to make it easier, latch on to it. Can you imagine how it was when they wrote with a quill pen?) You should have a routine and no expectations. Just see what happens.

WIATER: Can you give an example of something occurring with "no expectations"?

FARRIS: *The Axman Cometh* began as a story. I thought of the premise the day before I started to write. Originally it was two short stories which came together in my mind as one, and which I planned for the expanded paperback version of *Scare Tactics*. I conceived the story on the fourteenth of August, sat down to write it on the fifteenth, and on the twenty-fourth of October, it was done as a full-length novel. I didn't know when I sat down this would happen! Although I always had a notion of where I meant to go with the idea, I didn't know who most of the characters were until they popped up while I was writing. My expectation was only that I wanted to find out what happened next.

WIATER: Since you've been writing horror for more than twenty years, have you yet to find any boundaries which you feel shouldn't be crossed?

FARRIS: It's all in how you approach the material. In *Son of the Endless Night* I had a sex scene between a twelve-year-old girl and the protagonist, which could be interpreted as pretty gamey. But one of the keys to the scene is that she's *not human*, which some critics seemed to overlook. Also, at that point in the novel I needed to get about as far down into the depths of degradation and evil as it is possible to go. In the thousands of horror stories that have been published, how many scenes truly make the reader's skin crawl?

We've had an abundance of things crawling out from under beds and popping out of closets. Even though my novel dealt with supernatural themes, I had to be very careful and choosy about graphically illustrating the point I wanted to make. No way to try to handle the scene tastefully. So I did not. It was about as pornographic as you can find in fiction. I haven't had too much feedback on it; a couple of fellow authors thought I really had gone too far. They're right! I think I really extended the boundaries about as far as anyone's going to in this century.

WIATER: Do you purposely set out to go beyond what's already been done in the genre?

FARRIS: I don't try to go beyond any limit in particular; I try to approach what I'm doing in a particular project—in a particular scene—and to give it a twist. To write it in such a way that people have never encountered before.

WIATER: You're certainly aware of the splatterpunk movement, in which one of the primary reasons for the story's existence is precisely that: to see how far the boundaries of sex and violence can be pushed.

FARRIS: There are writers out there—I know of a few and I've read a few—who pile on the gore. But it's not particularly creative, and a lot of talent is required to make it work. I do believe I have a knack for describing the horrible without belaboring the point.

WIATER: Yes, but you're not a shrinking violet at describing explicit scenes of violence. In the story "Horrorshow" from your *Scare Tactics* collection, the scene in which the girl is attacked is incredibly brutal.

FARRIS: Go back and read it again and find all the brutal paragraphs. I think there's a total of *one*. The rest is anticipation of that specific paragraph. It's not as if I spent eight pages having the killer jump up and down on her head. That's precisely the point I'm trying to make. When you lead a reader up to that moment, you've got to give him something—you just can't cut to the corpse lying back at the morgue. Doesn't work anymore. It's a scene which has to be shown somewhat graphically, but there's a degree beyond which you don't have to describe it any further. I think I reach that middle ground. I'm not particularly fond of long scenes of bloodshed; how many ways can you really do it, anyway?

When I get into violence—something that's really terrible—I want it to be memorable. Because I can bring considerable power to bear on just such a situation, I do. I want the reader shaken and helpless not to continue reading. I don't pull any punches, but I don't look for opportunities just to gross people out.

WIATER: So you believe it truly takes a special talent to be a writer of horror, over any other kind of writing?
FARRIS: Sure! It's not easy to evoke a scare in somebody. It's not easy to take tried-and-true material and make it fresh. You're working in a form that is just about as rigid as the Western story, and they aren't publishing Westerns anymore for a lot of reasons. And one of them is that the public got bored because there wasn't anything more to say. This may happen to horror fiction, though I think the latitude is wider.

But working up to a good scare scene is difficult to do, and that's the heart of it. At this point, it's simply a case of talent coming into play; some people can do it, some people can't. It's like the difference between Julius Irving on a basketball court and some kid in high school. Dr. J has the moves, and the kid doesn't have them. He can try to emulate them, he can do a pretty good job of dribbling... but going one on one with Dr. J, he's going to get killed! And there are very few writers who have got the moves—I don't care what genre they're in or whatever it is they're trying to write.
WIATER: Before turning to horror, you had a successful career as a writer when many of your colleagues in this genre were still scribbling with crayons. Just how old were you when you published your first novel?
FARRIS: Eighteen. I sold my first book the summer I was out of high school. It was published under a pen name about a year later. I had three novels published in 1956. I was involved in playwriting in New York for a time, and I've done a hell of a lot of screenwriting. But I try to produce at least a novel a year.
WIATER: Why so much work, besides the obvious reasons of supporting yourself and a family?
FARRIS: One, I still like to write. Two, I try each time I sit down to write something to make it especially challenging—something I've never done before.... When writing becomes boring or difficult or unnecessary to do anymore I'll stop, but I don't foresee that happening. I enjoy working on something—a poem, story, novel, screenplay—every day. Maybe in a way I'm obsessed. That's probably part of it. Maybe in five years I'll retire and take up painting again [*laughs*]. If I get the chance to make a movie again, I will. But writing is the main thing I do, and everything else is just a break or change of pace that's refreshing.

Charles L. Grant

You can say a lot of things about Charles L. Grant—that he's an award-winning author; that he can write in just about any genre (even though he clearly enjoys horror the most); how he's acclaimed as one of the most stylish writers working today. What you can't say about him is that he's lazy. For even though he did not start writing professionally until he was twenty-six years old, since 1975 he has published more than seventy-five books: over forty novels, some two dozen anthologies or short story collections, and more than one hundred short stories.

How has he done all this? you might ask—he'd have to be several writers working simultaneously. And so he has been—not only is he Charles L. Grant, but he has in the past been "C. L. Grant," award-winning science fiction writer; and "Felicia Andrews," best-selling romance novelist; and he is currently "Lionel Fenn," author of humorous fantasies; and "Geoffrey Marsh," pulp-adventure fictioneer as well.

Of course, under his own name, Grant is the very popular writer of several superior horror novels, including *The Sound of Midnight, The Nestling, The Tea Party, The Grave, The Pet,* and *The Orchard.* For some reason, his most recent novels have longer titles, such as *For Fear of the Night.* Besides winning the World Fantasy Award twice for his own work, he has also won a third coveted Howard (named after H. P. Lovecraft) as editor of the landmark *Shadow* series. Beyond those honors, his wife, Kathryn Ptacek, is also a fine horror novelist and anthologist.

Born in 1942, Grant has long been recognized as one of the leading exponents of a style which he and other critics have termed *quiet horror*. Although he is not the only writer in the genre to share in this philosophy, it has made for some interesting discussions in the small press and at various conventions such as Necon and the World Fantasy Convention. Especially when the exponents of quiet horror are purposely put on a panel with others who prefer their horror served "loud." He is also a past president of the Horror Writers of America, and like so many of the veteran dark dreamers, has spent countless hours advising young writers. (Not to mention giving several a start to their professional careers in one of his many anthologies.)

Since he has spent a large part of his career weeding through the very worst in horror fiction, Charles L. Grant certainly knows what qualifies for the very best, no matter what "volume" others may label it. He neither leads the pack nor cares to run with it, just so long as he can continue to bring his best nightmares and fantasies out before the public.

WIATER: A fairly obvious question—why so many books? Don't you have a credible enough following under your own name?
GRANT: In 1968, I sold my first short story, and in 1975 my first novel. Why [*laughs*]? Money!
WIATER: Come on—it can't be that cut-and-dried!
GRANT: No? [*long pause*] No—in the beginning, when I decided I wanted to write for a living—and realized I wasn't Ray Bradbury or Theodore Sturgeon or James M. Cain—I knew I had to write novels to make it. The first couple of science fiction novels came out while I was still a teacher, and then I wasn't teaching anymore. And when I started writing horror, horror wasn't a big-paying field yet. So I had to see what else I could write to support me while I wrote the horror novels. And that's why I got into the gothic and romance novels for a time. But eventually the horror novels were beginning to sell well enough so that I could support myself with them. But I was also trying different kinds of writing. *A writer writes*. And I really think it's a crime that writers restrict themselves to only one kind of writing. I've tried mystery novels, contemporary novels, suspense novels—they just didn't work.
WIATER: But why still write in other genres using other names—surely

you have enough clout by now to write only horror novels if you wanted to?

GRANT: Yeah, I could. But you can only have so many "Charles L. Grant books" out in the stores at one time. I'm getting a little nervous now because the *Shadows* anthology series are all being reissued in paperback, plus the other original paperback anthologies—so there's a lot of books out there with my name on them—and I didn't write 'em. And a lot of my novels *are* coming out again; but let's assume for a moment they aren't there. Let's talk about just new books: You can't have three new books coming out a year, every year. In ten years that's thirty Charlie Grant books. So if you have one main book coming out in hardback, and then it's followed the next year in paperback; well if I just write those, that leaves me eight months out of the year to sit around and go crazy! So I write the other ones under pseudonyms to keep from going crazy. *I write because I have to write.* I can't go three days without writing something, even a sentence or two. All the books are different, and they're all hard to write. But I just enjoy writing.

WIATER: Considering your prolific output, a fair statement to make, what's your work schedule like, and does it differ greatly from your wife's?

GRANT: It pretty much dovetails with my wife's, except she gets up earlier than I do. I don't know about anything before ten-thirty in the morning. I'm out of bed about ten-thirty in the morning, but I don't really wake up until about noon. I'll work from then until about five or six o'clock and take a couple of hours off for supper and to watch the news. Then I'll work from about eight or nine until one or two in the morning. So it's about a ten-hour day. Every day—Monday through Friday. Most of the time I'll work Saturday night and Sunday nights, too, for three or four or five hours. Especially when I'm working on a novel.

WIATER: You once told me that you quit writing science fiction because you felt you had a lot more ideas in the horror genre. Do you feel your "well of ideas" is still running deep?

GRANT: I will never live long enough to write all that I want to write. [*long pause*] That's the truth. I've never had a writer's block; I never worry about running out of ideas.

WIATER: I know that you're always reading new stories for your various anthologies. But for pleasure, who do you enjoy in the field?

GRANT: I read the writers I always like to read: Ramsey Campbell, John Farris, James Herbert, Bernard Taylor. And Robert R. McCammon— I wouldn't pass up a Robert McCammon. Ever. I think he's great. Of

course, it's understood that none of these authors is as good as I am [*laughs*]. But I also love to read "good bad books." It's usually badly written—but it's a lot of fun!
WIATER: Explain, please.
GRANT: It's like watching a B movie from the forties and fifties. I read a ton of those, especially the ones from Great Britain. Their "bad books" are better than our "bad books." I read Guy N. Smith and Shawn Hudson. I recently brought back a bunch from England, and one is called *Maggots*. You know—"bug books." *Slime. Scum. Blow-Fly.* [*laughs*] I think they're wonderful.
WIATER: All right, but a lot of those novels, some of which are also referred to in England as Nasties, are quite explicit in descriptions of sex and violence. Yet your own work is highly regarded for a subtle atmosphere of quiet horror, as you've termed it, rather than gore for the sake of gore. What are your true feelings on all this?
GRANT: I really believe this: The most powerful books—not necessarily mine—are the ones that force the reader to use his imagination. Because there is nothing more powerful than the reader's imagination. Writers who spell it all out—let it be the sex act or, more specifically, violence—are cheating the reader. I think it's an insult to the reader's intelligence and imagination to spell it all out. But as Ramsey Campbell has said, *everybody's* imagination is under attack because television doesn't permit us to have an imagination. Good films always do. But the splatter films are a lot like television: It's quick scenes, punch go, punch go, with no room to think. But when you're sitting down to enjoy yourself with a good book—or a good film—explicitness is lazy writing. I really think it is. They don't know how to suggest it, so they spell it out. It's a lot easier to spell something out than it is to suggest it. Let the *reader* fill in the rest! It has a greater impact than a whole paragraph describing entrails one by one.
WIATER: Could you state an effective example?
GRANT: I once had a fan letter from a woman in Montana about *Night Songs*. She told me she enjoyed the book, but she deplored the explicit violence in it. There is *no explicit violence in the book.* She specifically mentioned one scene where a cop is sitting in a car, and Tess Mayfair, the woman from the boardinghouse, comes up, and she reaches in the car and struggles with him—and she pulls off his arm. That's all I said: She pulls off his arm. Period. She mentioned that scene specifically because of all the blood and gore. I did not mention the word blood *once*. But the way I did it I guess must have been right because she filled it all in. *That's* the best way to do it, I think.

WIATER: Some of your colleagues, such as King, Barker, and Farris, have directed motion pictures from screenplays they've also adapted from their work. Have you ever had the itch yourself, if ever given the chance, to direct a motion picture?

GRANT: No, no, no, no! Right now I'm working on screenplays for *The Pet* and *The Nestling*, but I'm only doing those to see if I can work in that form. But otherwise, I don't want any part of those people in Hollywood. No thank you! They can take options on my work, and that's fine. And they can do what they want with it—because they can never wreck my original novel. And if a good movie comes out of it anyway, that's a bonus. Of course, if the opportunity ever came along, I'd like to write the kind of horror movie that *I'd* like to see... which they're not making anymore.

WIATER: Knowing your tastes, we have the feeling it won't be another sequel to *Friday the 13th*.

GRANT: I'd like to make a Val Lewton-kind of movie, is what I'd like to make. I want to make the kind of movies that will scare the hell out of people, without once showing someone getting their heart torn out of their chest. Lights and shadows. *Lights and shadows*. Even today, even in a color movie, the best scares—not shocks—come from lights and shadow. *Fright Night* is a great more recent example of that—it was so much fun, and it was obvious that the people who made that movie really loved the field! Tom Holland... bless 'em! That kind of film is far more chilling than, say, the new *Cat People*. Yech! Transforming and then licking the slime off the skin... that's bullshit.

WIATER: It's an established fact that you're *the* anthologist in the field. The *Shadow* series, the *Midnight* series, the *Greystone Bay* series, and so forth. Perhaps someone reading this might be a young writer wishing to submit his or her stories someday. What advice do you have?

GRANT: "Serious Advice for Young Writers Who Want to Break into the Field?" [*pauses*] The first thing they have to do is *read*. Not just the horror field; that's the worst thing they can do! They have to read *everything* they can get their hands on. They've got to read Dickens, and Twain, and Shakespeare. And poetry. And they've got to read the contemporary masters. Before they can write, they've got to learn good writing. They have to learn what makes a good story, and what makes a good novel, first. *Read!* Watch less television! Exercise the imagination! Learn to use the goddamn language. Stay away from manuals of style and creative writing classes—they don't do a goddamn thing for you.

I get a lot of submissions after a hit movie comes out—and there'll be tons of stories that are *almost* the same as the movie. But those people can't write—and they never will. Not without an imagination. And you have to know the rules before you can break the rules. Somebody who wants to write something different can't do it any differently until they know how it's done *right*. Then they can twist and turn and learn to develop their own style and voice.

WIATER: Although you've threatened to quit doing them at some point, why do you continue to edit original anthologies?

GRANT: I'm not. I started *Shadows* because I wanted to see more of the type of story that I like. And there weren't enough markets in the field in those days. I just thought it would be neat to be an editor. I didn't have the slightest idea of what I was getting into! I did it because it was fun. I like to do those kind of stories because I like to read them—and keep them alive. It also gave new writers a shot—there's more new writers in each volume. It's not for the money. It's also not that much work—the work is writing those stupid headnotes before each story—God, I hate those [*laughs*]! But after twelve years, I'm tired—and I don't want *Shadows* to just dribble away. It's time to end it; the final *Shadows* will appear in 1991. That's it.

WIATER: Speaking about your own short stories for a moment, why do you continue to write them when you know there's so few markets, and the pay will always be negligible?

GRANT: Well, writing short stories is infinitely harder than writing a novel. But you get ideas that just won't support a novel, and besides, I *like* to write short stories. They're fun. And they make you practice your craft with a lot more diligence than a novel does. In a novel you're tempted to run around a lot, but in a short story every word has to count. So it's good practice. And practically speaking, it helps keep your name out before the public when there aren't any of your books out. I know there're people who don't read novels—

WIATER: —because they don't have the time?

GRANT: Because they *think* they don't have the time—so they restrict their reading to just short stories. I've met people who haven't read any of my novels but have read most of my short stories.

WIATER: To ask you again for Advice for Young Writers, how should they approach that first novel?

GRANT: Well, the tried-and-true method is to outline. But I don't outline, so I'm really being hypocritical here. But that's the way my work methods evolved. I can't outline. But for new writers, I would suggest they write themselves a ten- or fifteen-page synopsis. Write it all in the present tense. In that way you've at least got some guidelines to work with. But as I said, I don't—the book's in my head when I'm ready to write. And I don't start writing it until I'm ready to, and then I just write it. Not every blessed little scene—but the basic structure is in my head, so I know what's going to happen. I see it as a movie up there in my brain, and I just write down what I'm looking at. I don't see it as a narrative flow; I see scenes. Specific scenes. I've got a bunch of scenes in my head now for the new novel; if I can put them into words, it'll be really great stuff [laughs]!

WIATER: A good deal of your horror novels and short stories take place in a mythical town in Connecticut known as Oxrun Station. How did its creation come about?

GRANT: I had to write a novel, and I needed a town, so to avoid comparisons to Lovecraft's Arkham, I made it an upper-class community. That's about as far away from Arkham as you can get. And that novel became *The Hour of the Oxrun Dead*. And right after that came *The Sound of Midnight*, and I thought, "Well, I've got this neat town—I might as well use it again!" So it just went on from there, with short story ideas that also seemed to lend themselves to the town.

WIATER: Why did you choose to become a writer relatively late in life—your mid-twenties? How long did it take you to sell that first story, and then the first novel?

GRANT: Two years. I started writing seriously to sell in 1966. I sold my first story in 1968—but I didn't believe it because it was another two years before I sold the second one. I don't think it was until I sold my fifth story that I believed I could really write well enough to sell. Then I thought, "Well, can I do a novel?" And it was five novels before I sold the first one. The others will never, ever see print. One was science fiction, one was fantasy, and three were mainstream. And they were all *bad*. Absolutely dreadful!

WIATER: From your own work, which would you recommend to someone who's never read you before?

GRANT: Okay. Hmm. [long pause] *The Pet, The Nestling. The Grave*. And for the short work, *Nightmare Seasons* and *The Orchard*. That should give you a pretty good idea of what I'm working on. But I am no judge of my own work, as my wife Kathy will tell you. Which is to say, I know I'm good—without sounding egotistical—because I sell. Consistently. How good I am, I leave that up to the critics. Some people think I'm very good, others think I'm a phony Ray Bradbury—I know I used to be, when I first started, but I believe I've outgrown that. While Bradbury was one of the writers who influenced me, he wasn't the primary one. That was Nathaniel Hawthorne—and I want to do more like Hawthorne, especially in my shorter work. I want to do a story like "The Black Minister's Veil" or "Young Goodman Brown." God, how I love those stories! But I really don't know how good I am. All I really care about is that if somebody spends good money on one of my books, reads it through, and gets a good chill now and then, I'm satisfied.

WIATER: But in disclosing your pseudonyms, aren't you ever concerned how some genres have more "respectable" reputations than others?

GRANT: One of the big problems that new writers have, especially those whose star rises really quickly, is that they get the idea they're writing "art." Well, anybody who sits down to write art is deluding himself. I always use the same examples, and I don't care if they're now regarded as geniuses: Shakespeare didn't write art and neither did Charles Dickens. *They wrote to make a buck.* And to entertain their audience—so they could continue to write and make a buck. It just so happens that they *were* both geniuses, and their work has lasted. But nobody knew that at the time. The test of time is the only way to judge if anything is a classic.

Now I have things to say in my books—but it's all below the surface, and I don't set out with a conscious theme. I just set out to tell a story. That's *it*. If there's anything else in there, that's cool. If the reader gets it, that's great. If the reader sees something I didn't intend to put in there, that's *wonderful*. But the important thing is that they get to the end of it, and they don't feel that I've cheated them.

WIATER: When I first interviewed you back in 1979, you told me that if a horror story didn't scare you when you were done, then you didn't send it out. Is that still the case?

GRANT: That's right. I never send it out unless I can give myself a chill. As my agent has told me, I write word by word. Every single word has to count—even in the novels. Every word in the book has to work toward *that last line*. Like on *The Pet*, I worked on the last scene for I don't know how long to get it just *right*. Only then was I ready to send in the manuscript. I still have to go . . . [*breaks into maniacal laughter*] or I won't send it out.

WIATER: Any other secret you care to reveal which enables you to go back to the word processor, day in and day out?

GRANT: You have to think—to trick yourself into believing: "I'm the best writer I know." You *have* to think that way. If you think you're lousy, you'll never improve, never get anywhere. In other words, you have to *believe in yourself*.

James Herbert

"People expect us to look like Christopher Lee and wear a black cape, don't they?" James Herbert wondered out loud as his wife handed him a drink in his barren study. Of course, his huge study was not in its usual working order, as he explained that the office equipment hadn't arrived since adding a new wing to his country home in Sussex, England. Regardless, Herbert appeared quite comfortable sitting within a most ornate, and unusual-looking, chair. ("It's the first time I've sat in it, so it may give me some good vibes.") A chair that once belonged to the infamous Aleister Crowley (1875–1947), an occult writer and reputed sorcerer who was once termed *the most evil man in the world*.

Herbert doesn't even look moderately evil, and in fact has a lovely wife and three daughters to prove that he is just an ordinary husband and father. Of course, he is much better known as one of the world's best-selling horror writers. The author of such novels as *The Rats, The Fog, The Survivor, Lair, Fluke, The Dark, The Spear, Shrine, The Jonah, Moon, The Magic Cottage, Sepulchre,* and *Creed,* he commands a popularity in his native England that is second to no one—not even Stephen King.

As Herbert was one of the first contemporary writers in the genre to "tell it like it is," he was initially condemned by the critics as going too far over the edge with his particularly grim and violent visions. Yet whatever the critics might say, the public has always embraced his work, as evidenced by how all fifteen of his novels remain in print with more than twenty million copies of his works published worldwide.

About the only area where Herbert hasn't been overly successful is with motion pictures. Only two lackluster adaptations of his novels have appeared so far—*Deadly Eyes* (based on his 1974 novel, *The Rats*) and *The Survivor*. Herbert was justifiably not happy with either film and was actually pleased when they were such box-office failures that they had no detrimental effect on his career. Just as unfortunate, he wrote an original teleplay for the BBC, which ultimately has never been produced. Fortunately, he decided to take the idea and transform it into a recent novel, *Haunted*. Presently, no less than four of his later novels have been optioned by various producers.

Born in the East End of London on April 8, 1943, Herbert is now surrounded by the material wealth he never imagined he would have as a youngster growing up in poverty. Although he repeatedly prefaced his remarks with the hope that he wasn't speaking too pompously or self-consciously, I found James Herbert to be a genial yet always direct man who believes he has worked hard and now is simply enjoying the fruits of his labor as a dark dreamer.

WIATER: In spite of the present condition of your study, what's your daily writing schedule like?
HERBERT: I'm a late riser. I'm one of those people that for me to go to sleep, it's like another day's work. I dream very heavily, in full technicolor. But I get into the study at ten, and I work through to lunchtime, at one o'clock. I'll have lunch, read the morning newspaper, and get back to the study about half past two, and then I'll work through to six o'clock in the evening, and if it's going well, until seven. But that's my deadline; I never work beyond that. Sometimes it's seven days a week, but generally it's six days a week.
WIATER: You mentioned to me earlier that your wife does the physical typing of your manuscripts. So you prefer to write in longhand?
HERBERT: I do. Because years ago I used to be an art director in advertising. And art was my favorite subject as a kid—I loved drawing and painting. So for me, nowadays, writing is like drawing pictures on the page. I use a medium-thick Pentel pen and a jumbo exercise pad, and I've worked that way from day one. It seems to work for me. You know at the moment I'm working on a desk—it's not even a desk, it's one of those coffee tables which has a strange hydraulic system where you can have it high or low—and it's the table that I did *The Rats* on,

my very first book. And *The Fog*, years ago. Because at the moment I'm waiting for my office equipment to come in, I'm actually working on this old table again.

WIATER: Well, between the table and the Crowley chair, some sparks of inspiration had better occur!

HERBERT: The thoughts that must be ingrained in that table—it must be quite remarkable by now.

WIATER: You mentioned your dreams as being particularly vivid. When you're writing, have you already visualized the entire novel in your mind, or is each day a new adventure for your imagination?

HERBERT: Each day is a new adventure. I sit there and just let it pour out. If I'm lucky, it pours out!

WIATER: After fifteen novels, do you find that the horror genre still fascinates you? Or are you growing tired of it?

HERBERT: It is *endlessly* fascinating, it really is. But there's a lot of humor in my books as well. So both ends fascinate me: humor and horror. And they often walk hand in hand. To put it more basically, I just find that you can write about a very mundane situation, and you can get into that; but after a while, it can become tedious for a writer—and certainly for a reader. When you find that boredom is approaching, you can take that mental leap—and invite the reader to take it with you—and take that one bound into horror that transcends everything you've written before that. You know, it really stops you getting bored with what you're doing.

You're only limited by your own imagination. So you can—I don't know. So you can . . . dig into areas that nobody else wants to dig into. Or they didn't use to want to—now everybody wants to [*laughs*]! You see what I mean? It gives you a lift. It gives you a metaphorical erection, if you like. It just gets the blood flowing and the thoughts flowing. It's wonderful.

WIATER: But how seriously should we take horror? For some writers, it's just a series of scary scenes, while for others, it's what they seem to be literally born to do with their lives.

HERBERT: I know what *I'm* doing, and I know that Steve King knows what *he's* doing, and Peter Straub knows what *he's* doing; whether anyone else can understand what we're doing is another matter. I find one of the dangers nowadays is that we can get very pompous about what we do. It's almost a defense mechanism. When people want to put down horror, we tend to try to explain it too much, and give too much motivation for what we're doing.

I think we do it by instinct alone. One critic said of me a few years back that "James Herbert could make Scunthorpe on a wet, dreary afternoon seem interesting." Now Scunthorpe is one of our dreariest, worst, seaside resorts. So that was a great compliment for me. It's something that's within us.... I have great difficulty explaining what I do. I work by instinct. Others are very articulate about this, but I try not to be. I really try not to be. Because I don't want to open that box. I don't want to see the mechanics of it.

WIATER: But if you could think of yourself as a magician, shouldn't you know better than anyone in the audience how the mechanism, or the tricks, operate?

HERBERT: But see, I don't know how the tricks work! And I'm determined to keep it that way. I'm a magician by instinct. To me, it *is* magical. In the true sense. Writing is not a mechanical thing; it's not trickery. And as soon as you analyze, and as soon as you give reasons, and as soon as you get pretentious about it, or try to explain it, I think it evaporates. It disappears. You know? Or at least it dissipates.

WIATER: So what you're saying is that true horror writers cannot be manufactured, that you have to be born with this fascination for the dark side?

HERBERT: I firmly believe they are born this way. The trouble with the genre at the moment is that there are too many horror writers who are manufactured; not natural horror writers. It's a booming industry, it's an exciting industry, and a lot of these guys don't work by instinct, they work by process, if you like. They've read a lot of good horror over the years, and a lot of *bad* horror over the years, and they emulate it. It doesn't come from deep within. With me, there must be some twisted side of my nature that just *loves* horror. And I think that's true of the best of us, it really is. There's something within us that is, I think, a bit warped, and you're born with that. It's not manufactured.

WIATER: Back in the 1970s, you were one of the first modern horror writers to purposely not restrain yourself in terms of scenes of explicit sex and violence. Now you're no doubt aware that many writers have surpassed you in both areas. What are your thoughts on that subject?

HERBERT: At the 1988 World Fantasy Convention, Charles L. Grant said to me, "Really, Jim, you're the Godfather of splatterpunk." I was a bit taken aback by that! Then I understood what he was saying. And it is true. It's a reputation I've had a lot of trouble shaking off over the years because when people think of *nasty* horror, they do think of *The Rats* and *The Fog*. Now these books were written fourteen, fifteen years ago, and my style has changed. There's still the same ingredients; but the more you do something, you have to improve.

I liken it to punk music. You remember punk music? There were these so-called musicians whose whole attraction was their sheer, raw energy. That is what carried the music through. Now, the more they played, the better they got. They actually learned how to tune their guitars, for a start. They learned a few more chords. They got better. They got more refined.

And of course they faded as time went on. The secret for me has been to maintain that raw energy, *but* learn my craft. Learn to play that instrument without losing that energy. You see what I mean?

WIATER: I do. But for a long time you didn't receive any serious critical recognition because of your willingness to describe the undescribable. You were roundly condemned, in spite of your ever-growing popular success.

HERBERT: I *still* am condemned for it. (Although my first review in *The Times* [London] used terms like "brilliant" for *The Rats*.) One of the problems I have with America is that the critics still think I'm doing that sort of stuff; they don't think I've changed. What happened was they picked up a few of the earlier books, and not bothered to read the later ones. So they can't see how I've developed as a writer. They just think of me as splatterpunk, if you like. Whether I'm responsible now for those kind of books, I don't know. I really don't. Do you think I am?

WIATER: I would say you were more or less responsible for the subgenre of "creature" books that appeared after *The Rats*. Stories dealing with monstrous bugs, slugs, and various slimy members of the lower orders gone suddenly homicidal.

HERBERT: That is true, but it goes way beyond that. Think of how certain scenes in *The Fog* and *The Dark* have been copied over the years.

WIATER: Some writers believe it's their duty to try to go beyond what's been previously done before. To make the shocks even greater than ever before. What do you think of that concept?

HERBERT: That's the mistake they make. "Let's go farther; let's go way over the edge." When I did my first books—yes, I did know I was breaking new ground—but it was a natural thing for me to do. It wasn't me self-consciously saying, "I'm going to be outrageous. I'm going to do things that nobody's ever done before." It was a very subtle thing—I was aware that I was doing it, but it wasn't a conscious decision to do it. It just happened that way.

WIATER: I know that in England you've had the opportunity to design the entire package: artwork, typography, and so forth, that go into the physical production of one of your books. If you were asked to design the cover for something called, say, *Dark Dreamers: Conversations with the Masters of Horror*, do you have any ideas how would you go about it?

HERBERT: Absolutely! I'd have a *huge* photograph on the front of James Herbert. And it would be the most dominant name, "James Herbert," as well. That's how I would do it.

WIATER: And I suppose everyone else's name in half the size?

HERBERT: What? Do they have to be even half size [*laughs*]?

WIATER: Like Anne Rice, you're one of the very few major horror authors who doesn't do short stories. Why not?

HERBERT: One of my problems—if you can call it a problem—is I run away from the herd. If everybody else is doing it, I don't want to do it. The only short stories I've done—one of them was for charity, and that's been used in various anthologies and publications, until everybody's probably sick of it. And that was taken from a novel that New American Library, who used to publish me, they knocked it out. And rather than waste it, I offered it up as a short story. It was called "Breakfast" and was about the final holocaust. The other reason is I don't have time [*chuckles*]. I really don't have time to sit down and write a short story when I'm too heavily involved in doing, you know, full-length stories.

WIATER: Over the past few years, many critics have had to do an about-face regarding your work, and now you're recognized as a true master of the genre. Any specific instances which have been especially gratifying?

HERBERT: My books have been used in exams, they've been used in universities—and not just here, but in Europe as well. [*long pause*] People are actually being educated in some way by my books. It's another reward for me. It's nice to be appreciated in your own lifetime. I mean, having said that, I'm still knocked all the time, particularly by teachers with young students, because I know the younger kids just want the blood and gore. There's not too much of that in my later books, you know, so some of them must be disappointed.

But for instance, I was invited to Oxford University, to give a talk to the students. Now, no amount of money can actually equal that! Just the joy of actually being asked, let alone doing it. To go speak to the Art Society was for me—remembering my background from the East End of London—it's a *tremendous* compliment. And I can't help but feel very proud of that. So it is doing other things than just "entertaining the masses." There *is* another level to what we're doing, and that's important.

WIATER: Some of your books are quite bleak and unrelenting, such as *Sepulchre*. While others, like *The Magic Cottage*, are noticeably lighter and more humorous in tone. Is there any reason to believe that one type of horror novel is easier to write than another?

HERBERT: They're all difficult, though some appear to be less difficult than others. For me, *The Magic Cottage* was a breeze. *The Fog* wrote itself. Books like *Domain* were very, very difficult because there was so much research. *Sepulchre* was very, very difficult because it was so dark, and I had to keep myself in that mood all the time. I didn't want to enjoy myself while I was doing it. I had to remain very dark and sinister so I could give myself no relief with humor or sheer enjoyment. The research aspects come into it as well—it's very difficult to stop your imagination from running away and just collate all those facts that you have, and make sense of them.

So it does vary from book to book. The one I'm doing at the moment I'm finding easy to write, because again it's very humorous, though it's a very wicked humor. It's not written in the first person, though it very well could have been. I'm making the reader very conscious of the narrator. I'm telling it in a very, very relaxed tone of voice—

WIATER: —almost as if you were writing in an Aleister Crowley chair and getting these particular vibes....

HERBERT: Yes, I'm still trying to get relaxed, but it's just not working [*laughs*]!

WIATER: How wrapped up do you get emotionally with your characters while you're writing? Do you laugh when they laugh? Cry when they must die?

HERBERT: I don't cry when they die, but I do get totally wrapped up in the characters, the plot, the whole thing. It's a very draining experience, yet I do have control over it. It takes a *lot* to frighten myself nowadays. When there's a scary moment—yes, I'm very, very tense. I find I'm more scared if I relate that scary moment in that book when I'm talking to people.

For instance, if I was in a pub and was asked, "What did you write today?" I would actually go through this scene of horror. *That's* when I would find the hair on the back of my neck standing up—when I'm doing it verbally. That's when I get that chill. When I'm writing it, I get a certain kind of chill, but I'm in control. But when I'm describing it, it's like I've reverted back to Jim Herbert—not James Herbert the writer—and it's almost like me telling a scene from a movie I've just seen or from a story I've just read. The audience part of me comes to the fore, not the author part. It's quite a weird thing, actually, but it does happen.

WIATER: To what degree do you use your own personal fears or real-life experiences in your fiction?

HERBERT: You have to remember that the hero of the book is usually the author's alter ego, so therefore your hero is thinking thoughts that you, the writer, would think. You can't avoid that, and your worst sort of phobias and fears come out. One phobia I do avoid is anything happening to children. It's one of the areas that Steve King and I differ on—he would always write about horrible things happening to kids. It's Steve's way of exorcising those fears. And I try to avoid that because it's too meaningful for me, you know? I'd rather run away from it. I've got three daughters, and I find it too painful to write about nasty things happening to kids. I have done it—and I've regretted it afterward.

I did try once, with a book called *Moon*. The hero had a daughter who was, at that time, the same age as my daughter. And the whole story was leading up to something really terrible that was going to happen to this child. And I couldn't do it! So the dreadful thing that happened, happened to her best friend next door. The reader never got to meet her, and nor did I as a writer—it had to be once removed. It was too horrific. I couldn't get into that terrible emotion of writing about the hero's daughter, because it would have been my daughter. And so I just avoided it. Very cowardly—but it was for a reason; it was too much to take.

WIATER: I know your religious upbringing was as a Catholic. Does a writer truly have to believe in the concepts of Good and Evil to write effectively about them?

HERBERT: I can only answer for myself: I do. I really do believe in Good and Evil. I asked a priest once, "Do you think Evil is an actual force?" And he said, "Yes. Undoubtedly—it is an actual force." Of course, being a Catholic, you're brought up with the supernatural. Because if you believe in God, it's as a supernatural being. It's instilled in you. I find it very valuable now as a writer in our genre. Of course, the Catholic Church is supposed to frown on the sort of thing that I do, but it's given me so much information and insight on the supernatural!

WIATER: Do you think you've ever reached the true "heart of darkness" in your work? To fully explore and perhaps ultimately understand the pitch-dark core that is the heart of evil?

HERBERT: I've never even scratched the surface. [*long pause*] It's just beyond us all. I thought I had in a number of books. Certainly with *The Dark* I thought I got pretty close. Again, with *Sepulchre* I thought I was very near. But I've come to realize I've never even scratched it. There's so much going on—yes, people like me have more of an imagination than the majority. And so we can either rise to great levels or sink to deep levels. I feel that I've sunk about as low as anybody [*laughs*]. But I still haven't even scratched the surface.

Whether that remains an ambition for me to do just that, I don't know. Maybe that's the next step for me, to *really* get as far as I can in presenting Evil as it really is. Evil is such a tenuous thing; in some sense it's very, very subtle, and in other ways it's very obvious and very overt. It's a wonderful, mysterious, mystical area. And that's why we do it. That's why we keep striving to reach for that understanding.

Stephen King & Peter Straub

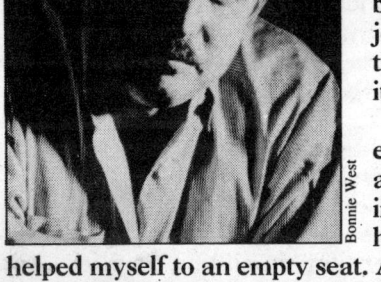

On a personal note, let me first say that I'll never forget the first words that Stephen King ever spoke to me, when, as a reporter on assignment, I introduced myself by immediately asking him for an interview: "Sorry," he said as he brushed by me on the way to the hotel bar, "I'm not giving any interviews now."

The occasion was the Fifth World Fantasy Convention, held in Providence, Rhode Island, on October 12–14, 1979. King was one of the guests of honor, and owing to the fact that *The Dead Zone* had just gone to the number-one position on *The New York Times* best-seller list, he was wearing jeans and a black T-shirt with the logo "USA #1" printed on it.

Like all brash young reporters who never take no for an answer, I of course kept walking right behind him, and when he sat down at a table in the bar, helped myself to an empty seat. Already seated at the table was a man impeccably dressed in an expensive suit. I recognized him as someone who had recently returned from living in England after his novel *Ghost Story* became an international bestseller. He politely introduced himself as Peter Straub.

Since it appeared I was not going to go away, both men agreed to talk to me then, and we have repeated such encounters on many occasions since over the years.

If there are any dark dreamers who need, as the toastmaster would say, "absolutely no introduction," it would be Stephen King and Peter Straub. Since their accomplishments are well known to anyone who has the slightest interest in horror fiction, let the simple biographical facts state that Stephen King was born on September 21, 1947, and currently lives in Bangor, Maine, with his wife and family. His books include *Carrie, 'Salem's Lot, The Stand, The Dead Zone, Firestarter, Cujo, Christine, Different Seasons, Pet Sematary, Misery*, and *The Dark Half*. His latest automatic best-seller is *Four Past Midnight*. Many of his novels have been adapted into major motion pictures, and King himself has written the screenplays for several, including *Creepshow* and *Pet Sematary*.

Peter Straub was born on March 2, 1943, in Milwaukee, Wisconsin, and currently lives with his wife and family in Westport, Connecticut. He is the author of such novels as *Julia, If You Could See Me Now, Ghost Story, Shadowland, Floating Dragon*, and *Koko*. His latest automatic best-seller is *Mystery*. To date, two of his novels, *Julia* and *Ghost Story*, have reached the screen.

In 1984, Straub and King collaborated to create the epic horror-fantasy, *The Talisman*. No less a cinematic talent than Steven Spielberg has purchased the film rights.

There is very little I can add to these bare facts, except that King and Straub remain the best of friends, and when it came time to include their interviews, I found it nearly impossible to separate their conversations. Indeed, the best sessions I have had with these two dark dreamers have been when talking with them at the same time. Therefore, from those dual interviews, I have excised the comments which are most in keeping with the general themes of this book.

I will add that, in person, I have found Stephen King to be extremely down-to-earth and not in the least affected (as far as I could tell) by his enormous success. Usually dressed in jeans and a work shirt, he would appear at first glance to be a truckdriver or a garage owner rather than an author. Stephen very much tries to keep as close as he can to the image of the writer as just another workaday man. As for Peter Straub, he is a very refined and dignified man who clearly knows what is the best in the arts and popular culture. Peter would also inevitably appear for our interviews in the most perfectly tailored of designer suits. An intellectual in the true sense of the word, Peter nevertheless approaches writing from his gut instincts and his heart, just as much as he does his well-trained mind.

I owe a special debt of thanks to these two authors, not only because they have always been forthcoming with answers to my unending list of questions, but for the other kindnesses and considerations they have extended to me along the way. In many ways, if it were not for the incredible success of these two authors—unquestionably the most famous dark dreamers in the world—the horror genre would probably never have become as accepted as it is today. And I probably wouldn't have managed to be one of the first journalists to specialize in this area. But I digress—without further ado, let's talk to Stephen and Peter.

WIATER: Why do you think horror finally took off as a truly contemporary genre? It's never really disappeared from the literary scene, except perhaps in the 1950s. . . .
KING: Well, they're around. Even if you go back to a period like the fifties when this stuff was very—I mean, *Weird Tales* magazine died from lack of interest as much as anything—but the stuff was there, and it would crop up every now and then. There was *The Search for Bridey Murphy*, which was the fifties' answer to *The Amityville Horror*, and just as hoaxy, apparently.
STRAUB: That's right.
KING: And it's just that people have to have this stuff! You need it—like a little salt in your diet.
STRAUB: Yeah, I think that's right: People have always enjoyed it, and always *will* enjoy it. But I have another little theory—which I've just invented—that the whole fiction market, the whole publishing world, changed a couple of years ago when the price of paper went so high. Publishers started turning down books that they normally would have accepted. It got much harder to be a first novelist. There was a certain handwriting on the wall, and I think one by-product of this is that many younger writers read the writing on the wall and wanted to exercise their talent in some form that would be acceptable to publishers. If you're very, very good—if you're *really* good—there's always a place

for you; you're always going to be read, and you're always going to be published.

WIATER: In other words, some writers embraced the horror genre specifically because they figured they had a slightly better chance of seeing that first novel getting published?

STRAUB: That's right. I think so. I'm pretty sure that's what's been happening. Barry Malzberg said the reason he wrote science fiction was because he wanted to make sure he got into print. I think that once you get into a genre, you discover how rich it is, and how varied it is. And just how much you can do with it! And of course you gravitate toward that genre which you feel close to anyhow, so it's not an act of hackery. It's an act of prudence.

WIATER: Peter, the first novel of yours I read—*Julia*—could actually be taken as either a mainstream or a horror novel, depending on the reader's own expectations.

STRAUB: That's certainly the way I thought of it! But I certainly wanted to write a book that was going to do me some good and would not have the problems that I had had with an earlier novel, *Under Venus*. So I just knocked at my imagination and that kind of story came up. But I *was* curious as to how I was going to write it. I remember writing the first sentences of *Julia*. I sat there, and the words came out, and I thought, "Well now, this is nice [*laughs*]. I'm writing this just the way I write everything else." I could still be happy with myself.

WIATER: Steve, before you made it, when your early novels were still being rejected and you were just starting to sell stories regularly, how was it that you kept going?

KING: For two reasons. Number one: You think you can do it. You think you have the talent to go over the top and earn your living that way. In a way, you feel that's what God meant you to do, you know? You don't feel satisfied with what you're doing because you *know* that's not what you were meant to do, you know?

I won't say I've led a grim life, but it was—and still is—sort of a humdrum life. It isn't any big deal. I don't go out and ride around in a limousine, sniff cocaine with a babe on each arm! And neither does Peter—you've probably changed a few diapers and I know you get up at six o'clock every other day with the baby.... But it's *fun*—you can go and get away from all that shit. And it's escapism. It's the same reason why people watch TV. But this is like "mind TV" or "mind movies."

STRAUB: That's right! There are really two aspects, and they're contradictory. One is the enormous *fun*, and anybody who is a writer does

it because that's what he likes to do. You enjoy it. But there is also the unutterable *tedium* of it, and I don't think most people can take it!
KING: They can't, man!
STRAUB: When people say, "Gee, I wish could do what you do . . ." [*laughs*] You know? I wouldn't wish it on anyone—because you spend most of your life alone in a room. And that's hard to adjust to at first, but you *do* adjust to it.

There really must be a love of just working the language. A delight in making sentences. There's a wonderful character in this Philip Roth novel that I enjoyed very much, *The Ghost Writer*, who's an old writer. He says, "I get up in the morning and I write a sentence. And then I turn the sentence around." You really have to like doing that! That's essential—that's the nuts and bolts. You really have to get a deep joy out of writing itself. And out of other people's writing, too.
WIATER: Did you ever sense that, like Stephen, you were destined to write? That even if you had to put X amount of novels on the shelf, the next one was going to be *the* one?
STRAUB: I never put anything on the shelf—but I *was* scared at the thought of writing because it seemed to me that it was impossible to make a living out of it. And I was also scared of the commitment—that I knew once I started doing it, I would be *ruined* for anything else. So I stayed away from it for a while. But . . . I'd be walking down the street, and I'd think, "A thirty-year-old, sandy-haired man named Jack Dugan stood in a telephone booth trying to dial his wife." And I thought, "Hey, I could go somewhere with that." You know? Little bits of dialogue would come in, and I realized that I *had* to do it! It was on my mind all the time.
KING: The other thing that was always in play with me was I was convinced—*deeply convinced*—that somewhere, deep inside me, was a money machine. Waiting to be turned on. And that when I found the dials and the combinations, the money would just pour out.
WIATER: But was there any motivation to write so as to say, "I told you so," to those early critics who didn't share that faith?
KING: [*hesitates*] Well . . . a little bit of that. But, really, not that much. It was never a question of I felt I had anything to prove to anybody else. But, in a way, with those early novels, I felt like a guy who was plugging quarters in the machine with the big jackpot. And yanking it down. And at first they were coming up all wrong. Then with the book before *Carrie*, I felt I got two bars and a lemon; then with *Carrie* bars across the board—and the money poured out. But the thing is, I was never convinced that I was going to run out of quarters to plug into the

machine. My feeling was, I could stand there forever until it hit! There was never really any doubt in my own mind. A couple of times I felt like I was pursuing a fool's dream or something like that, but they were rare. They were moments of real depression....

WIATER: Now that you've achieved major financial and critical success, do you still feel any pressure to produce more or any better or any differently?

STRAUB: I think you'll always feel a real pressure to write better, to do better, to try to do more. But that's all part of the fun. It's scary also, because you can't let yourself down. You want to do something that's bigger and better; you want to take on more. I know Steve does—and I do too.

WIATER: Peter, any restrictions self-imposed on your work?

STRAUB: I don't know. I suppose there would be... generally I try to be as awful as I can be. At certain times I want there to be real *shocks*, because in a way that's part of the appeal. And this is something I learned from Steve—that there's no point in exercising too much restraint in this field because it's enormous fun to be scared in a big, gaudy, splashy way.

WIATER: Steve, would it be fair to say you've been writing adaptations of your own works because you've been dissatisfied with the results of other screenwriters you've dealt with to date?

KING: No, that wouldn't be fair at all. It's done because sometimes it's fun, and because I want to see what that's like. And a lot of times, I felt like a high school kid who is almost getting laid, but not quite [*laughs*]. Like when you're a high school kid, and you say to yourself— if you're a boy!—you say that one of the major factors working in wanting to get laid is that once you do it, you don't have to worry about *worrying* about it anymore!... And I sometimes think that if I could get a screenplay that was actually produced—whether it was good or bad or indifferent—then I could say, "Yes, I *am* capable of doing that. I don't have to worry about *that* anymore!"

WIATER: Peter, have you ever had a similar desire to adapt your own work to the screen?

STRAUB: Not really. I never wanted to take the time because I figured there were other things I could do with my time that I knew *would* work. And I also figured there are people out there who would probably do a lot better job than I could. And also, no one ever asked me!

WIATER: Could you tell me the origins behind your only nonfiction book, *Danse Macabre*?

KING: Sure. There was quite a bit of research involved in it, but I don't think it shows in the book a lot! That is to say, hopefully it shows in the sense that the facts are right, the facts are straight. But what happened was Bill Thompson, who edited the first five novels that I did—*Carrie* through *The Stand* —went to Everest House. He called me up later and said, "Do you want to do a book about horror in movies and on TV and radio and all this stuff over the last thirty years or so?" And I said, "No." And he said, "How many times have you been asked why do you write that stuff?" And I said, "Billions." He said, "How many times have you been asked why do people read that stuff?" And I said, "Billions." He said, "Write this book. And whenever anybody asks you those questions, you can just say, 'I wrote this book.' And then you'll sell books and never have to answer those questions again!" So I said, "Okay, I'll write the book." I got into it in a very casual way, and found it very difficult to write.

It's got some autobiography in it, because in discussions like this, they always want to go back to Freud: They want to know what your childhood was like....

STRAUB: Sometimes they say, "Didn't you have a really rotten childhood [*laughs*]? You *must* have had a rotten childhood!"

KING: I told a story—this is in the [*Danse Macabre*] book—at a convention, a mystery convention. And we were on a panel about fear. There was myself, and there was Robert Morasco—who did *Burnt Offerings*—and there was Janet Jeppson, who is Isaac Asimov's wife and who is also a psychiatrist—a clinical psychiatrist. So you know why *she* was there. And that shows where they come from when they set that panel up!

Somebody in the audience said, "Did anything ever happen to you in your childhood that was really horrible?" And I told a story that I thought would satisfy them. I mean, it isn't anything *I* remember, it's something my mother told me. She said I was out playing one day with this friend of mine. I was about four. I came home, deadly pale, and I'd peed in my pants. And I didn't want to talk. She asked me what happened, but I went upstairs and closed the door and stayed in my room all afternoon. She found out that night that this kid I had been playing with had been run over by a train, okay? I can remember her telling me that they picked up the pieces in a basket. A wicker basket.

I don't remember anything about it; the chances are very good that by that time he had wandered off on his own somewhere, and then I wasn't anywhere around. There's a small chance that maybe I *did* see it happen, maybe the kid chased his ball onto the tracks or something. So I told this story and said, "I don't remember it at all," and immediately what Janet Jeppson said was "And you've been writing about it ever since!!!" The whole audience applauded—[*claps hands together*]—because they *want* to believe that you're twisted!

WIATER: But it would seem to me that you're slighted either way—first because you both don't appear to follow the cliche of what a horror writer should look like, and then because you appear too "normal" to *be* one. It's as if the public really wants you to run around in a black cape, acting crazy.

STRAUB: Yeah—absolutely nuts!

KING: But these things . . . it's odd that it should work that way. One of the things that psychiatry—the Freudian brand—is supposed to do is to allow you to open up lines of communication from your subconscious to the outside, where you can finally externalize it to the world. So, on the one hand, we say that psychiatry allows us to talk about our innermost fears, and that's wonderful, it helps you to get "normal." But if you do what Peter and I do, you *must* be "weird" because those channels are *open*. If they were closed, people would say you're normal, because you *can't* talk about your fears. You're all fucked up! Situation normal: all fucked up!

STRAUB: On the other hand, there's probably a great deal of truth to the proposition that books like this come out of conflicts which are imperfectly resolved. And I suppose these conflicts—if we presuppose their existence—are things that we actually are not aware of, but they seek their resolution in our books. You really want to protect those problems!

KING: That, for somebody like me, is what's so frightening about what's happened to somebody like Ray Bradbury. I read his collection, *The Stories of Ray Bradbury*, because I reviewed it. And basically what happened is you begin with someone who's totally—apparently—fucked up, if he had these imperfectly resolved conflicts, and I think he did. Little by little he works them out, and his fiction ultimately becomes very boring.

STRAUB: In general, I think one of the most satisfactory things of writing novels is that you do improve—and as you get older, you do tend to get better. And I can't see that kind of . . . banality happening to Steve. And I can't see it happening to me, either.

KING: No, I don't believe so either. One of the things that has comforted me about my own work is that, in almost all cases, I've begun with a premise that was really *black*. And a more pleasant resolution has forced itself upon that structure. Like in *'Salem's Lot*. I was convinced that everybody was going to die! That's what I wanted to happen in that book. But when it didn't, I didn't try to monkey with that fact because I knew in the end that it was *right* that they not all die.

STRAUB: Oh, of course! It would have been disastrous if they all died.

KING: Yeah, I think so. So that's okay, I think. It works both ways.

STRAUB: However, I think part of what our work is trying to do is to celebrate aspects of humanity which are worth celebrating. Courage. Gallantry. Humor and steadfastness.... These things ought to be celebrated.

KING: It's the only place you can write anymore, it seems to me, where you can still deal with romantic notions and not seem impossibly corny. You still have to be really careful though, or people will laugh.

WIATER: How important is it for you to really get under a reader's skin? To really getting close to the actual fears someone may have?

STRAUB: That's an important part of the job. You are supposed to burrow under the readers' skin. And unsettle them. Steve sometimes uses the word *hurt*, which is a wonderful word, in a way, because it sounds so violent! Sometimes you want to hurt these readers. But at the same time you don't want to hurt them too badly—I mean, you *do* want to hurt them very badly at a couple of points—but I don't think you want to leave them that way.

KING: No, not really.

WIATER: Critics are now reading all sorts of things into your work. Have there been some "underlying meanings" purposely placed in your work which readers might have missed along the way?

STRAUB: Well, especially in the case of reviewers! People sometimes construct meanings that I had never seen, and never intended. In a way it's interesting, and I don't mind it at all. And they can make elaborate structures, and when I come to meet them, I look like an absolute idiot because that stuff has never crossed my mind. But very rarely do people actually fasten on what I thought of as the center of a book. Either they talk about their own peculiar theory or they talk about the scares. More or less ignoring what I was actually doing in various books.

WIATER: Steve, the vast majority of your short stories deal with horror in supernatural rather than psychological terms. Any reason for this preference? "The Man Who Loved Flowers" is one of the very few stories that falls into the latter category.

KING: I like to make stuff up [*laughs*]! There's a scene in *Shadowland* —it's my favorite single moment—where this guy looks up from an examination and there's this pencil floating in the air, and Delmar Nightingale sees it and snatches it away because he doesn't want anyone else to see it. But that's the essence of the attraction the supernatural story has for me: that pencil just floating there in the air. It's like those Magritte paintings where trains are coming out of fireplaces, Dali paintings where clocks are lying over branches. In [my novella] *The Mist*, for instance, the great attraction in a story like that to me was I really don't *care* what causes it, or anything else. It's the idea of that train coming out of the fireplace. The familiar juxtaposed with the unusual and the strange. That, to me, is the attraction. The psychological stories just seem . . . nastier, somehow.

WIATER: It seems that Charles Beaumont—one of my personal influences—has always been one of the great unsung horror and fantasy writers. What did you think of him?

KING: I think he was great. I think he was wonderful, and I think—if he had lived—he would have been just an *amazing* writer. I just wish I had gotten to meet him sometime! I think he was amazing . . . wonderful. *The Magic Man* and *Night Ride* and all that stuff. It was good.

WIATER: Since you must read horror as much as you write it, is there anyone out who still is capable of giving you a chill or two?

STRAUB: There's only one place I can go—and that's my friend here. But most of it I find so ham-fisted, unsubtle, and badly written that I really have a lot of trouble reading it. That's not the case with Stephen King, anyway.

KING: Well, I like Peter's books better than anyone else's, so I guess I'm stuck with that [*laughs*]! I read a lot of horror novels, but I don't get a frisson from too many of them. Every now and then I get a book that scares me, that is not supposed to be in the genre—at least it *says* it's not in the genre. I can't think of an example right now. Oh—like people ask me what's the scariest book you've ever read, and my answer has always been *Lord of the Flies*. That's what scared me the most. But I usually just go to a movie—it's easier to get scared in a movie.

STRAUB: Yeah, it's easier to get scared in a movie. What I said was probably too harsh. Like Steve, I'm sent a lot of galleys, and I don't have time to read about half of them, but sometimes when you read those galleys, you find something that is very, very good by some first novelist. I don't think I've ever been *scared* by one of those books, but I've certainly read a couple that I liked a lot. But the reason I'm not scared when I read these things is that I'm too conscious of the technique. Because I *know* what he's doing—I just want to see how well he can dance.

Which is not to say I'm immune to shocks. But I think really, that if you think about that kind of thing all day long, you're less open to purely literary fear.

KING: But good writing in itself is a pleasure, and it can seduce you into the story. I'm not very concerned with style or anything like that, but I *am* concerned with the balance. Language should have a balance, and it should be a balance the reader can feel and get into, and feel a sort of rhythm to the language as it moves along. The language should be able to carry you into the story. And that's *it*. Because if the reader is seduced into the story, then it carries him away.

WIATER: Speaking of language, should the horror writer not only seduce the reader but terrorize or enrage him as well?

STRAUB: Not as far as I'm concerned. You mean, to fling an outrage in the public's face? No—I can't find any echoes there. That's not what I'm trying to do. It's not the same as *scaring* someone, because we definitely do want to scare. But gross-outs? I'm not interested in that.

KING: [*enthusiastically*] Oh, I am!!

WIATER: There's a scene in the film version of *'Salem's Lot* where the young hero is shown to be "monster-crazy." At least in the sense that his room is filled with monster models, posters, and so forth. A lot of people, including myself, went through that phase as kids. Was your room anything like that when you were that character's age?

KING: No. I think maybe I had an Aurora model werewolf at one time that I put together, but that was all. I wanted to try to set up a situation where we would be able to believe in the kid dealing with this. I knew that there were kids who were—and are—big monster freaks. You know, about the only thing that still amazes me about Forry Ackerman's *Famous Monsters of Filmland* was the letters' page. And they have something that says: "Wanted—More Readers Like Sean Beatty of Camden, New Jersey!!" And there'll be a picture of some smiling, beautiful little boy. They always look beautiful, and you think to yourself, "Here's this kid, and he's wild about monsters. But he doesn't *look* like he should be wild about monsters."

WIATER: Peter, did you go through any similar phases growing up?

STRAUB: I didn't surround myself with the accoutrements of monsterdom, but as a kid I certainly read those horror comics, those E. C. Comics that were so awful that my parents really objected to these kind of things! But I thought there was some kind of marvelousness to them. But I didn't have stuff like that on the wall....

KING: You said on "The Dick Cavett Show" that your imagination was powerful enough that you had to put down "The Rats in the Walls" once or twice. It was in that big collection....

STRAUB: Did I? Oh . . . the *Great Tales of Horror and the Supernatural*. Yeah, it was very scary. That was a great one. And there was one that

had something to do with cancer . . . ? Where these awful, wormy white sluggy creatures flowed down a staircase and into a man's room, and two years later he died of cancer.
KING: [*almost jumping out of his seat*] Holy shit!! Isn't that awful! I don't remember that one—I've blocked that one out!! Wow!
STRAUB: I remember the Arthur Machen story, "The Great God Pan," and that *really* affected me.
KING: Yeah, me too!
STRAUB: In fact, I cribbed from it unmercifully in *Ghost Story*.
KING: Oh, that's an amazing story. That's just a *good* one!
STRAUB: Yeah, that's a good story. So I definitely had a predilection for that stuff. But what I did say on the Cavett show that was true was that as a small boy, and as a preadolescent, I told ghost stories to my friends. At camp . . . every boy had to do something. Some kids did skits, and some kids did little plays, and some sang, and I stood up and told horror stories! Which I made up on the spot.
KING: [*in a psychiatrist's voice*] And you're still doing it!
STRAUB: And I'm still doing it.
WIATER: How do either of you feel about the slasher films in which seemingly only defenseless women are the victims? The media has made a lot of this, and since most of these slasher films are typically lumped in with all other horror films, the entire genre takes a bad rap.
KING: I think we have, but I don't think anybody points the finger at either one of us with any real authority. Because neither one of us has ever treated women in that stereotypical fashion. Peter, for instance, writes the most well-rounded female characters of just about anybody in popular fiction. But I think a lot of this has always been there, and will continue to be there. Peter was talking about imperfectly resolved conflicts, and I think that a lot of what this comes from is imperfectly resolved sexual conflicts. And it's involved with sex as a power trip rather than sex as a manifestation of love, where a man and a woman stand on pretty much equal ground, and each has something to give to the other. It's some kind of imperfectly realized conception of where sex is in those relationships.
WIATER: What's a typical workday for you both?
STRAUB: Well, in my case it's what I do; it's my job. And I do it in a way people do jobs. . . . I suppose my usual writing day is from about eleven to about six. But if I am "warmed up," and it's getting toward the end of a book—and I'm writing in my head all the time—then I might write to very late at night. But in general, it's just like, "Daddy's going to the office," and then Daddy comes home.

KING: I start at about eight-thirty—I try to get out and walk two or three miles first—and start to "write" as I'm walking around.
STRAUB: Walking is so wonderful for that! I don't know why, but it's just magical.
KING: Yeah. And you see things. A lot of times I'll see things while I'm walking that will turn up later that day at some point in my work. Not as a major thing, but I'll come back and have a big glass of ice water, and then I'll write from, say, eight-thirty until eleven o'clock. Then I'll stop, and then for the rest of that day and that night I'll go in there with two quarts of beer and rewrite for about two and a half hours. So I work maybe five hours a day.
STRAUB: That's about what I do. . . .
WIATER: But you don't let the work sit there—you go back at night and rewrite what you've just done in the morning?
KING: No. I always let it sit—the rewrite that I do is always on something else. What I'm working on in the morning is what I'm *working* on. The other material that I'm rewriting, that's a different function altogether for me. That's a very—"mechanical" is the wrong word—but it's a nuts-and-bolts kind of operation. You get down there . . . it's like adjusting the carburetor or something to make it right. That's what you do. But I always like to drink beer with that because it's fun, and it's not as demanding of something in me that says in the morning when I sit down, "I'm really working!"
STRAUB: "Invent!" Get in there and invent—work!!
WIATER: Okay, so when the muse tells you to go "invent," do either of you need a special room or setting in which to get your creative gears turning?
KING: Both Peter and I have our special rooms.
STRAUB: Yes, we have our rooms, but that's not what triggers it off—because if we were stuck on a boat, we'd write on the boat.
KING: Maybe not as well . . . !
STRAUB: But it's internalized—there's an internal lightning bolt or something that one is very grateful for . . . it just comes up and slams you on the head! You set up this little universe, and you order it just the way you want it and then you get hot.
WIATER: Peter, what do you enjoy most about horror fiction?
STRAUB: Steve was talking about those images of Magritte and Dali. I've always thought that the real advantage to the kind of books we write—over other genres—is that they have a deep vein of surrealism in them. It's that aspect of the field that I really find most valuable. I don't mean that in any pretentious way, but I mean that in the heart of

very good books in the "gothic" manner, there is this basic question about the nature of reality. Like the juxtaposition in Magritte of two ordinary things that creates some kind of spark of disquiet and unease. There is a shaking up the material world that supernatural fiction *has* to do—it has to jolt reality, and slice into it.

WIATER: Not only the unease in our perceiving reality, but the idea of what is sanity versus what is termed *insanity*?

STRAUB: Insanity *is* real, actual horror. And of course a depiction of it only works if it's coming as much from inside the characters as from outside. It really must do that, or it's childish. There has to be some kind of "echo" in the characters of the basic situation, and there be some kind of "rhyme" between the situation and the characters.

I think you really should have characters for whom you feel deeply, since you want to have characters who have "worlds" inside them, because everybody you know has a world inside them. And you want these people to be as complete as possible—and *then* subject them to whatever godawful thing you subject them to!

WIATER: Is there such a thing as making a work too depressing to still be considered entertaining?

STRAUB: It shouldn't be *too* depressing. I also don't see any point in depressing people. I see the point in scaring them.

WIATER: Yes, but what about the concept of unhappy endings—to have everyone die at the climax, or to have the creature of evil ultimately victorious over the forces of good?

STRAUB: I can understand the reason for doing that—because it adds another "fillip" at the end. It's a trick of technique, really. But I don't think all gothic or supernatural stories should end that way. It would be terrible—they'd all be downers.

WIATER: Recent comments have been made about "rock 'n' roll horror." Didn't you once say that you've compared writing in this genre to playing the blues?

STRAUB: That's really the way I feel about it. The analogy is that there is an incredible amount of richness and variety in what seems to be an extraordinarily limited stock of situations. But it's only limited to the extent that your imagination is limited! You know there's only a certain chord progression, and that's the blues! It goes twelve bars and repeats itself. But—what you can do with that chord progression is staggering.

WIATER: Considering the millions of words you two have published over the years, are you still—

KING: —friends [*laughs*]?

WIATER: —bubbling over with new ideas? And are you still at the stage

that the more stories you do, the more that occur to you?
STRAUB: Certainly I think Steve and I both have many, many ideas yet. I'm conscious now that I'm in a different stage in my own approach, and maybe working on *The Talisman* had something to do with this. That is, I'm much more levelheaded about it and I rewrite and revise much, much more than I ever did before.
KING: It's the word processor, I think.
STRAUB: I don't think so....
KING: [*sighing*] I revise—I mean, it's *insane* how much I revise!
STRAUB: But I think it's also that I've become more conscious of my errors than I used to be, and I can then see them much better. Maybe this means I just grew up a little bit as a writer. When I read over a page or four or five pages I wrote during the day, I can see right away the goofy spots and the errors and the dumb passages and the unnecessary parts. And I didn't used to be able to see it that well. The only other change I feel, right now, is that I'm not very interested in supernatural horror anymore, and I'm not going to write it for a while because I figure that I pretty much did it. I did what I could with that.
WIATER: But aren't your publishers saying, "Look, you're doing just fine writing chillers—don't risk it all by changing"?
STRAUB: No. I felt that particular pressure much more strongly several years in the past. And I understand that I have a duty, if I'm going to get large advances, to be entertaining and to supply a lot of narrative tension. To tie the reader to the book. So I'm going to continue to do that. I think I do that naturally, anyhow.
WIATER: Steve, are your publishers ever afraid that you might someday not want to frighten your readers anymore as well?
KING: No. No, I don't really think so. I do think that it's true that "if we give you enough rope you'll hang yourself." I think now I have enough rope so I can hang myself in Times Square at high noon with three-network coverage. If I told somebody I wanted to rewrite the Bible in common prose, I could probably get six figures for it at this point. And that's the problem—I'm not saying that to be a hot shit or conceited or anything else. But for me, that's the problem.

As far as I'm concerned—*It* is my final exam. I can't say any more about monsters. I don't *have* anything else to say about monsters: I put all the monsters in that book.

But then I never had any interest in horror to begin with. *I never did!* I just wrote all these horror novels because that's what came out. I mean, I didn't write it to make money, because, Jesus, when I started and when Peter wrote *Julia*, you *couldn't* make any money writing this stuff. It's ridiculous—the money came to us, we didn't go to the money! Like *Pet Sematary*—I didn't know what that was going to be, I thought it would be so much fun to write that book, because I didn't know what it was going to be! You just follow it along, and I think that a lot of times my mind goes down this path. People who like my stuff and the people who like Peter's stuff will come along unless you shortchange them.

WIATER: You both have already achieved an incredible degree of success in your careers—

KING: And I have enjoyed it!

WIATER: —but do you have any other goals beyond writing? Has this success opened other doors for you?

KING: To be a good husband and a good father . . . to try to stay alive . . . try not to get too fat, try not to drink too much beer. . . . I'd love to hit the inside fastball. . . .

STRAUB: I don't know. I couldn't tell you. I'd love to be able to play "Cherokee" on the tenor saxophone at a real fast tempo.

KING: Guys like me, you know, and I won't say guys like us because I won't presume for Peter, but guys like me, we were duds in high school. . . . Writing has always been *it* for me. I was just sort of this nerdy kid. I didn't get beat up too much because I was big, played a little football and stuff like that. So mostly I just got this, "King—he's weird. Big glasses. Reads a lot. Big teeth." I've thought about stopping—sometimes it seems to me I could save my life by stopping. Because I'm really compulsive about it. I drive that baby. . . .

STRAUB: I *don't* want to be a schoolteacher. I don't want to be an IBM executive. For me, that's boring. One advantage to this position that we have is that we can meet people we like, whose work we admire. Steve can hang around with rock-'n'-rollers and I can hang out with jazz musicians that I just cherish. Somehow we've got a mysterious access, and they sort of believe in us!

KING: I don't know exactly what it is, but they treat you like maybe you were . . . *smart* [*laughs*].

WIATER: Steve, we're always under the impression that writers are supposed to lead some kind of private and sedated life-style. Of course, we realize that when you become a best-selling author, you're obviously going to become a little more accessible to the public. Yet you acted in *Creepshow* and did a television commercial for American Express. . . .

KING: "Do you know me? Instead of saying, 'I wrote *Carrie*,' I carry the American Express card."

WIATER: Isn't it coming to a point where you'll be recognized whenever you walk down the street? Was this a conscious decision to get your face known as well as your name . . . ?

KING: No, it wasn't. I mean, if only people knew—this idea that somehow you have a career planned. But we were sitting around the living room and George [Romero] said to me, "Do you want to play Jordy Verrill?" Because I did this redneck in *Knightriders*. George has got a certain sense of humor and it tickled him. He thought it would be funny—and so I did Jordy.

I did the American Express commercial . . . because I thought, "Jesus Christ, that's really flattering. I must have arrived." So I did the commercial. I also did it because I thought it was a chance to do something amusing that was diametrically opposite to Jordy Verrill—sort of a late-seventies gay Hugh Hefner! Then, you have to draw a line someplace; the other day these people called me up from some other ad agency: "Saw your American Express ad. Loved it! You wanna do a Miller Lite ad?"

And I went, "Jesus! Yeah, I *do* want to do a Miller Lite ad—those are really cool!" Then I thought to myself, "You know, you're a *writer*. You do about three more of these things and you can go on *Hollywood Squares*, for all the reputation that you've got." Not that I've got much of a reputation anyway. But there had to be a point when, before you sell, you say, "I'm not a huckster, a commercial object." So I did the American Express spot and I can't explain why any better than that. But it was not for the money and it wasn't specifically for the fame so much as it was, I guess, because we get to be such commercial creatures of our time that I started to feel like, in some perverse way, that it was an *honor* to sell their product.

WIATER: Have you two reached a point where you still can stop and say, "No, it's not good enough," and start over, or do you just say, "Yeah, that's good enough to make the grade because my name is on it"?

STRAUB: I'm *less* satisfied than I used to be. I think I work harder to get it right. And I see it as a part of the obligation.

KING: [*solemnly*] I'll tell you what: It's getting later and I *want* to get better because you only get about so many chances to do good work. There's no justification not to at least try to do good work when you make the money. I mean, there are guys who are starving, just about. And they're trying to do good work. Some of them are.

STRAUB: Some of them—some of them don't know what it is.

KING: And that's why they're starving, in some cases.

WIATER: Do you two feel any responsibility for "double-handedly" raising the public awareness of the genre so that it's now far more acceptable—and respectable—than it ever was before?

STRAUB: I think we wrote "horror" novels that were actually novels. They were different from most previous horror novels. In a way, they kind of redefined what it was. Then others came in and started pushing away at the idea of what a horror novel was, too. And then commercial success gave what we were doing acceptability. Part of it is that we obtained the commercial success because we gave people the horror in a flavor in which they could take it and *believe* in it.

KING: And they were not expected to say, "Well, this is a horror novel so I have to expect all of this junky characterization and unbelievable developments and everything." I think that's what Peter means when he says we ask them to accept it as a novel first. I'm not sure how much we raised the awareness of horror or gave it any kind of a cultural cachet. I'm sure that we allowed a lot of contracts to be signed by a lot of writers, put a lot of money in a lot of pockets, that otherwise wouldn't have gone there. And I think that's a wonderful thing and I'm delighted because most of the people who are doing it aren't in it for a free ride. They're really serious about it. I think now—and I didn't used to think this way—but I think now that we might actually have a serious place in American literature in a hundred years or so....

STRAUB: In a kind of a queer way, yeah....

KING: Well, I think that we might first look to people like "Monk" Lewis or Ann Radcliffe, or neo-Gothic revival, or something like that! But maybe we'll still do a lot of good work and people will say, "Hey—they weren't so bad."

STRAUB: And the answer to the other question is "Yes, every word is autobiographical!"

Dean R. Koontz

In discussing this author, critic John Gilbert has stated, "Who, amongst modern writers, can be in fantasy, horror, science fiction, romance and thriller genres all at the same time and yet be in none of them?"

The answer: Dean R. Koontz.

What do such best-selling authors as "Leigh Nichols," "Brian Coffey," "Owen West," and "K. R. Dwyer" have in common?

The answer is Dean R. Koontz.

Once described by the *Los Angeles Times* as "the least-known, best-selling author in America," Koontz has emerged as one of today's most respected and popular writers—after a twenty-year bout with obscurity via genre paperback originals and from publishing much of his work using names other than his own—pseudonyms such as "Leigh Nichols," "Owen West," "K. R. Dwyer," and "David Axton," to list only a few. (Koontz is in the process of bringing back into print, under his own name, the best of his pseudonymous work.)

An admitted workaholic, Koontz launched his career writing science fiction stories and novels in the mid–1960s. It was not until the 1980s, however, that he began to make his mark with a series of remarkable horror and dark-suspense novels which include *Whispers, Phantoms, Darkfall, Strangers, Watchers, Lightning, Midnight*, and his latest release, *The Bad Place*. His immense popularity is indicated by the fact that, with *Midnight* (1989), he reached the number-one spot on *The New York Times* hardcover best-seller list, based on sales during the book's first week in stores. His worldwide sales total more than fifty million copies. So far, motion pictures have been produced from three of his books: *Shattered* and *Demon Seed* in 1977 and *Watchers* in 1988 (which Koontz called "hopelessly dreadful"), with several slated for production.

In his early forties, Koontz lives in southern California with his wife Gerda, whom he credits for "invaluable emotional and intellectual support during the dark days" of his career. He divides his time between writing sixty to seventy hours a week and turning down requests from motion picture studios and publishers who wish he'd write even more. His office is a fantasy come true for most writers. One corner is composed of floor-to-ceiling shelves which contain one copy of every edition of the more than fifty books Koontz has written, totaling nearly six hundred editions. He works at a magnificent, custom-made wooden desk, with every drawer designed to fit precisely his needs. Along the walls are advertising posters and framed originals of the cover artwork for several of his novels. "I can look around and see that somebody *does* buy this stuff, and likes it. When things get really gloomy, or I can't think of the right word, this helps."

A modest yet decidedly humorous man, Koontz has done more behind the scenes for other writers than he would ever be willing to admit. And in spite of the fact that he strongly dislikes the term *horror* used in conjunction with his work, he was the first president of the Horror Writers of America.

WIATER: For many years you employed a pseudonym for practically every other novel you wrote. Yet didn't the pseudonyms only hinder your becoming a recognized brand name author?
KOONTZ: Sometimes there are legitimate reasons for using them. If your publisher wants you to have only one book a year under your name, yet you have the ability to write two, you might need a pen name. But I also used them for the wrong reason because of bad advice. I wrote in a wide range of styles, and I experimented with style, so I was told that every time I did something different from what I'd done before, I had to use a different name in order not to alienate or confuse the reader. After a while I figured out this wasn't true; readers will stay with an

author, no matter what the variations in style and genre, as long as they get that sense of story, of character, of empathetic involvement that the work provides when it's functioning at its highest level. In fact I've learned that readers appreciate a writer who will risk fresh approaches, book after book—as long as the stretch the writer is making actually works.

I began to realize that all these books, which were being well reviewed under pen names, were doing absolutely nothing to build *my* name. Nobody knew those writers were me! If all the books had been published under one byline, and those good reviews had reflected upon me—not upon a motley group of pseudonyms—the reading public would have been aware of me far sooner. So I dropped all of them.

WIATER: Isn't it true that of your first three best-sellers, two of them were under pseudonyms? For example, your "Leigh Nichols" books sold well worldwide and had a reputation of their own.

KOONTZ: You always risk the danger of your pen name becoming more famous than your own. Two of my first three million-seller paperbacks were under other names. And look at Evan Hunter. He's a wonderful novelist, but more people know "Ed McBain" than know Evan Hunter now. The first book I had on any best-seller list was *The Key to Midnight* by "Leigh Nichols." And *that* was an unsettling event because I couldn't go around in bookstores grabbing people and saying, "Hey, this 'Nichols' is really me!" [*laughs*] I'd look deranged! The second was *Whispers*, which was under my own name, but then the third was *The Funhouse* under the "Owen West" identity.

I now recommend that writers avoid pen names. If you have to pay the bills, and you write something you're not proud of, use a pen name for that. But if you're proud of your books—as I was of those under many of my pseudonyms—put them out under your own name and to hell with what the wisdom of the business is! Because if the books are written with care and passion, publishing them under other identities softens your impact. And if you want to publish two books a year under your own name and your publisher doesn't, maybe you need a different publisher.

WIATER: You began your career in science fiction, though you have no plans of reissuing the novels you wrote in that period between 1966 and 1972. But did you go into that genre because it was what you enjoyed writing at the time, or because you felt it was the easiest market to break into?

KOONTZ: Never, never try to scope the market. If you say, "They want science fiction, so I'll write science fiction," or, "They want mysteries, so I'll write mysteries," then you're *doomed*. You've got to write what you're passionate about. Otherwise you'll produce juiceless, flavorless fiction. I sold my first story when I was a senior in college, and to some extent I regret that I started selling so young. Because *young* and *naive* are two words which go together, as are *young* and *stupid*—at least in my case [*laughs*]. A lot of that early work is so poorly formed because I was inexperienced and floundering, but I *was* passionate, all right. Because I began that early, I was writing what I'd read as a kid, which was science fiction. It was my favorite form of fiction then, so I wrote it out of sheer love. But I eventually burnt out on it.

WIATER: Around this time you began writing a wide range of novels, including horror and suspense. Apparently the "powers-that-be" felt this was another bad career move, since you had already spent years to establish yourself in one genre.

KOONTZ: I had become a heavy reader of suspense of all kinds, and a great admirer of John D. MacDonald, Donald Westlake, James M. Cain, Raymond Chandler—a whole host of people. That reading influenced the direction of my work because I began to enjoy *that* kind of fiction over any other. When I made the switch, I was advised that the suspense genre was really moribund, that there were other things I should have been writing. But I happily moved into what I was told was a dying form because, dying or not, I loved it.

WIATER: I know that you went so far as to buy back the rights to your early novels so you couldn't be classified any further as a science fiction writer. Yet isn't that part of the reason why you have equally strong feelings about being labeled for a time as a horror writer, because readers might mistakenly believe you can only write in that genre, once again incapable of transcending it?

KOONTZ: Exactly. There are many reasons why I don't want the label, and that's one of them. I don't want to be limited as to what I can write; I want to be able to write what I want. For example, when I signed a recent three-book deal with Putnam, the most appealing clause in the contract was that they wouldn't know anything about the contents of the books, not even the titles, until the delivery of the manuscripts. That's the only way I want to write. I write what I want to read, what appeals to me, and what excites me at the moment.

A second reason is that I don't exactly like a lot of what usually carries the "Horror" label. Any time there's a boom in the genre, you find yourself mixed in with a lot of writers who are grabbing what's popular at the moment, and who are writing it because there's a market for it, not out of true passion. So you end up being tarred with that same brush.

WIATER: What caused you to break away from this fairly rigid genre identification—for now a Koontz novel is not "just" a science fiction or a thriller or a horror novel, but a seamless melding of many diverse elements?
KOONTZ: Something clicked with me about 1974 or 1975 when I wrote *Night Chills*. I still had a love of fiction of the fantastic, and I began to blend certain SF and horror elements with the suspense novel.
WIATER: What elements exactly?
KOONTZ: Well, scientific extrapolation from SF. For example, *Night Chills* deals with possible new developments in mind control, and the plot of *Watchers* springs from genetic engineering. SF is in part a fiction of *ideas*, so I took that aspect of the genre for my blend. From horror I borrowed mood more than anything—that cold sense of foreboding, eeriness, ineffable but frightening presences at the periphery of vision, which is always a part of good horror writing. From the suspense genre I took a contemporary setting—all my books are set in the present or the past, never the far future—as well as headlong pace and tension; few SF novels and fewer horror novels are tense and swift moving, so I felt that I'd really have something if I coupled SF's ideas with horror's mood in a story with a suspense novel's taut pace.
WIATER: Sounds easy enough. But seriously, did you set out to achieve this blend intentionally, or was it something you did unconsciously and noted in retrospect?
KOONTZ: A little of both. I was dissatisfied with the possibilities offered by any one genre, and I knew that I wanted to bring various genres together and knit them up into a mainstream novel, so some of my decisions were conscious and calculated. But creativity is as much an unconscious process, and many of the techniques and approaches I came up with were not obvious to me until I had been using them awhile. You can't coldly calculate and *plan* a new style. All you can do is determine what you hope to achieve, then create the mental environment that will let art happen on deeper levels of consciousness.

Anyway, my current style and narrative approach were arrived at by evolution. I said earlier that I wish I hadn't begun publishing so young. But on the other hand, I wouldn't have become what I have become if I had undone those early years. After putting in time as a science fiction writer, with my imagination running wild, I was able to approach the suspense novel with a background that other suspense writers never had. Therefore my plots tended to be fresher—or at least stranger—than theirs [*laughs*]. More off the beaten path. For example, I can't think of another suspense writer who would come up with a plot like

that in *Midnight*, which deals with the development of silicon microspheres that can be injected into the human body, there to link up and form a computer that actually overrides the brain in the interest of "improving" the species. The book doesn't have one spy in it, not one serial killer, not one of anything you expect to find in a traditional suspense novel, yet it is most certainly suspense.
WIATER: You've clearly made your point. So how would you best describe your own work?
KOONTZ: Back in 1974 or 1975, I coined the term *cross-genre*, and no one could figure what I was talking about, but now the term is getting wider usage. In my case this means the aforementioned melding of elements of mystery, suspense, science fiction, horror, adventure—even the love story. But most important to me is telling the tale from *a mainstream point of view*, with mainstream sensitivity.
WIATER: Yet you certainly had a viable genre reputation even before you broke through into the mainstream. Wouldn't it be advantageous for some new writers to establish a career by becoming closely associated with a particular genre, such as horror?
KOONTZ: It depends on what kind of writer you want to be; what you're going to be satisfied with. I'm not talking money now. I'm talking about the size of the audience that will satisfy you. Will you be happy with a small audience, a middle-size one? If you're really serious about your writing and have a view to impart that you think is important, then you're *never* going to be satisfied with the size of the audience you'll get as a midlist genre writer.

If, however, you'd be happy to make a comfortable—though at times uncertain—living with a medium-size genre audience, then you will approach your career totally differently. You'll write smaller, less-complex books. They might be brilliant books, you understand, but they'll be different because you'll be seeking a different niche. The problem is that some people say they'd be happy with that, then they discover they aren't happy when they're stuck in such a career. I know many writers who have spent twenty years developing a fine genre reputation with which they are completely dissatisfied. They have done excellent, admirable work—and they're miserable. Now, after all these years, they're so typed they can't escape the jail they've built for themselves. Publishers see them as writers with a limited audience, and they're never given the chance to do the broader work when they're ready for it.

It's wise to plan early on where you'd like to go, do serious self-analysis to determine what you want from a writing career. Now, I made the same mistake. When I began I thought I'd be comfortable as a straight genre writer. I just kept switching genres as my interests grew! I have since been fortunate that—with a great deal of effort—I have been able to break the chains of genre labeling and do larger and more complex books. But it's very difficult, and very few people who develop straight genre reputations ever escape them.

WIATER: But what do you say to someone who truly enjoys writing dark suspense or horror—how can they thrive in an established field and yet not be swallowed up by it?

KOONTZ: Let's say your primary area of interest is in suspense fiction. Then I think a new writer, starting out, should realize there are two approaches. He can come up with nice, simple suspense stories about two people harassed by a psychopathic killer—like my own early book, *Shattered*—and he can sell things like that steadily. The other approach is to say, "I want to write suspense. What has nobody done before? I want to come up with an idea that is staggeringly original, no matter how much sweat and blood it takes."

Start out that way, and you've got a much better chance of breaking into a bigger career. If you're going to be a novelist, you might as well start out as Scott Turow and Tom Clancy did. They created something new within a form they loved. Clancy virtually single-handedly created a subgenre of suspense; and whether or not you like his stuff, you should realize he guaranteed a place for himself in the history of popular fiction by writing something which didn't exist before him.

WIATER: But how *do* you form and explore these fresh ideas?

KOONTZ: There may be other ways, but I only know one: You have to read enormous amounts of material of all kinds; you have to be constantly feeding the subconscious, giving it material from which it can devise story ideas. First you must read nonfiction of all kinds, not just in areas that already interest you, but in a wide range of subjects. I regularly read books and magazines about the latest developments in genetics, physics, medical technology, forensic medicine, police technology and procedure, and much more. I read a daily newspaper, three Sunday newspapers, and scores of magazines every month. I never take notes, and I never consciously look for story ideas; it's a much subtler process than that. You pour the information into the subconscious, dump it all in like meat and vegetables into a stewpot, then let it cook until the ideas boil to the surface. They *will* boil up, I guarantee, and they'll be far better than the ones you arrive at by conscious manipulation of story elements, better because they're not forced.

Then you have to read fiction, too, lots of it, and not only in one or two genres. I read mysteries, suspense, science fiction, horror, Westerns, mainstream, everything. The more you read, the more you become aware of the techniques that are special to every genre, and the more you begin to see ways to meld the strengths of the genres into a whole that is, one hopes, more than the sum of its parts. Finally, you have to live a life of broad interests. You can't acquire the breadth of experience that makes for good writing if you spend most of your weekends at writer-fan conventions. Get out, get around. See and do!

WIATER: Like many novelists, you use a word processor. Do you believe it truly aids a writer to learn how to work on one, or doesn't it make that much difference, creatively speaking?

KOONTZ: It all comes down to the writer. You should learn how to use a word processor. If you approach it as a wonderful tool that allows you to do extensive revisions and a lot of polishing with ease, then it's going to improve your writing. If you only approach it as something that will make your work go along faster, the result will be sloppier writing. If you're passionate about language and *driven* as a writer, word processors will serve your passion. If you're lazy, they'll just encourage laziness.

WIATER: Do you ever need any special trick to jump-start your creative engine?

KOONTZ: I love what I do, so I don't have to motivate myself. But here's one thing—there's a handful of writers whose influence on me has been greater than anyone else's. So I tend to keep their books nearby: John D. MacDonald, James M. Cain, Ray Bradbury, Dickens, several others. I'll sometimes start the morning by picking up one of their books, a particular favorite, and read a few paragraphs at random to appreciate the use of language. Writers I tend to use this way had a terrific sense of the language and could write a sentence that really moved, that had a dazzling shine to it. I'll say, "Damn, that's good!" and it motivates me to want to do something that might approach the imagery and musicality of prose that I admire in them.

WIATER: Perhaps it can be safely assumed that some writers are following that very same pattern of inspiration with a favorite Dean R. Koontz novel?

KOONTZ: It'd be a lot of fun to think so.

WIATER: I'm aware of the amount of fan mail you receive and how you do your utmost to respond to most of it. What is so special about fans to you?

KOONTZ: They are the concrete evidence that you touch people's lives.

Like the guy who called me and said, "Last year I had a leg amputated and was in the hospital for that and related problems dealing with cancer for a period of several months. In the course of that time I lost my business, and my wife left me." And he told me, with his voice breaking, "The only thing that got me through that year, and made me want to go on, were two books of yours, *Strangers* and *Watchers*, which were scary novels but were filled with so much hope, and so much faith in human beings, that by reading them repeatedly got me through times I don't know how I would have otherwise gotten through."

That for me is what writing is all about. If something in your writing gives support to people in their lives, that's more than just entertainment—which is what we writers all struggle to do, to touch people. Entertainment is just a vehicle to reach them on a much deeper level.

Also, a woman wrote me and said, "My father is dying of cancer. He is the most wonderful father anyone could have had, and he's only in his fifties, with six months to live. I'm not articulate enough to say all the things I want to say when I speak at his funeral. There's a long passage in *Twilight Eyes* about how what we really fear is not our own death but the deaths of those we love. Would it be possible for me if I could read that at his funeral service and reprint it in the program?" Man, you can't answer a letter like that fast enough!

Something you've written has clearly touched someone on a deep, personal level and speaks directly to their lives. *Those* are the moments when you think you're doing something worthwhile.

Joe R. Lansdale

Karen Lansdale

Like his friend and colleague Dean R. Koontz, native Texan Joe R. Lansdale is possessed of an enormous and varied talent which can't be locked into a single genre. With such controversial and violent novels as *Act of Love*, *The Nightrunners*, and *Cold in July*, it's obvious that Lansdale is on his way to becoming a master of psychological horror and suspense—even if he doesn't like to be labeled as favoring any genre. With such plain weird novels as *The Drive-in* and *The Drive-in 2 (Not Just One of Them Sequels)*, Lansdale also shows a penchant for the utterly outrageous which is second to none. His Western-horror novel *Dead in the West* reads like Zane Grey's (and George A. Romero's) worst nightmare in its unflinching descriptions of mutilation and mayhem. Then again, a small gem like *The Magic Wagon* is poignant enough to bring tears to anyone who reads it and can still remember what it's like to be a child.

If his novels weren't enough to insure his reputation, then the short stories (over one hundred to date) would certainly qualify this plain-talkin', straight-shootin' Texan for at least cult status. Just three stories like "Tight Little Stitches in a Dead Man's Back" (*Year's Best Horror Stories XV*), the Stoker award-winning "Night They Missed the Horror Show" (*Silver Scream*), and "On the Far Side of the Cadillac Desert with Dead Folks" (*Book of the Dead*) were enough to declare to the critics that he had arrived. A collection, fittingly entitled *By Bizarre Hands*, was published in 1989 by specialty publisher Mark Ziesing.

As a writer, Lansdale is possessed of the ability to make you laugh out loud and then retch in disgust—sometimes in the same sentence. His voice as a writer is unmistakably his own. In person, Lansdale is both funny and profane, and the last person in the world to think he deserves some special status on this earth just because he thinks and writes differently from just about anyone you'll ever encounter in the field.

WIATER: There was a time when you were grouped in with the lads half-seriously referred to as the splatterpunks. It was a title that you didn't seem too pleased to carry.
LANSDALE: I didn't like to be called a splatterpunk writer, *at all*. I was doing what I was doing long before anyone decided to call anything splatterpunk. I don't think it's a fair term anyway, in the sense that I do a wide variety of things. I don't mean to imply that I dislike splatterpunk or the people who write it; I don't like the title merely because I find it *limiting*. If people start thinking of you in that way, then they always expect you to write that sort of fiction. I don't like any kind of label at all—I don't even think of myself as a horror writer. And I don't mean that in the way those film directors say, "Oh my God, this isn't a horror film . . . !"

I, by God, *like* horror. And I write horror. But I write other things, too. It's no more fair to call me a horror writer than a Western writer or a suspense writer, because I'm those, too. I'm a writer. So it doesn't bother me at all to be called a horror writer; the only thing I'm saying is I don't want to be referred to just as a horror writer, because I don't want to mislead people into expecting that all the time. But it is the largest percentage of my work. And I think a lot of the novels and short stories I've written, which may not be thought of strictly as horror, always have *horrific* details. In my suspense work it's the same way.
WIATER: You may not use the term *horror*, but there's a great deal of intense violence in your work, and for many critics, violence can often be equated with contemporary definitions of horror.
LANSDALE: That's true. A lot of stories I've written have no violence or your usual "action" in them, but I do lean in that direction. I'm fascinated by violence—I'll be the first one to say so. But my fascination with it doesn't necessarily mean I enjoy violence or that I'm a violent person any more than anyone else. But I suppose that all people who

are involved with horror, action-adventure, suspense, or crime are in some way connected with that interest in violence. But then, that's what sells newspapers and television programs. So most of us—who are at least willing to admit it—are in some way or another interested in violence, even if our interest is to be incredibly repulsed by the whole idea of violence.

WIATER: But few writers seem to deal with violence so intensely; you almost gleefully rub the reader's nose in the sight and smell of it.

LANSDALE: There is a certain glee in my work, I'll admit. But for me, it heightens the horror. It's really a little trick I learned from Robert Bloch. I think my approach and style is very different from Bloch's, but he is really the one who taught me—and so many others—that horror and humor are opposite sides of the sword. When I was growing up, Bloch was undoubtedly my favorite horror writer—and is still one of my favorite horror writers. Maybe the favorite horror writer of them all.

The hard-boiled mystery writers influenced me in terms of style and approach. In many ways, I consider Robert Bloch a hard-boiled writer, with *Psycho* and *The Scarf*. Those are masterpieces. I think the hard-boiled voice has influenced me a lot more than horror writers. In the same way, Flannery O'Connor has been an enormous influence. So I like that straightforward, here-it-is, "fuck you" attitude. Bloch gave me an attitude. He was an original I-don't-know-what-you-would-call-it, but he would always cackle on about the most unpleasant things in the world [*laughs*]! And I always liked that posture, because if I was going to read horror, I wanted it to be scary. For me, he *was* scarier that way. And when he wasn't scary, he was at least always interesting and entertaining.

I think there's nothing more frightening than to find horrible things somewhat amusing. Any horror movie or book—even a good one—if you stop and think about the majority of 'em, the idea's *stupid*. Unless you really believe in vampires and witches and werewolves. Of course horror has moved in considerably different directions from that, which I believe it has to—we've outgrown it for the most part. Which is not to say people shouldn't write about these supernatural creatures—I'm not saying I wouldn't do it. But in modern times, they become more representative of modern themes rather than simply being vampires and witches and werewolves. They may have had some psychological representation in the past, but they must have even more now if they're to be used effectively. They represent today's society.

WIATER: That's why the traditional label of "Horror" doesn't quite fit you—your work is more concerned with the terror man has in fighting his inner demons rather than any supernatural forces from beyond.

LANSDALE: Yes, I really am. I find as time goes on I'm more and more bored with supernatural elements—a large percentage of my work doesn't contain them at all. I hadn't thought about it before, but it's almost Lovecraftian in that I often deal with the breakdown of what you think are the expected rules of existence. In a sense, I guess that's what H. P. Lovecraft was doing with his Cthulhu Mythos, except he had them explained as aliens or entities.

WIATER: Where do you feel your strength lies as a writer—in novel or short story form?

LANSDALE: I prefer the short story medium. I think if I could make a living as a short story writer, I would do that primarily. I do like to write novels, though, and I'm proud of all the novels with my name on 'em. But I feel better about the short stories in general, though I'm very proud of *The Magic Wagon* and *Cold in July*. They're my favorite of my novels, for whatever reason.

WIATER: *The Magic Wagon* is unique among your works to date; it's all but impossible to shoehorn into any one genre. What compelled you to write it?

LANSDALE: I feel a strong connection to that one because it's very much about East Texas, and it takes place the year my father was born. My father's "voice" is the voice I tried to capture, with my own voice mixed in. By that I mean it contains some of the stories and attitudes that he told me when I was growing up. And I added in my own tendencies toward fantasy and oddball elements. But I am also a great fan of Westerns. I wish I had written more Westerns, but fate just didn't work out that way. I have a great big Western novel that I would like to do at some point.

What I've begun to realize, and I could be wrong on this, is that one of the things that makes my horror work interesting is that I do come at it from the perspective of thinking of myself as a Western or suspense writer writing horror. So the blend comes out more interesting for me. If you analyze a lot of my stories, you'll see they are very Western oriented or have Western elements.

WIATER: *The Drive-in* and its sequel *The Drive-in 2* are again two novels which seem to fit into no set genre, but rather use elements of every fantasy-related genre one can imagine, plus some elements no sane person should be able to imagine.

LANSDALE: I usually enjoy every line when I'm writing. But I didn't enjoy writing either one of the drive-in books. And they're the ones that seem the lightest and the "frothiest" in many ways. I had a very, very hard time writing them. I think the universe I set them in was confining. Also, I work better when I am dealing with normal situations that are screwed up, instead of abnormal situations that get screwed up even more! Because in a universe where anything can happen you have to rely very strongly on humor and on characters, and that just takes a lot out of you. Writing those two books was very much like being a stand-up comic. You're on stage, people paid their money, and by God you'd better be funny—cause they got tomatoes....

WIATER: Stephen King has often stated the theory of the three levels of horror, the third and most outrageous being "to go for the gross-out." Some of your critics would state this is the level where Joe Lansdale typically begins.

LANSDALE: [laughs] I like to go for the gross-out if it has some irony. I'll probably put my foot in my mouth for saying so—and then they'll say, "That pretentious asshole!"—but I think of myself as a satirist a lot of times. Not every time out, but I often see what I do as being that way because some stuff is so over the top that it is humor. Like "Cadillac Desert...." A number of people I'm told were deeply offended, which in one sense makes me feel real good. And in another sense, I'm not out just to write something that will offend. It's very easy to offend—but it's not easy to offend deeply [laughs].

WIATER: Organized religion seems to be one of your favorite targets as a satirist, again most obviously in *The Drive-in* and its sequel.

LANSDALE: I seem to have this thing about religion. I step on it every chance I get. But it's not that I'm stepping on people's beliefs in religion. I'm stepping on the *smugness* that people have about religion, about how everybody's got to believe in this to be a good person. I think that I'm a good person, and lead a good life, and don't have to go to church or necessarily believe in a Christian God—or any God—for that matter. I can believe that I live this life, I die, I go belly up, I'm meat for the worms. And if I can be a good person knowing that, that can be an accomplishment that may be greater than expecting some reward in the next life.

WIATER: Any boundaries you've set on yourself as a writer? You don't appear to be the sort who "pre-censors" his work to insure easy acceptance from an editor or publisher.

LANSDALE: No, I don't think so either. Much to the dissatisfaction of a lot of publishers, and to the audience, too, at some point. I'm sure I have some subconscious boundaries, like everybody else. Most of my boundaries would be in that I would write about almost anything—

except in an area where I feel it's already been overworked. Or this particular subject is something I can't give anything new to. My boundaries are: Try to avoid stupidity. Or trying to repeat what someone else has done because you like what they did. Those are the only real boundaries I have in mind.

WIATER: Do you ever use any of your personal fears or experiences in your stories?

LANSDALE: I use a *tremendous* amount of autobiographical material, and I use a lot of my own fears. I use a lot of the fears of other people, that they've told me. But usually if I can't put something of myself into the stories, I can't write them. Which is not the same thing as saying the stories represent all my beliefs, but they are boiled down from my subconscious. Mainly it's autobiographical elements from personal attitudes and beliefs or experiences. A lot comes from newspaper headlines.

WIATER: It's well known you had some trouble early in your career with publishers being afraid to deal with such violent and uncompromising novels as *Act of Love* and *The Nightrunners*. Is this still the case?

LANSDALE: You know, it's funny, but when I started out, I sure did have trouble. Now, publishers always expect for me to be over the top, and don't even think about it anymore. Maybe they should [*laughs*]. No, I hope it doesn't get to that again. I've had editors say, "I like the story, but I just can't... because I'm afraid it'll ruin my magazine." I had one story called "Boys Will Be Boys" which caused subscriptions to be canceled.

WIATER: Could you tell me what your typical workday is like?

LANSDALE: I usually get up with the wife and kids around seven-thirty and I try to get down to work within thirty minutes of when I get up, and work till about noon. I take off an hour, hour and a half, for lunch, then go back to work till about three. And I do that seven days a week. Sometimes I'll pull a double-shift if I get a little behind. But mainly I'll do only that, because I have a family and I have interests other than writing. I just don't live to put paper in the typewriter. I like to spend time with my wife and my kids. There's a lot of things I'm interested in that I try to devote time to because I think you can get very stale as a writer. Those people who just live to write eventually repeat themselves. Besides, what kind of life is that? Go out and get a life!

WIATER: I can see you now: practicing martial arts in your backyard, followed by a half-dozen Lone Star beers, right?

LANSDALE: I'm not much of a drinker, contrary to what people always

assume—that I'm a big, two-fisted drinker. I very seldom ever do. There goes the image! I'm an iced tea and Diet Coke man.
WIATER: Speaking of image, what advice do you have for someone who imagines writing fiction to be an easy road to fame and fortune?
LANSDALE: Learn to be a plumber. I'm serious. You need to learn something where you can make money, set your own hours, and then spend your spare time writing as you see fit. A plumber makes pretty good wages, doesn't have to work all the time, and doesn't have to take a specific job if he doesn't want to. I was a janitor, and found that was good for me. The rest of the advice is put your ass in a chair, put some paper in a typewriter, and write.
WIATER: Early on in your career you ghostwrote some novels, and also did some pseudonymous work. For what reasons?
LANSDALE: First of all, there haven't been many ghostwritten or pseudonymous books. Oddly enough, there were a number of projects where I was hired to do writing on them, was paid, and then the projects were eventually canceled for a variety of reasons. I once wrote *one* chapter for an action-adventure novel. Don't ask me why [*laughs*]. One of the pseudonymous novels is fairly common knowledge, though I don't think it's much of a book. It's a Western by "Ray Slater." There's very few copies of it, so I don't worry about it, though I would never reprint it. But the reasons I did them was simply to put food on the table, and also just practice.
WIATER: You've also edited a few very strange Western anthologies. Like your own work, they are a wild collage of Western elements, science fiction, horror, fantasy, mystery—you name it. What was the inspiration behind them?
LANSDALE: In many ways they were attempts to interest people in the cross-pollinization of genres. *Best of the West* has perhaps more traditional Western material than the others. My love of Westerns is there, but I didn't hold anybody to any strict guidelines and cliches: "Just take some idea of the Western in your mind and take it from there." It's the whole idea of blending genres and becoming a little less genre-conscious. Which is not a comment that I don't like horror or Westerns or science fiction—I like all of them—but I think one of the things that is wrong with all those fields is that they become *predictable*. They become what's *expected*. And that's the main reason I did the anthologies, and each one's a little bit different from the others. *The New Frontier* is the one I'm most proud of.
WIATER: I understand you're also anxious to become more involved with screenwriting, or at least adapting your own work to the screen?

LANSDALE: *Dead in the West* has been optioned. The book itself was optioned—I've done a screenplay, and we'll see what happens to it. I've had a tremendous amount of film interest in all of my work. I haven't written a novel yet that there hasn't been film interest in. So we'll see what all pans out. But I like the idea of writing original screenplays, and might even adapt a book someone else wrote. But I don't feel driven: "My God, I've got to work in the movies!" I want to do it, but I believe I can pick and choose the projects I want to work on. A few years ago, things might have been different; I might have needed the money and said, "Sure, I want to write the next sequel to *Piranha XII*."

WIATER: It was once said about Charles Beaumont that he was the sort of writer who wouldn't be remembered for the titles of his books, but for his name being *on* the books. Does this seem to hold true as well for you?

LANSDALE: I generally just think, "This is the story I'm telling now. I will tell it to the best of my ability." I don't worry if I'm topping the last story or not. I don't worry if my audience is going to accept it or not. I don't think about my audience, and that's not an insult to the readers. I certainly care about the readers. But when I sit down behind the typewriter, *fuck the readers!* What I'm interested in then is *me* as a writer, or otherwise I cannot get this story down. And if I start worrying about my readership, then I'm going to repeat myself and burn out either me or my readers. Or I'm going to bore myself, which in that case, why not dig a ditch?

I'm just not going to open new gates if I say, "I've found what works!" I don't think I've ever found what works. There's a certain voice that comes through most of my stories, but I'm sort of like a weathervane—there's no telling where I'll point next time! I want to keep it that way, because I think in the long run I'll get more readers and the readers respect that more. I don't ever want to be a predictable commodity.

Richard Laymon

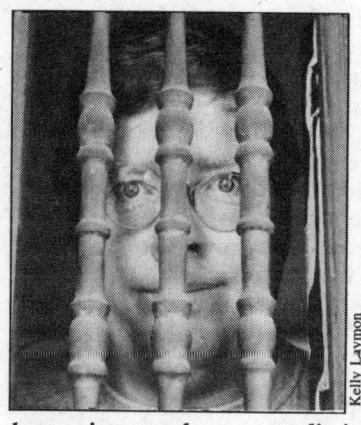

By this point, the reader is no doubt familiar with the popular buzzword regarding the "new wave" in horror—the infamous *splatterpunk*. Some writers like the term, others who have been labeled with that name energetically reject it, while others whose work truly fits the description have never seen their name and *that* word used in the same review. A case in point: one dark dreamer who actually *has* written truly gory, sadistic, and blood-drenched tales, years before the term which perhaps best describes him came into its current usage.

The case in point is Richard Laymon.

Right from the start, with the publication in 1980 of a no-holds-barred chiller called *The Cellar*, Laymon has shown that he is not afraid to hit below the waist. Laymon writes in a style that leaves little to the imagination, and yet he deals with ordinary details and people in such a way that the reader almost always imagines an even worse fate for his terrified characters.

Born on January 14, 1947, in Chicago, Illinois, Laymon's family moved to southern California in the early sixties. He still lives in that state, but now with a family of his own. Like many writers, he has served time as both a librarian and a high school teacher. He has written in a variety of genres (Westerns, romances, juveniles, mysteries) under several pseudonyms. He has published some fifty stories, many of them for straight mystery magazines such as *Ellery Queen's Mystery Magazine* and *Alfred Hitchcock's Mystery Magazine*. (I am also pleased to say that I obtained his services in this form as one-third of the lineup for *Night Visions 7*, which I edited in 1989.)

Horror, of course, has always been his primary interest, and remains the focus of nearly all his novels. In addition to *The Cellar*, they include *The Woods Are Dark, Out Are the Lights, Night Show, All Hallow's Eve, Tread Softly, Flesh, Midnight's Lair, Beware, Resurrection Dreams, Funland*, and *The Stake*. Several show a pronounced influence of a steady diet of horror movies, particularly the low-budget splatter variety.

In person, Laymon actually does remind one of a high school teacher, or more closely the stereotype of a quiet, pleasant, unassuming physical education coach. Like all the dark dreamers, he does not appear to be in any way as sadistic and warped as his imagination. An imagination which he will admit he keeps in check because his visions are so dark they often would be stomached only by the most hard-core horror fan. About the only way you can tell that Laymon enjoys his work is that he can't help grinning from ear to ear whenever he comes up with a particularly repulsive idea. Whatever buzzword you may give his style, Richard Laymon is a killer with words.

WIATER: I imagine your work has been rejected by more than a few editors who might otherwise be receptive to more "standard" horror fare?
LAYMON: I'm pretty sure that it has been [*laughs*]. I have a letter from a publisher which has its own horror line, and though the editor doesn't spell out exactly why she declined my work, says something to the effect, "In all good conscience it wouldn't be right for us to publish these novels." I also have a great rejection slip from a literary agent. The first time I ever sent out a novel—one that's never been published, by the way—I got back a letter from this old, established agency saying, "The book shows a lot of talent, and we wish you success with it elsewhere, but we found it was too sadistic in subject matter and don't think we could handle it." I framed that letter.
WIATER: The critical perception that you write stories with sadistic themes has been with you since the publication of your first novel. In *Fangoria*, for example, your early novels were praised for the way your characters often ended up drenched in blood. Which is leading to, do you think you deserve—or do you even want—to be thought of as a splatterpunk?

LAYMON: Speaking of *Fangoria*, there's a lot about the magazine in my novel *Night Show*. You might want to check that out. I did a lot of my research for the book by reading *Fangoria*. In fact, the magazine itself plays a key part in the plot, which deals with a special-effects makeup artist. But you asked about splatterpunks. Well, I don't like the "punk" part of it because you picture people with spiked hair and razor blades in their ears. Now, if you want to call it "rock 'n' roll horror," I might go along with that.

My real problem with some of the splatterpunks is that their main characters often seem to be the real punks. I don't think readers appreciate protagonists who are obnoxious assholes [*chuckles*]. Yet I certainly have no qualms against writers getting down and dirty. Or bloody and gory. Not if it's done well.

In spite of the way I feel about the so-called splatterpunks, I do sometimes resent it when I hear about them and I'm not mentioned. I was writing graphic, erotic horror novels when some of those guys were still in high school. But I really don't want to be identified with a group, anyway. Especially not that one.

WIATER: It would seem undeniable that you truly like to get "down and dirty" in your work. Do you ever restrict your imagination, or pre-censor yourself to give the story or novel a greater chance of acceptance with a publisher?

LAYMON: Oh, I've started restricting myself considerably.

WIATER: [*taken aback*] Why—for what good reason?

LAYMON: It depends on the market. I did pull out *all* the stops when I wrote my story for the anthology *Book of the Dead*. But I think this a factor that horror writers have to deal with: If you want to try for major success, you can't be too far out. To have that "blockbuster mainstream" novel, you have to temper the nastiness, gore, sex, sadism—all that fun stuff [*laughs*]!

WIATER: Now why am I not surprised to hear you say that [*laughs*]!

LAYMON: So I've been going more in the direction of toning myself down. I still try to come up with some real nasty material, but I have been self-censoring myself a little bit lately. It's not just me, though. I've seen this trend going on with most horror writers whose careers I've been following: A *lot* of them start off real gritty, and then taper off as time goes by. I don't think it's because they're mellowing with age. I think it's because they have an eye on the marketplace, and they're looking for a wider audience.

WIATER: But are you saying this is good or bad creatively, in terms of the direction horror fiction may be taking?

LAYMON: It makes it harder to find well-written raunch [*laughs*]. But I think the average citizen doesn't really want a hard-core pukebag brand of horror. In a way, neither do I. I think the main thing about horror is that it should be fun.
WIATER: Explain please? How can blood and sex and death be fun?
LAYMON: I don't like to read stories which are actually *upsetting*. Real life is upsetting. I think that reading a horror novel should be a trip to the fun house, not the charnel house. I don't want to feel like I'm taking a tour through Auschwitz. I want to be scared, but I want it to be that fun kind of scare. That carnival kind. You know it's make-believe. When I'm writing, I want to frighten you and sometimes gross you out, but I don't want you to feel as if I'm putting it to you in a torture chamber.
WIATER: But what of those dark dreamers who do take their horror extremely seriously? Who actively seek to bring the reader into a charnel house, and not a fun house, as you phrase the difference?
LAYMON: Well, I think if you do go into a charnel house, you should still try to make it as much fun as possible. I mean, in a way I'm wading through a charnel house all the time, but with a sense of glee, not depression. I don't see the fun in it otherwise. I read for fun, and I write for fun. Now, by saying all this, I don't want to give the impression that I don't take horror literature seriously. I do. It can be the structure to tell any kind of story, and for really getting to the heart of the human condition. It's just there are other writers who seem to take the matter much more seriously than I feel comfortable doing.
WIATER: You wrote in other genres before making a successful career in horror. Any regrets with now being universally identified in this genre?
LAYMON: Oh, no! I'm proud of it. I wouldn't want to be known as anything but.
WIATER: Did you always secretly want to be a horror writer?
LAYMON: Yes, that's how it was for me. The first story I ever wrote was something about a witch. It was in the sixth grade, I think, and the teacher read it out loud to the class. I ended it with a witch's cackle. I think the story I did after that was about werewolves. So my heart was always in there. I was also reading *Famous Monsters of Filmland*—I wish I had kept those suckers! What I did was tear out the articles I was really fond of, and save them, and throw away the rest of the magazine [*groans*]. I've learned my lesson though—I keep all my *Fangoria* intact.
WIATER: There's an obvious cinematic influence in your work. Many

of your early novels in fact seem like the prose equivalent of low-budget splatter movies. How much of an effect did horror movies have on you as you were growing up?

LAYMON: Growing up in Chicago, I used to stay up late and watch "Shock Theater." The host's name was Marvin, and he had a wife named Darling. He kept her head in a box and tortured her during the commercials. They usually showed these terrible movies—like Elvira did—that were so bad you couldn't even watch them. But they also showed a lot of the great old movies like *Frankenstein, The Wolfman, The Mummy*. That was always the high point of staying up Saturday night.

WIATER: Of the stories you did for *Night Visions 7*, the gory novella *Mop Up* is a good example of your highly cinematic style. Would you explain its genesis?

LAYMON: I had a vision of a young, scared soldier in the ruins of a city, who, with a few buddies, were getting their asses ripped by these vile creatures in this postapocalyptic world, and then meet this nice young lady survivor somewhere along the way. I thought of the general situation a long time ago, but couldn't figure out how to make a novel out of it. Then I realized this would be my opportunity to flesh it out. It took me about three weeks to do it.

It was inspired in part by George Romero's movies—*Night of the Living Dead, The Crazies*. And I think maybe a little of John Carpenter's *Assault on Precinct 13*, and some of the movies that have been spawned by Richard Matheson's *I Am Legend*.

WIATER: Your stories and novels rarely possess many happy endings, do they? Usually, just about everyone is dead or dying at the conclusion.

LAYMON: My first horror novel had a real downbeat ending, and a lot of people were upset by that. But I think an ending where things don't turn out rosy is pretty appropriate to a horror story. I'm not obsessed with downbeat endings, but I do have a real appreciation for endings that deal with a sort of poetic justice.

WIATER: In spite of your reputation, the violence in "Madman Stan," another story of yours in *Night Visions 7*, is noticeably softer.

LAYMON: It's true the others have a lot of hard-core action, and with this one I wanted something a little more subtle. I came up with the idea for the "Madman" long before there ever was a story. As I recall, my daughter Kelly left the front door unlocked one night. And to break her of the habit, I told her there was a guy who wandered the neighborhood at night, trying all the doors, looking for one that wasn't locked. While I was making that up, it occurred to me that it even scared *me*.

Months later, she had a friend staying over for the night, and I told them both the story. The girl started crying, and then called up her mother to have her take her home!

When it came time to make it into a story for *Night Visions*, I thought up the angle of the babysitter telling the tale to give it a structure. I did have some trouble giving the madman a name. I remember a movie [*Madman*] where a guy told a spooky story around a campfire, though I can't remember the name of it. But in early drafts I called the character Madman Marz after the character in the movie. Then I simply called him Madman.

WIATER: Do you think anyone will ever learn how you settled on the final choice of a name?

LAYMON: Well, Stan is such a nice name for someone who's a total lunatic [*laughs*]. It just sounds so all-American.

WIATER: No comment. Did you begin your professional writing career with short stories or with a novel?

LAYMON: I was one of those "Ellery Queen: First Story" writers. In fact, because of that, I had a long segue into the mystery field. Which was certainly not a waste of time because I learned a lot about writing short stories, though it did sidetrack me away from horror for a few years. I came back when I read King's *'Salem's Lot* in paperback. Shortly after reading it, I wrote my first horror novel, *The Cellar*. Actually, I had been writing novels before, in the suspense-thriller genre, but none of them sold. With *The Cellar*, I turned away from the bleak crime story to a supernatural-type of situation.

WIATER: Do you have any preference to writing supernatural horror over psychological horror? You seem to go for the latter.

LAYMON: An awful lot of supernatural material—it just doesn't wash [*chuckles*]! I've used the stuff on occasion—things like black magic— as a way to create suspenseful situations. But basically, I don't care for such stories unless they're really well done.

WIATER: Do you have any personal beliefs in the supernatural or the occult? Most horror writers I've met are surprisingly conservative in such beliefs.

LAYMON: [*pauses*] I don't disbelieve in much of anything. I'm not into the "New Age" or anything, and I don't follow astrology or any of that. But I do think there may be more than a grain of truth in what's being presented to us as superstition or the paranormal. I do think there's such a thing as extrasensory perception. I even half-believe there may be things out there such as ghosts. And UFOs.

WIATER: Do you advise breaking into professional writing with short stories, or should one leap headfirst into a novel?

LAYMON: In terms of trying to make a living, I don't really advise short stories, but it depends. It's a good way of learning your craft, but you don't get a lot accomplished by only writing short stories. It does seem that there are several writers in the horror field who believe they *can* have a career writing short stories. Maybe they just can't write novels; I don't know what their situation is, but they're in almost every anthology.

WIATER: Do you go along with the old theory that "you should write what you like to read"? Or, "write about what you know"?

LAYMON: I try not to write about subjects I don't have firsthand knowledge of. For example, about ten years ago I had a great idea for a novel set in Vietnam. But I missed that war. I figured no amount of research was going to give that story the ring of truth, so I didn't do it. I think it's okay to just write about the areas in which you've lived, and the type of people you've been surrounded with in those areas. You get closer to describing things the way they really are rather than hoping for the best by doing a lot of research where you don't have any personal experiences.

WIATER: You once told me you were inspired to write a novel simply by visiting the famous Howe Caverns in New York?

LAYMON: Yes, that was a case where we were taking a tour of the caverns. And the tour guide told us about the other end of the cave, which hadn't been developed, and was unlighted. He made some joke about, "If we get stuck down here, I'm the guy with the flashlight!" [*laughs*] I thought, "My, God! I've got to write a book about this!" So I did. It's called *Midnight's Lair*, and the whole story occurs over the period of one day. Less than a day, actually. It's about a tour group that gets stuck down there—and what's on the other side of the wall at the far side of the main cavern.

WIATER: That novel is currently published only in England. It's certainly an odd situation, but why is Richard Laymon currently much better known there than in your native America?

LAYMON: There are a couple novels which haven't been published here yet that have been published in England. I really don't know how people think of me in England, but my books have been published steadily there, and my reputation has been improving constantly. My past several books have come out in both hardbound and paperback, whereas I've never had a hardbound in the United States. I guess they just appreciate me there more!

Graham Masterton

One of the most popular—and prolific—dark dreamers on both sides of the Atlantic is England's Graham Masterton. Born in Edinburgh, Scotland, in 1946, Masterton has had a lifelong fascination with both writing and horror, having completed his first epic work—a 550-page vampire novel—for the amusement of his friends at the ripe old age of twelve. After first working as a reporter, then an editor for such lofty British publications as *Mayfair* and *Penthouse*, Masterton struck the right vein by returning to the supernatural with his first published novel, *The Manitou*, in 1975. (The film, starring Tony Curtis and Susan Strasberg, was released three years later, directed by the late William Girdler. According to the author, "I think every one of my novels has been optioned at one time or another." However, it remains the only Masterton novel produced to date.)

Since that initial success, Masterton has been quite busy at his word processor, having published more than thirty novels. These include *Revenge of the Manitou, Death Trance, Sacrifice, Ikon, The Pariah, Charnel House, Tengu, Condor, The Wells of Hell, Night Warriors*, and *Mirror*. He has also written two sequels to *Night Warriors: Death Dream* and the forthcoming *Night Plague*. Under the pseudonym of "Thomas Luke," he has written three books, *The Hell Candidate, The Heirloom*, and the novelization of the John Huston film *Phobia*.

Interestingly enough, he divides his talents into two distinctly separate camps: first writing a horror novel, then writing a mainstream or historical novel, then back again to horror. Published under his own name, his mainstream novels include *Railroad, Lords of the Air, Rich,* and *Maiden Voyage.* However, he has recently gone on vacation from the epic historical novels to concentrate on writing larger and more-complex novels of horror.

He is also writing a new series of adventures for an American comic book firm, Northstar, based on his popular *Night Warriors* characters and themes. Although he travels to America to gather research for his novels, Masterton resides at Epsom Downs, Surrey, with his wife Wiescka and three sons. He confesses only to preparing a "huge cup of extremely poisonous coffee" and a sincere attempt "to do the *Daily Telegraph* crossword" to get his own creative juices flowing every morning.

WIATER: Frankly, from reading several of your novels, I first believed you had to be an American just living in England—most of your novels take place in this country, and they certainly read like they were written by a native-born American.
MASTERTON: Yes, it's an odd characteristic in some ways. But right from the very start, when I wrote *The Manitou*, I found that the acceptance for that kind of horror story was very much stronger in the United States than it was in England. Also, I really wanted to get away from all the gothic and traditional horror forms that had been around at the time, and so the idea of having an ancient horror that was rooted in the New World was very powerful to me. So the summers when I become "Graham Masterton: horror writer" I just look for that sort of audience—not so much American these days, but certainly international to that extent. And because of the universality of American television in particular, everybody all over the world seems to be able to accept a story set in America.
WIATER: Many of your early novels revolve around ancient cults and religions—you must enjoy creating your own mythologies as the origins for your monsters and demons. H. P. Lovecraft was famous for doing this sort of thing.
MASTERTON: I think I'm slightly moving away from the ancient demon type of book, but there were so many interesting and unusual terrors of the past! One reason I wanted to go back and look at them is because some time in the past they really *did* terrify some cultures. It's quite interesting to explore what it was about them that made them so fright-

ening. Exploring certain fears like being visited by the dead; that comes up as zombies and ghouls. Fears of being dragged under by strange maidens, fears of being made love to in the night by disgusting creatures!...

I also like to have something of an intellectual game with the reader, with those who have a long-standing interest in horror stories, and have knowledge of their background. By getting in little jokes and wordplays which refer back to old Lovecraft stories or other stories they may have read. It's kind of a "shorthand of horror" in that you *know* it's going to be frightening once you start mentioning Arkham or going the wrong way by the Miskatonic River [*laughs*]! You just add layers to the horror. And to those who know these mythologies, it's an added pleasure.

WIATER: With the obvious exception of the sequels, no two Masterton novels deal with the same kind of fear. Clearly you believe you have more to explore in the field?

MASTERTON: It's gotten so that there are so many fascinating things that one can do. And the discipline of it alone is so interesting. Because you're dealing with the occult and the supernatural—remember we were just talking about mythologies?—well, there have to be some kind of ground rules. Otherwise, there is no fear. Without ground rules, your hero cannot overcome the demon, or the other way around. So in some ways, writing horror is *much* more difficult than writing any other kind of book because you have to create your own discipline, your own ground rules, and then have to stick with them.

WIATER: Yet the whole point of working in this genre, some of the critics say, is to keep going forward, to keep breaking rules. What boundaries or censorship do you put on your work—or aren't there any?

MASTERTON: I don't think I'm going to receive any medals as Prude of the Year, after eight years of working on *Mayfair* and *Penthouse*, and editing *Forum* for four years. And I contributed to an anthology called *Hot Blood*. Certainly it's a question of taste more than anything else. I personally don't like watching movies where people get chopped up into pieces. I didn't like *The Fly* [1986] very much—I thought it was just plain disgusting. And I thought *Hellraiser* went well beyond the bounds; it wasn't frightening because it was just... tasteless. The extraordinary thing is, the more overt the horror is, the quicker the fear factor drops. There's no particular fear in having somebody's head chopped off or blown off or anything like that. It's jolly good special effects, and it was all right the first time that David Cronenberg did it in *Scanners*.

But if you just want butchery, you might as well go along and visit your local meat counter. It's about as frightening as that. And, it seems to me, that those writers who are becoming really successful at developing this genre are those who are exploring ways of making you *frightened* rather than ways of making you disgusted. Anybody can write a "meat story." You can write a factual piece describing a liposuction operation and that would be sufficiently disgusting. Anybody can do that, and it's not clever or impressive. And it doesn't take the genre anywhere. I don't deny that there's still an audience who wants to read about such things; otherwise there wouldn't be the kind of sensationalism we've always seen in the past.

WIATER: What about sex in horror—is there any reason to be squeamish about that any longer? Haven't most writers gone beyond the idea of just putting it in a story to be merely sensational?

MASTERTON: I would be inclined not to include any particularly sadistic sex. It's one of the reasons I didn't like *Hellraiser*, actually. I thought the sex in it was sadistic. But certainly a story can be erotic. And it can be frighteningly erotic. And there can be strong hints of sadomasochism in it; it's simply a question of the intelligence of the writer and how he or she handles what they're doing.

WIATER: Do you ever incorporate any of your personal fears?

MASTERTON: I'll tell you what one of the strongest fears is that runs through my books. When you're a father, and a parent, and a husband, and a lover, you have very strong protective feelings about your family. I've been asked about the novels I write in the first person; not many horror novels are written in the first person because you give the game away right from the beginning, that the hero is going to survive. But what you can do is transmit the fear and the anxiety that the main character has for the people he loves and is responsible for. It's become one of the strongest themes running through all of my horror novels. I think it's a lot more terrifying than the fear you feel for your own survival. So I have a wife and three sons that I care very much about, and if there's any personal experience that comes through my work, it's that constant feeling of looking after them.

WIATER: When you write in this genre, do you purposely try to frighten yourself? In other words, have you any way of judging if your work is coming across as effective?

MASTERTON: I *have* to be frightened by what I'm doing. There has to be at least one moment—hopefully it's underlying through the whole experience—when I shut off that word processor at the end of the day, and the house is dark and quiet, and there is a true feeling of fear in me. Hopefully, I've transmitted it to the reader as well. That effect, I think, is very important. It's like when you're writing a sexual story, there should be a strong feeling of eroticism. When you're writing an adventure story, you want to be thrilled by it and want to know what will happen next. So I think it's very, very important for a horror writer to be frightened by his own work.

WIATER: This leads to the question of what novels of your own would you recommend, going along with those qualifications?

MASTERTON: In some ways, I think the first one I did was the best one I did in terms of story—*The Manitou* would certainly be a good introduction. Another would be *Charnel House*, which in some respects is a reworking of *The Manitou*, except the fear was rather more sharpened and developed. *Tengu*, which was a sort of thriller-horror novel, had some moments of fear in it intermingled with more everyday life than just the purely fantastic. I would also recommend *Picture of Evil* as it was called in America.

WIATER: Getting back to *The Manitou*, what was your reaction to the film version?

MASTERTON: I liked it a lot, actually. It had all the right elements of humor and fear in it, and I thought for the time, 1978, the special effects were very good. I think the director, Bill Girdler, got a little bit carried away by *Star Wars* toward the end of the film—remember *Star Wars* had just come out then and was influencing a lot of the people who were making movies. But it had all the right wry elements in it that I believe made *The Manitou* what it was in many respects.

WIATER: Under the name of "Thomas Luke," for example, you did a novelization of the film *Phobia*. Probably more people read that book then saw the actual film.

MASTERTON: Oh, yes, that was just a novelization. That was done in four days. People are always asking that question: How long does it take to write a book? You just look at them and say, "I don't know!" Some books are very quick, though. *The Manitou* was written very quickly—in about two weeks. I don't know if having a word processor now has speeded things up; I don't use as much correcting fluid [*laughs*]. The word processor *has* made my desk tidier, though. I'm usually quite fast as a writer, in any case. But it depends. You can labor all day over a single paragraph, and sometimes you can't write anything at all. I've never really suffered from writer's block, but one is confidently trying to drag the very best out all the time.

WIATER: Considering your long list of publications, it appears that you've never had to worry about writer's block.

MASTERTON: I have an idea for a new horror novel practically every day. I thought of one this morning, actually. A guy buys this old Zenith radio, and hears on it these old radio programs. He also hears the most grisly things going on, like he's witnessing these ritual murders. He hears something that was in the past, with someone begging him for help. So how does he go about dealing with it—with going into the past? It would be a horror story set in some sort of 1930s' motor court, with all the historical detail and atmosphere of that time. And so on and so forth, and so on and so forth. . . . [*laughs*] But right now I don't have the time for it; I'm doing something else.

WIATER: It must be somewhat frustrating to have your imagination always brimming over with new ideas?

MASTERTON: One way I can productively use this brimming over of ideas is to get into different fields, like comic books. I've also been writing more short stories lately for various anthologies. It's a different way of expressing the same ideas which may eventually make novels, but which will certainly help develop the terror—and develop my own techniques. You never stop learning; you never stop expanding your techniques and ideas.

WIATER: Besides having a family to support, what else compels you to write? More than thirty novels since 1975 would seem to most like a lot of time spent locked away in a room.

MASTERTON: As I said, I *do* have a lot of ideas, so this in some ways is the problem. But it's also the joy of imagining these other realities and possibilities and other lives. Imagining new fears, exploring various frights. Being able to convey this to other people is a joy. My biggest axe to grind is with publishers who fail to see the author-editor-publisher-distributor-reader as one direct link. There are so many good books published today (and some of mine are included amongst those) that are badly published. They just don't reach the public that they ought to. Unfortunately, too many writers today are writing for the publisher, and not for the reader.

WIATER: Tell me the story behind *Scare Care*, where the stories were donated by many of the top writers in the field. Even its American publisher, Tor, donated the hardcover profits of the book to the various charities involved.

MASTERTON: Well, *Scare Care* started off as one of those five-o'clock-in-the-morning inspirations. I thought, "There are a whole lot of very good writers out there in 'horrorland,' and it would be a whole lot of fun to put some stories together and send the profits off to charity." One of my favorite charities here in England has always been the National Society for the Prevention of Cruelty to Children, not to mention other charities such as cancer research for children, and so on. I started to write blindly to writers I knew—I asked Ramsey Campbell for help on writers he knew—and it started off from there. It's quite a large collection—there are thirty-eight stories—that covers the whole spectrum of what's being written today, from new writers to quite experienced writers.

WIATER: It's undeniably an impressive lineup, and worth purchasing for more than the obvious reason.

MASTERTON: Roald Dahl is represented. Ruth Rendell. James Herbert. Peter Tremayne. Kit Reed, whose work is gently grotesque. J. N. Williamson. The great thing about Jerry is the tremendous inspiration he's given to other people. He's really got that professorial quality about him. In fact, he was practically my bureau for getting in contact with American writers. C. Dean Andersson is in it, who, once he stops writing such sadistic work, I think is going to be tremendous.

But the anthology forms an extraordinary cross section of working writers. I think the most spectacular aspect of all is the amount of work and good wishes I got from all these writers. Even those who didn't have anything to submit sent their best wishes. I think I had over one hundred fifty stories submitted, which, considering that some of those writers don't make very much money on their own and gave this work away freely, I think it's absolutely marvelous.

WIATER: What other projects are presently under consideration?

MASTERTON: I want to continue to develop the themes I started with *Mirror*, and have other ideas based on historical events, with horrific explanations for more recent literary creations. *Mirror* for example is based very much on *Through the Looking Glass* by Lewis Carroll. And I have a very horrific story coming up which is based on Richard Wagner's last unknown opera. He's a great character—he had such bad skin.

WIATER: You mentioned that new novel idea about the 1930s' motor court. Rumor has it that you're an automobile buff and are still in pursuit of the car of your dreams.

MASTERTON: Yes, I've finally got the car I've always dreamed of. It's a Fleetwood Brougham, in white, with an interior the color of Joan Collins's toenails. Being an author, you lead such a solitary, monkish life. But as soon as I get onto the street, I'm immediately visible. You know the size of most of the cars in England—everyone's stuck to the windows like those suction-cup Garfields. It was Liberace who said, "It's awful being stared at, but not being stared at is worse!" The car is wonderfully inconvenient [*laughs*]! You don't get much notice being a writer; it's not like being a motion picture star, because they don't recognize your face. And several of the writers I know have vulgar cars.

WIATER: I confess that I share that passion, since I own a black Mustang GT, which gets me to the bookstores at nearly one hundred fifty miles per hour. When people ask why such a "vulgar" car is needed, it can only be said that it's obviously a car designed for writers.

MASTERTON: That's right [*laughs*]! There's a very interesting article in that somewhere.

WIATER: All modesty aside, what influence on the field do you believe your work has had?

MASTERTON: If my work has had any influence—or if it's had the influence I hope it's had—I can only tell from the feedback I get from my readers. (A) That my novels are literate, and (B) they've brought a large measure of believability to the supernatural and to the far-out. This is achieved by technique, by believing in what you're doing and having respect for your reader.

If a novel of mine was to have the ultimate effect on the reader, it would be a novel in which the reader would be reading the story, and look up, and find out he is reading it *for real*. Then they would have to put down the book and deal—for real—with the terror to which they've been introduced.

WIATER: And of course the only way they can survive the terror is to somehow manage to finish your book!

MASTERTON: If they can survive long enough to finish the book, that's the only way they'll do it. How I would love to do that! I try to write books that deliberately encourage involvement, that have atmosphere, and smells, and strong believability. I always aim to write a book that you're not conscious of having read as a book. Because the greatest compliment I've ever been paid by my readers is when they write or call up to say, "What happened next?!"

What really happened next was that I shut off the word processor and went to bed. But if that world I created for them existed long enough so that they believed something *did* happen then, then I've gone a long way toward that ultimate Graham Masterton novel that I hope someday to be able to write.

 Richard Matheson

Although many of the dark dreamers will readily admit to having read *Dracula* or the works of Edgar Allan Poe in their youth, it's just as likely they were also influenced by someone who has been quite involved with a world full of vampires and the works of Poe. In various mediums, Richard Matheson's words have had an effect on literally millions of people because, as he has described himself elsewhere, he is in fact four writers.

First, Matheson is the author of such classic novels as *I Am Legend, The Shrinking Man, Hell House, Bid Time Return*, and *What Dreams May Come*, among others. His most recent, published so far only in England, is *Earthbound*, originally published in the 1970s in a botched and heavily edited edition which he disowned and had issued under his pseudonym, "Logan Swanson."

Second, he is a marvelous short story writer, recognized as one of the most talented in the field. Indeed, his best work was issued in 1989 by the specialty publisher Scream/Press as the *Collected Stories of Richard Matheson*, though they first appeared in such treasured paperback volumes as *Shock!, Third from the Sun*, and *The Shores of Space*, to name only a few.

Third, as screenwriter, Matheson was responsible for a number of fine horror movies released in the 1960s which were inspired by the stories of Edgar Allan Poe, directed by maverick director Roger Corman, and starred Vincent Price. Beyond the Poe films (*House of Usher, The Pit and the Pendulum, Tales of Terror, The Raven, Comedy of Terrors*), Matheson also worked on a number of films produced in England: *Burn, Witch, Burn* (based on the novel *Conjure Wife* by Fritz Leiber), *De Sade, Die! Die! My Darling*, and *The Devil's Bride*. He also adapted his novel *The Shrinking Man* as well as *Hell House* (released as *The Legend of Hell House*), and *Bid Time Return* (released as *Somewhere in Time*). Two unsuccessful film versions of *I Am Legend* have so far been produced.

But Matheson, who was born in New Jersey in 1926 and has lived for many years in southern California, is perhaps best known for his work in the medium of television. Besides the teleplays for such memorable movies as *Duel*, directed by Steven Spielberg, he also wrote the teleplay for what would become (at that time) the most successful made-for-television movie ever, *The Night Stalker*. It, of course, later inspired a sequel and the series starring the unflappable reporter Kolchak.

He also, incidentally, was one of the top writers (along with creator Rod Sterling and Charles Beaumont) for a half hour, black-and-white series known as "The Twilight Zone." Which is another way of saying only the surface has been scratched of this mountain of talent, Richard Matheson.

WIATER: Admirers of your work will say that you've written far too few novels in your career. One of your most popular, *Hell House*, was reportedly written over a ten-year period. Why so long?

MATHESON: Well, it wasn't because I was writing it for ten years! I had so much other work to do out here that I would put it aside, then go back to it. It doesn't sound like much money, compared to what they're paying for books now, but at the time I had gotten a five-thousand-dollar advance, and I was too cheap to give it back [*laughs*]. Even though I just wanted to drop the whole project—so I just kept laboring at it through the years.

The first version of *Hell House* that I submitted was told in the first person—each of the characters writing their own story. Which is kind of interesting, but it's very difficult—if not impossible—to get suspense that way. Because everybody who's writing can only write about something that's already taken place. Therefore, if somebody's writing a book, you know that no matter what they go through, they already got through it, because they're writing the book! This may be picayune as far as logic is concerned, but that bothers me.

WIATER: When you mean "other work," you're of course referring to your numerous television and film assignments?

MATHESON: Oh, sure. Of course. Although I've had success in novels, I sometimes think maybe I should no longer keep trying because, although they work out reasonably well, none of them has sold a lot. Maybe *Hell House* did. But their only value to me financially was that they sold as motion pictures. I suppose it's nice to have a couple of novels that people call "classics"—*The Shrinking Man* and *I Am Legend*—so obviously I'm going to keep on writing them. But I do feel that the film medium is a tremendously powerful one, if used properly. Of course, it is very rarely used properly.

WIATER: I'm far from the first to tell you what an enormous influence you've been on an entire generation of young writers and filmmakers. Do you think the influence has come mostly from your published writings, or your "Twilight Zone" episodes and the horror and suspense movies?

MATHESON: I know Stephen King has said this, which is very gratifying. King said that because of reading *I Am Legend*, he realized it was not necessary to write everything like H. P. Lovecraft; that you could have a contemporary shopping mall, housing-tract setting and still do a horror story. So that was very crucial in his decision as to what he was going to write.

But now of course, people probably don't read books or short stories that much anyway, and there are producers out here who only know me—there is ageism out here in Hollywood and I would qualify for it—except a lot of young producers and young executives know me because they grew up on "The Twilight Zone." Which is understandable, because that's all they could know, because I don't have anything in print in particular, except an occasional reprint.

WIATER: In spite of the influence you've had on others in the field of horror and dark fantasy, the term *horror* is one you've never appreciated having associated with your work.

MATHESON: If things like *Friday the 13th* and *A Nightmare on Elm Street* and *Scanners* are "horror," then I've never written horror. I don't think I've ever written anything—except maybe a scene here and there in *Hell House*—that was gruesome, ghastly stuff. It was explicit sexually, yes, but I don't know if it was anything more "horrible" than had been written before. But sex and horror is all the rage now.

WIATER: Certainly none of the films you wrote in the 1960s would qualify as what most young people label as *horror*. Nowadays the popular theory is that we must see *everything*. With no shocks left to the imagination.

MATHESON: I think what it is now is that the viewers are anesthetized; they've seen so much of it that the only way to reach them is to stick the needle in further every time. To get any kind of a reaction. This is not a good thing, by any means.
WIATER: Do you think that today's horror writers and filmmakers have to do this because audiences today are so jaded they won't accept anything else but the explicit blood and gore?
MATHESON: Oh, sure. They don't *have* to do this—they do it because it's what sells. It's bullshit if they're trying to say it's anything else.
WIATER: Yes, but what about the classic philosophy of the catharsis—we purge our evil intentions by seeing others act them out on stage or in a book or movie?
MATHESON: Like everyone, I used to believe in that old theory that by experiencing these horrors vicariously, you are able get them out of your system, and are therefore able to cope with the horrors of reality more efficiently. I don't believe that now. I believe everything you put in your mind stays there. The more crap these kids and young people are putting in their minds, the worse their minds are going to get. Because it doesn't trickle out while they're asleep. It's always in there. It's rooted. And one of the proofs is that the only things that will scare them are things that get worse and worse all the time. *More* horrific.

I don't want to blow up an entire field of literature, which would be ridiculous. But we are living in a very violent period of time—with the drugs, and the street killings, the driveby shootings. . . . New York is like a nightmare, a jungle. Washington, D.C., is a total horror. And Los Angeles is apparently now the number-one drug center in the country. There's been a general deterioration in society—there's no doubt about it. The horror movies are just a reflection of that. It's symbiotic: The public wants it, and Hollywood therefore provides it. It's a circle which just goes on and on—they keep making pictures like that knowing they'll succeed, and if some of them don't succeed, they assume it's because they're not horrific enough. So they'll make it even worse.

Even *that's* not working now. I think there's actually a change in the attitude of the mass viewers because pictures are making money now at the box office that didn't for a while, films like *Parenthood* and *Dead Poets Society* and *Rain Man*.
WIATER: Has your work been of any benefit to society through the mass media you try to communicate through?
MATHESON: Beyond entertainment value? Probably not. I can't think of any. Just the fact that I've been able to scare people doesn't make me a great guy. I've entertained them, that's about all you can say.

WIATER: Is that enough?
MATHESON: No! It's not enough for me now. That's why I'm trying to get into projects that have something more to say.
WIATER: Is part of the reason you've never had a chance to work on major mainstream projects because you've always been identified strongly as a genre writer? As you know all too well, you're best known to the public as "Science fiction writer, Richard Matheson."
MATHESON: I still don't understand why. I haven't written any science fiction. But I can see my own obituary: "Science fiction writer Richard Matheson succumbs to ennui." But this labeling hasn't helped my career at all. Not at all. Years ago I wrote a movie for television on alcoholism called *The Morning After*, and it worked out beautifully. I was told that it was so definitive that it was shown in medical schools. (Whether they still do, I don't know.) It was a marvelous study. But there was a reviewer of that who used words almost like, "This is a true horror story, and who better to write the script than . . ."

And I thought, "Oh, hell! I'll never get away from it." They don't want you to get out of your category! You try to get out of your cubbyhole, boy, they smack you on the head and say, "Get back in there!" God knows what the reviewers are going to say now about the television movie I just wrote on the life of L. Frank Baum called *The Dreamer of Oz*—there's not a scare in it.

WIATER: I think I speak for many when saying that your fantasy novels *Bid Time Return* and *What Dreams May Come* are truly your finest.
MATHESON: I feel that, for sheer writing, *Bid Time Return* is the best book I've written. I've created in a sense a whole society of people out there who responded not only to the film but to the book, the music, everything. I feel very good about that. I feel extremely good about *What Dreams May Come* because I've had letters from people saying, "My mother was dying, and I let her read this book, and she faces her death now with peace." And I think no writer can do more than that. But the critics didn't like it. They wanted me to do horror.

I once gave a speech at a writers' conference on why I hate genres. Do everything you can to destroy genres. *A good story is a good story*. If you tell a love story, and you set it on Mars, then it's a science fiction story. You tell it set in the Old West, and it becomes a Western. You tell it in the midst of a detective story, and it's a detective story. And so on and so forth. This idea that there's this "genre" that exists like a steel coffin, and you've got to jump inside it to write your story. . . . In many cases, it's not that these writers, including Robert Bloch and myself, have not attempted other fields. It's just that there's not a welcome mat in these other fields and they've got to *batter* their way into it if they're going to do it. And even if they do it, the longtime readers are going to say, "Aw, gee, why don't you do the old stuff?"

WIATER: But marketing labels aside, certainly you can't deny that you're a writer of the "fantastic"?

MATHESON: Oh, sure. On my tombstone they can put, "Fantasy Writer." I don't mind that. "Off-beat writer." That's fine.

WIATER: I know you've written a few stories in collaboration with your son, Richard Christian, as well as a screenplay. Any chance that the rumor's true that it's in the horror field?

MATHESON: We're working on a rewrite now of a script that we sold that is in that specific area, so we're both guilty there. The first screenplay we wrote and sold was in the detective-action area. This script is sort of horror and action, but it's comedy, too. Richard is very good at that.

WIATER: What was it like to work with the late, great Charles Beaumont? Had he lived, he undoubtedly would have been included in this book.

MATHESON: As a matter of fact, Richard and I were discussing him just last night. The scripts that I wrote with Chuck did not involve comedy. They were all straight dramatic or suspense-action types. We usually just split it in half. Like the picture we wrote from Fritz Leiber's *Conjure Wife*—I wrote the first half, and Chuck wrote the second half. I don't even recall us looking at each other's halves and making any big changes. In that respect, we wrote pretty similarly. We didn't really collaborate for that long a period of time; we did it in television, mostly in the beginning, just so we would have each other's company in a strange world. When that became unnecessary, we broke up and went on our own individual paths.

WIATER: When you were writing for "The Twilight Zone" and various other television and movie projects in the late 1950s and early 1960s, alongside such talents as Beaumont, did you have any idea what effect your work would eventually have?

MATHESON: We enjoyed what we were doing. Certainly we were trying to earn money and support our families, but we were doing it in a way that interested us and in a way that we could do our best. We were pretty good at it. But when I started writing books like *Bid Time Return* and *What Dreams May Come*, a lot of readers in the fantasy, horror, and science fiction world thought, "Well, Matheson's brain has turned to mush. He doesn't write that nice lean, hard, scare-'em-to-death stuff anymore." But you know, who cares [*laughs*]? If that's where you want to stay fixated at, that's your privilege.

WIATER: Any idea why there's always been a certain audience who remains fixated with the fantastic, no matter what the medium?

MATHESON: Oh, I don't really think about it, but I suppose the best of our work taps some sort of undercurrent in people's thought processes, in the mass psyches of humanity. That may be going too far—but something like that.

WIATER: You've worked in many different mediums—novels, short stories, screenplays. Then you claim to get tired of the form and try your hand at something else. I understand you've also done your share of plays?

MATHESON: Now *that* I'm really tired of [*laughs*]! I took my shot at that. I had a play all ready to open on Broadway, and that fell through. I've been working for some time on a musical based on the film *Somewhere in Time*. But the theater is fascinating, and at one time I was real involved in it and wrote play after play. I guess I finally realized I could only do so many projects. I'm at the point where I really feel I had better write something that *says* something now. Not that I want to get preachy, but there are things to be said, and I would like to say them. I tried to do that in *What Dreams May Come* and, to a degree, succeeded. I would like to do that again.

WIATER: In spite of the fact that many of the screenplays you've written have never been produced—which is the norm in the film industry—they've apparently always paid better than any novel you've written to date. You worked for years on a miniseries dealing with the paranormal that never got off the ground, worked more years on a still-unproduced miniseries based on Philip Wylie's *The Disappearance*, to name only two.

MATHESON: It's hard when you're making a living as a writer, and some producer comes to you with something that sounds interesting—you don't say, "I'm sorry, I think I'm going to be poor this year and write a novel." And I've never been in that category where millions of dollars have been made available. I obviously quit the field too soon—I may be ahead of my time, but I'm sure a poor judge of time! I give up fields just before they hit big. Consider that I sold *I Am Legend* for three thousand dollars way back when. But as my wife keeps reminding me, I was supporting four children, so I really didn't have that much in terms of options. But I look at all these screenplays that never got made, and they're just sitting on the shelf. No one will ever see them. No one has any idea of the wonderful work I did on them.

WIATER: Any of your film work that you're as proud of as your books, besides *The Morning After*?

MATHESON: There are a number of things. Obviously *Duel* was a wonderful piece of work. *The Night Stalker* was great, and its sequel, *The Night Strangler*, was also good, too. Quite a few episodes of "The Twilight Zone." The only pictures I am ever happy with are the ones that really follow my script, and amplify them, and do them even better. Like *Duel*—that *was* my script.

WIATER: One of the most frightening shows ever presented on television was your 1975 *Trilogy of Terror*, directed by Dan Curtis, with whom you worked on a number of other successful projects such as *Dracula* and *Dead of Night*.

MATHESON: Even though they were all three of my stories, I let Bill Nolan do the first two, which was very unkind [*laughs*]. One of them was a short-short, and the other wasn't much longer. They were very difficult, though he did a marvelous job turning them into scripts. But I took the flashy one, and of course that's the one everybody still talks about—that little Zuni doll chasing Karen Black around the apartment. Dan Curtis is a remarkable director . . . that was quite a piece of work.

WIATER: With all the frustrations you've experienced over the years, are you, ultimately, happy being a writer?

MATHESON: I've been out here since 1955, when I sold *The Shrinking Man* to films, and for all that time—and I've been successful most of that time—I've had very few true creative pleasures. Which is not surprising, of course. If I had had any brains I would have realized that, when you've got that many people working on projects—and the majority of the time most of them are not that talented—that is what's going to happen. Every once in a while there's a rare joining together of really talented forces, and then it turns out great. And then I'm happy.

But that happens *so* rarely. I've never knowingly written down to an audience; I always tried to write the best I can. And I still do. Somehow my numb head has never gotten over the fact that I have to keep doing my best.

WIATER: What advice do you have for the aspiring writer?

MATHESON: If somebody's really intent on being a writer, it doesn't matter what anybody says to them. When I was starting as a writer, people were always saying, "Well, how long are you going to give it?" And, "When are you going to get a job?" I would just stare at them, blankly. It's the ones who send me and other writers letters asking, "Tell me how to become a writer. Tell me how to get started." *They're* the ones who are in trouble! I never asked anybody how to get started! I corresponded in the early days with Ray Bradbury, but only to tell him how much I liked his work, and he wrote me back telling me how much he enjoyed my early short stories. But I wasn't asking for advice on how to become a writer.

There is no big secret. Just keep writing. And keep writing about the things you feel strongly about. You should not write anything that doesn't absolutely turn you on; that you love. I *love* writing. It's a hard field. It's very often unrewarding financially—and certainly creatively—for the majority. But if you *do* love it, great. Stay with it! You should love any field you go into. I love it, and I will stay in it until the day I die.

Robert R. McCammon

Unlike Stephen King (four novel attempts before *Carrie*) or John Saul (ten novel attempts before *Suffer the Children*), Robert R. McCammon apparently did it right his first time out. For even though he intended to make his career in writing as a journalist, no one was more surprised than he when that first attempt at a novel, *Baal*, was published in 1978. McCammon was all of twenty-six. Since that time he has published nine more novels and a growing body of acclaimed short stories, recently collected in *Blue World*. The novels include *Bethany's Sin, The Night Boat, They Thirst, Mystery Walk, Usher's Passing, Swan Song, Stinger, The Wolf's Hour*, and this year's *Mine*. Although his popular novels have yet to be filmed by Hollywood, two of his short stories ("Makeup" and "Nightcrawlers") were adapted for the television series "Darkroom" and "The Twilight Zone," respectively. In its original form, or as it was adapted for television, "Nightcrawlers" is one of the most terrifying examinations of the power of the human mind to bring into reality its own worst nightmares.

Regardless of the usual cliches that go along with being labeled a creator of tales of fear, in person the soft-spoken Rick McCammon more accurately represents the finer qualities embodied by the phrase *a Southern gentleman*. (Admittedly yet another stereotype, but certainly an admirable one.) His consideration of other writers in the field extends back to 1984 when he originated the idea for the Horror Writers of America, a professional guild which currently has some 400 members. (Further information may be obtained by writing Horror Writers of America, c/o Theresa P. Gladden, P.O. Box 1077, Eden, North Carolina 27288.) One of the reasons McCammon started the organization was the belief that horror writers needed to "have a place they could call home," in the manner of the Science Fiction Writers of America and the Mystery Writers of America. Like the organization he founded, McCammon's career has been growing at a rapid rate, with the end nowhere in sight.

He still lives in his native city of Birmingham, Alabama, with his wife Sally, and his work has often been critically recognized as possessing a depth and a maturity which belies the author's age. *Booklist* has described him as, "A true master of the gothic novel." Perhaps one of the ultimate signs of this writer's popularity is evidenced by the newsletter devoted to the man and his writings. Entitled *Lights Out!* it can be obtained by subscription in care of Hunter Goatley at *Lights Out!*, P.O. Box 30704, Knoxville, Tennessee 37930. Even though he feels he is just beginning to reach his stride as an author, book-length critical examinations of his work are already in progress.

WIATER: When you went to college it was to major in journalism. You had no intention at that point of becoming a novelist?
MCCAMMON: When I finished school, it was when *All the President's Men* came out, and *everybody* wanted to be a reporter, so I couldn't find a job as one. I found a job in the advertising department of a local department store. It was a terrible job and wasn't what I really wanted to do. So I realized the only thing I could do was to try to write a novel. I'd entertained the idea of writing one, but never thought I'd be successful at it. Because who really thinks they can be successful with a first novel? And whoever thinks they can write something someone will buy and *like*? So I was just astounded when my first novel was bought. And I'm still astounded, because I really don't think *Baal* is a very good book, though it was the best I could do at the time. It mirrored a lot of what I was feeling, because at the time I was very angry, very frustrated and upset about a lot of things.
WIATER: Was it a conscious decision to write a horror novel, or was that simply a subject you thought had a chance of selling?

McCAMMON: Yes, it was something that had always been my interest, and I think it's the most difficult question to answer: Why do you write horror? I don't know what went into me to make me write horror. But I had the same interests as you—I read *Famous Monsters of Filmland* when I was a kid, and loved collecting all those. I went to monster movies. But monster movies *scared* me [*laughs*]! They scared me to death when I was a kid—I just couldn't watch 'em! So maybe now, by writing horror novels, I'm forcing myself to watch—to sit and look at—things I was fearful of as a kid.

WIATER: Tell me some of your early influences.

McCAMMON: With the exception of Ray Bradbury, I can't honestly say I was influenced by anybody as much as I just liked to *read*. People may say, "I was influenced by this writer and I was influenced by that writer," but I believe horror writers are really influenced most of all by their childhoods. I wonder if most horror writers had happy childhoods. I wonder if things have happened that made us this way—it seems like we're always trying to get back to our childhood. Trying to find something we lost, or correct something we missed. Or purge it. Perhaps you *can* purge something in a book, and it seems to come back to you. I don't know what that is; perhaps that's just our bent as horror writers.

WIATER: Unlike some authors who have reached a noticeable degree of success in this field, you don't seem embarrassed to be primarily recognized as "Robert McCammon, horror writer." I ask this because I've had others tell me that what they really write are "novels of fear" or "dark fantasy." Anything so as not to be considered a writer of horror.

McCAMMON: Well, I'm *not* embarrassed. In fact, I'm very pleased to be associated with the field. I'm very pleased with what horror can be for its millions of fans. I think those labels like dark fantasy are glossing over what horror really is. I think it's a gut-level kind of writing, an on-the-edge kind of writing. Horror is also really neat because it's always redefining itself. So I'm extremely pleased to be a horror writer, and would be willing to shout it from the rooftops that I love horror and that I love what I do.

WIATER: That may work for you, but others have declared that they don't wish to be so labeled—that it limits their careers to be thought of as horror writers, even though they don't deny it's an area of fiction in which they excel.

McCAMMON: The problem is not in the writing, or in the writers. The problem is with the publishers. They see horror as primarily a book with some scary elements, and they market it from that narrow perspective. But there's so many different kinds of horror, and so many things going on in horror fiction, that it's very hard to define. But the publishers will try to define it in terms of the marketplace, and will push whatever works. I think it's the writer's responsibility to push the boundaries of what a publisher may feel is "horror fiction." It's the writer who should really get in there and try to do different things within the genre, and push those boundaries. And in that way he'll eventually reeducate the publishers—and the audience—as to what horror fiction is.

I'm not sure myself what horror is. But I know it's *not* just one thing; it's not just *Friday the 13th* or *The Shining* and it's not just *Weaveworld*. It's all those elements—and more.

WIATER: Critics say that the genre will never be taken seriously because it doesn't deal with real events or real people. You should be writing on a "serious" topic.

MCCAMMON: [*angrily*] Yeah, that really ticks me off. Because to me, hell, horror *is* real. I don't think I or my colleagues could write it if we didn't think it was a serious subject. I take that as a great insult when somebody says, "When are you going to write something serious?" But this *is* real—it's about life and death! You know, people who ask that question have never read horror—they don't know a damn thing about it! And they probably don't know much about . . . anything.

Because horror writing has always seemed to me a very liberal, forward-thinking kind of literature that is not afraid to shake things up. It's not afraid to be nasty. It's not afraid. It's just *not afraid*. And isn't that what art is all about? Horror fiction can be—is—art. Now art may not necessarily be pleasant or nice to look at. And yet, to me, the beauty of horror is that there's so many ways to go, there's so many areas still left undiscovered and unexplored.

WIATER: Are there any taboo areas that you won't touch in your own work for risk of being too offensive? In other words, can there be such a concept as "bad taste" in horror fiction?

MCCAMMON: I don't believe there can be such a thing as bad taste. There can only be bad writing. You can have the most outrageous scene with the most extreme violence and handle it in such a way that it'll be extremely excruciating—but there'll be no blood. So I don't think there can be any bad taste in creating a scene, only bad writing in handling it.

WIATER: A major theme in your work is that, no matter how awful the situation may be, your characters always retain the hope that they will somehow reach the end of the darkness or the chaos. But don't you feel the most effective horror lies in dealing with situations which eventually fade to utter black?

McCAMMON: But how do you mean "effective"? I tell stories which are effective to me in terms of hope. But then someone else might want to tell a story in terms of hopelessness. But my key word *is* hope; I think there's hope in any situation. And that's what motivates my characters to do what they do, because they think, "There's a way out of this mess . . . " or, "There's a way I can transform myself personally. . . . " Again, one voice may want to deal with horror from this perspective, while another may want to focus on the darkness. I have different tones in my stories, and hope is not always the right tone, but the element of hope is in most of my work.

WIATER: You've been described as a writer whose strength lies in bringing life to his characters rather than just finding the ways of gruesomely destroying them. Do you feel others are attempting to create more than just "books with scary elements"?

McCAMMON: You know, I think horror writers are now like that Bohemian society in Paris in 1920s, where everybody had their own style of art, and their own philosophy about art. This one was experimenting in cubism, and this one in naturalism. . . . But what they were really all talking about was the same thing—they were really talking about art. So it doesn't matter whether we talk today about quiet horror or splatterpunk because there's a great horror within all these voices. And I know I'm trying to sound diplomatic, but I'm not: I enjoy all these spectrums, and there's room for all of them. So to say, "Well, there should only be quiet horror, no blood and guts," or that it should be the other way around, diminishes the field. Diminishes the force of horror itself. It may be that horror is forever undefinable. It will always have these different voices and moods, and there may be no way to tame *or* define it. And that may be one of the great powers of horror fiction.

WIATER: Do you believe that perhaps the academics have given the field a legitimacy it didn't have even a decade ago? For example, science fiction and mystery are genres that have at last been recognized as worthy of legitimate literary acclaim.

McCAMMON: Well, I have to admit that my aged relatives don't read my books because they would find it very uneasy to be around me [*laughs*]! But I really do feel there's a change in the wind. I don't want to say that horror's become respectable—the great thing about horror is that most of it will *never* become respectable—but people are finally listening to what this kind of fiction can say about the human condition. And it's not only that people are being scared by the superficial elements of horror fiction. They really are beginning to realize that there is more to it than just the scare scenes.

WIATER: You've told me before how horror is in fact the oldest form of literature, both written and oral.

McCAMMON: Horror fiction has as its basis the human condition, and it can talk about that condition in a way that other types of fiction cannot. It's the idea that this literature that we do has worth—it's also fun, it's a hell of a lot of fun!—but it has *worth*. And I think it has enduring worth. People are beginning to realize that as well, and they're reading horror now as serious literature. I really believe that. (And I can hear the howls from that statement all the way across the Atlantic. But I really think it's so.) The longest running tradition in literature *is* the horror tale, and it goes back to *Beowulf*, and I'm sure it goes back to the oral tales of "You better not go by the swamp, because there's something in there...." These tales of warning, of danger—either in a physical or a mental way—which show the ways others have dealt with it, have been around a long, long, time. And will be around until the end of time.

WIATER: A personal favorite of mine among your early novels is *They Thirst*. Can you recall how that story originated?

McCAMMON: Well, I always wanted to do a vampire novel. So I thought, where would be a good place to set a vampire novel? First it was going to be set in Chicago, and be about teenage gangs who were vampires. I did two hundred pages of that book ... and you get to a certain point where it either takes off or it doesn't take off. Well, that was one that *didn't* take off [*laughs*]. I wanted an epic novel that I could take in a lot of different directions, so the first thing I did was have a detective who was originally from Hungary, who had a lot of prior experiences with these vampire forces. So, where? Los Angeles—a lot of different kinds of people out there, different nationalities. I mean, who says a vampire can't be Jewish, or whatever? So I went from there, and this time it worked out.

WIATER: It's no secret that, early in your career, some critics mistakenly dismissed you as imitative of Stephen King. Now, a decade later, some critics declare you're as good, if not better, than King. How do you and other writers respond to that kind of almost inevitable comparison in the media?

McCAMMON: Well, King is the best. He's the top of the list. And that's why, in a way, a lot of writers get compared to him. He's the best—

and most visible. People will come up to you and say, "What kind of work do you do?" I'll say, "Horror." "Oh, do you write horror stories?" And I'll say, "Yeah." "Oh, like Stephen King?" So what do you say? "No, I don't write horror like Stephen King!" [*laughs*] So King is the key to the translation between other people in our field and the public at large. But it happens all the time, and it's kind of a dilemma, to explain to them that you write horror stories like Stephen King, but you *don't* write horror stories like Stephen King [*laughs*]! But I am extremely flattered to be likened to King, and to be received well.

It was difficult for me because my first novel *was* published, and in a sense I learned how to write in public. And I was searching for my own style of expression, my own voice—in public—and I think that's where the idea that I was overly influenced by King comes from. Which was probably true because I was reading a lot of Stephen King, and even though I was reading a lot of other people, too, I thought this guy was at the top of the form! This is the person who has led all the others—so I think that's where a lot of the early criticism came from. It's an interesting situation because the public at large doesn't know authors, unless they're really serious about the field. Some of them just automatically put King and horror together. But I'm very glad to be getting out of that shadow.

WIATER: It may at last seem like an appropriate stereotype, but is it true you write at night and sleep during the day?

McCAMMON: I start work at about ten at night, and finish up at about four in the morning. When I'm finishing up a book, as I am now, I'll get up at about eleven o'clock in the morning and get right back to work. It takes me about nine months to write a book. I pace myself pretty well, in terms of doing only about five or six pages a day—and those are finished pages. When I'm completing a book, I'll double up on my shift, working seven days a week. I take my summers off. I do some short stories, but generally I just enjoy the summer.

I enjoy working at night—I just *do* better at night. I've noticed that the quality of my work changes somewhat: When I work at night, there's more of the fantastic and a horrific feeling to it. And in the daylight, that's when I go back and shape up what I've written the night before.

WIATER: Speaking of stereotypes—and since you founded the Horror Writers of America—why are people in this business often just the opposite of what the public expects them to be?

McCAMMON: Usually when I talk about fellow horror writers, I find that others ask me, "Aren't those people all weird???" It's amazing that most of the people in this field are so nice. Really! And I think it's because we're able to get all this acid out on paper. To get these bad feelings and impulses out on paper, which so-called normal people can't do. Everybody has violent impulses sometimes, where they'd just like to rip somebody to pieces; where they're inflicted by some kind of momentary madness. But we can get it all out on paper! And we're probably a lot more healthy, mentally, then a lot of these folks running around. I really believe that.

WIATER: Of course, not everyone is a fan of your work—or the genre in general. What do you say to those who charge that horror—in any medium in the mass media—is inherently bad for children, and is basically of no value whatsoever?

MCCAMMON: Well, *life* is bad for children, too. Life makes them grow up, and that can be bad. Like it or not, there are many aspects of horror fiction which offer clear and very penetrating insights into the human condition. Yet I can see some very prim and proper person saying that "Horror fiction is no good, and it should be banned." And that's been said to me before. After I gave a speech, I once had a person stand up who was very upset and ask me, Why was I forcing people to read this stuff? And I said I wasn't forcing anyone to read it. Because there is nothing wrong with reading horror fiction!

One of the reasons I like it is because there *is* an element of hope in most horror fiction; it doesn't all have to be dark. It can be a glorious human transformation as well as an unfortunate fall from grace. And a climb *to* grace. And that's what I believe the best in horror fiction entails. I think that's fantastic—I think that's fabulous! Of course, nothing I could say would probably keep anybody from censoring horror. But it'll never be censored in this house.

WIATER: But what about the critics who charge that, with all the real-life horrors around us, why dwell upon the subject even more?

MCCAMMON: Horror writers *are* approaching "real" horror, but we're doing it in such a way that is, hopefully, artistic and civilized. And in an educated and thoughtful way. We're not glorifying madness or murder or child abuse or any other of our twentieth-century horrors. We're simply trying to make sense out of the chaos, and in the process, exploring ourselves as well. We have to go all the way in, to conduct exploratory surgery. And some surgery is done with a laser, and some with a saw. We may not like what we find, but we still have to know what's there. For me, that has always been one of the valid reasons to write horror fiction.

WIATER: So again, you have no misgivings about being recognized and ultimately packaged as a writer in this genre?

McCammon: Absolutely none. Although some publishers may treat it as a second-rate literature, it is a first-rate literature, as far as I'm concerned. I don't believe there's any other kind of literature that has as much to say, or is as strong. Or as important. I think many *more* people should be exposed to the genre. Because when you consider the term "horror fiction," the average person says, "Well, it must be . . . horrible." Or, "Why should I want to read something that gives me nightmares?" But good horror fiction can be a wonderful way of stirring things up—of making you appreciate life all the more because there *is* so much death and suffering in this world.

David Morrell

It may seem odd to include a best-selling thriller writer (*The Fraternity of the Stone, The Fifth Profession*) and the creator of the incredibly popular adventure hero John Rambo (*First Blood*) in a gathering of dark dreamers. However, David Morrell is one of the best writers of fear and violence working today, and those are two key elements which are undeniably vital to creating what is commonly referred to as horror fiction.

Inspired by reading Stephen King's *'Salem's Lot*, Morrell has, indeed, written one novel firmly placed in the genre: 1979's *The Totem*. However, anyone who has read his first two novels, *First Blood* and *Testament*, will soon realize that what separates Morrell from every other writer of adventure and international intrigue is that he somehow bridges the gap between what is often accepted as the "thriller" with out-and-out "horror."

Even more than his novels, his short stories are quite overtly set in the horror genre. The fact that his stories have appeared in such anthologies as *The Dodd, Mead Gallery of Horror* and *Shadows*, not to mention his award-winning story—"Orange Is for Anguish, Blue for Insanity"—in *Prime Evil*, stand as evidence of that. Morrell was also one of three writers contributing to *Night Visions 2*.

In a way, Morrell has made his career as a genre writer who

has never been content to remain in the same genre. He has published action-adventure novels (*First Blood*), Westerns (*Last Reveille*), and Hitchcock-inspired thrillers (*Blood Oath*). Of course, Morrell is perhaps best known to the public as the author of a string of best-selling espionage novels, including *The Brotherhood of the Rose, The League of Night and Fog*, and the recently published *The Fifth Profession*. As far as the labelers in our culture are concerned, he is an acclaimed writer of espionage novels, most often introduced as the "creator of Rambo." He has also written a book on the tragic death of his teenaged son, *Fireflies*.

Regardless of what he writes, when you talk to the experts on contemporary literature in the horror genre, the name David Morrell comes up again and again....

Born on April 24, 1943, in Kitchener, Ontario, Morrell now lives with his family in a quiet neighborhood in Iowa City, not far from the University of Iowa. Formerly a professor of American literature until he resigned in 1986 to devote all of his time to writing, Morrell is that rare breed of writer whose work simply defies any quick or obvious categorization. This is partially because, like Dean R. Koontz, he comprehends the literary mechanics of both the "mainstream" and what is inevitably referred to as "genre" fiction. Whatever label the critics may put on him, what remains is an underlying sense that a pure, tangible horror resides within every one of his tales.

WIATER: Your short stories have always been more overtly horrific than the majority of your novels—why?
MORRELL: First, I like to believe my novels are thrillers with a difference. If you ripped off the title page, and put my novels side by side with a group of other writers' thrillers—so you couldn't know who composed what—you'd see that most thriller writers look as if they've been reading each other, and are all doing essentially the same kind of book. But with me, I think what you'd find would be a distinctive mix of the eerie, the insane, the horrific lurking alongside the action in the story and, at a certain point, the combination explodes upon the reader. Hopefully, with appropriately satisfying results.

Now, with the short story—and I pretty much decided that my short work would be in the horror field—there is nothing lurking; I have the horrific situation in mind, and I always try to keep that horror at the center of the effect that I'm trying for. I have found those stories come easiest for me when I write in the first person. I had a block for many years writing stories, and I happened to be rereading Browning and came upon what are known as his "dramatic monologues." I just loved the way he was doing these poems, and I suddenly said, "What if I made my short stories the equivalent of dramatic monologues? In which the first person addressed the audience to tell them what was going on?" On the face of it, this doesn't sound like a great revelation, but it was for me. The first person suddenly seemed a new technique.

WIATER: This is the stereotyped question asked all dark dreamers: Do you believe you're working out childhood traumas and fears in your work?

MORRELL: I would say that's the case with many writers. When I was still teaching, it used to be that when a student came into my office and said, "I want to be a writer," I'd reply, "What defect in your personality accounts for that ambition?" [*laughs*] It seems that many of us are writing, inadvertently, because of some inner turmoil that we're trying to get rid of. In my own case, one can find certain themes that reappear with remarkable regularity. There is, for example, the theme of a child and the parent, usually involving a father and a son, but not exclusively.

My biological father died about the time I was born, during World War II. So I grew up during those formative years alone with my mother. Apparently that was very traumatic for me, to find that other children had two parents, and I did not. I was utterly baffled by this, and I'm still trying to work out that bafflement in some of my stories. It isn't good to think too much about such traumas, because if you were ever to come to terms with whatever it was that's bothering you, then you wouldn't have anything to write about anymore. God knows, I don't want *that* to happen. So a little turmoil from my youth is probably a good thing.

WIATER: Considering that you were once a professor of American literature, I'm curious to know if you ever had the chance to read any literature of horror in your formative years?

MORRELL: I'm sure this is a familiar refrain, but Poe's work really did strike me as being so wonderful that I couldn't wait to get to the next story. I remember feeling the same way about Ambrose Bierce and H. P. Lovecraft. They all had a strong effect on my early years.

But we also can't ignore that I was a child who grew up watching television. What I liked so much were the monster films that were shown on television in the 1950s, and I'm thinking particularly of something like *Them!*, which is one of my favorites of that genre. And the Hammer films from England, particularly their Dracula series. I

found them terrifying! Of course, we can't ignore the Universal films which preceded them, with the Frankenstein, Dracula, Wolfman cycle they put out. And of course, that wonderful producer, Val Lewton, and the very subtle, moody horror movies he put out in the 1940s as well.
WIATER: What drew you to these kind of movies?
MORRELL: What I liked about them—and it was the same way with Westerns—is that I am drawn to narrative. I *love* to experience a very strong narrative. To some degree, I was seeing them to escape from real life—and again, that's no big news!—but I came to associate narrative with these kinds of stories. So when I made that choice to become a fiction writer, I was saying to myself, "What kind of areas turn me on?" It became obvious, looking at it from the point of view of that old gag, "Write what you like to read." Or, "Write what you like to watch." I knew immediately that I wanted to have an effect on my readers that would be equivalent to the effect the books and movies I've just mentioned had on me. I do it constantly now—attempt to distract my readers from reality.
WIATER: An admirable concept. Explain that phrase, if you would?
MORRELL: After my son died, one of the ways I was able to break my writer's block was by the numerous, very kind letters from fans asking, "When are we going to get another book? We can't wait!" Or they would say, "I lost my loved one" or "I've been in a car accident" or "My wife left me," or some other disaster. I was reminded of that wonderful line that Kris Kristofferson uses [as the title] in one of his songs, "Help me make it through the night." So these days I'm deliberately writing stories which I'm hoping will serve that function.

Horror, of course, is pure plot. Some people write "ooze horror," but I write "incident horror." It's one thing after another in a startling fashion, but without being so gross that the reader shuts the book.
WIATER: David, at the 1989 Horror Writers of America Conference, you told a very personal story about a book you were reading while you watched your fifteen-year-old son dying in a hospital room. May I ask if you could possibly relate that story again?
MORRELL: It's tough to talk about it, but I think it's valuable, so I'll give it a try. The basic situation was that Matthew had cancer, and I was convinced he was going to survive it. To my overwhelming shock, he did not respond to the chemicals he was given. And at a certain point he went into a coma. I sat with him in the intensive care ward, at the University of Iowa Hospital. Partially because of the lack of space, the entire family wasn't in there at once—we all took turns. We also took turns because if you spend more than eight hours in an intensive

care ward it can really, really have a disastrous psychological effect on you.

So we took shifts.

During my eight hours, I was sitting in a corner, looking at Matt while the nurses were doing what was necessary. At one time I counted that the poor kid had three IV poles, with every one of their several hooks filled with various fluids connected to the IV lines. That doesn't take into account the respirator they had down his throat, or the heart monitor that was patched to his chest. Nor the fact that his kidneys had failed and he was on a dialysis machine as well. This poor kid . . . you want to talk about horror: I was seeing the real thing.

Stephen King, being the generous and caring man that he is, had periodically been getting in touch with Matt, to try to cheer him up. Sometimes he'd call and sometimes he'd write, and sometimes he'd send a tape because he knew that Matt liked rock 'n' roll as much as Steve does. Sometimes Steve would send a new book. Now, Matt sure wasn't going to get to read the book, which if memory serves, was an advance edition of *The Tommyknockers*.

So I was sitting there. And what I would do periodically is read Stephen's book, and look up at Matt, and see all the tubes and the lights flashing on the monitors, and then I would go back to reading. And we all know the kind of wonderful thing that Steve does with horror: I was reading about people with their hair falling out, and their flesh rotting, and all that. In a certain way, the same sort of thing had happened to Matthew. So I'd read Steve, and look at my son—my poor, bald, puffed-up-with-steroids son.

Fake horror, such as in Steve's book—and I use the word *fake* with great respect—was somehow acting as an antidote to the real horror around me. It was allowing me to escape to this fantasy world that was believably depicted, but nonetheless *was* fantastic. It was like releasing the pressures that were within me. So afterward, I realized that rather than write an entirely different kind of fiction—a very realistic form of fiction that addressed very real-life concerns—I could, in fact, feel that by writing thrillers or horror that I was performing a very positive function for my readers. That I would be distracting *them* from real horrors with my fake horrors.

It was a revelation to me that what we do in this form has such social benefit that I have an obligation to continue doing it. Referring back again to those letters that I received, from people who were asking me to distract them from their problems, I said, "All right—let's get back to work." I guess I have to be very thankful to Stephen for all kinds of reasons, not only for his generosity to my son, but also just for the example that he provided.

WIATER: How actively do you search for the "heart of darkness" in your work? There is an ongoing examination of what is Good and what is supposed to be Evil in your work.

MORRELL: I suppose it's what we all, as horror writers, strive to do. The simple answer would be, "I haven't gotten to the end of the search yet, or else I would have run out of material." I continue to feel the need to do these stories and these novels because new situations occur to me which have striking implications. Embedded in everything that I've written is a major theme, religion and violence for example, which is lurking there for the reader who has eyes to see it. The juggling act I try to do is to keep the philosophical statements there, but at the same time keep the plot moving.

WIATER: But you're aware that in the perception of some readers, you inevitably come across as a horror writer? Does that bother you in any way, or is it actually a valid point?

MORRELL: I think it was Doug Winter who once said to me that he thought the last third of *First Blood* tripped over from adventure into horror. Because the characters become clairvoyant; they start to read each other's minds. And the bat cave sequence, even though it was a naturally horrific scene as opposed to a supernatural one, nevertheless evokes all the feelings that we normally associate with a supernatural horror scene.

Testament, the next novel, had very, very *strong* horror overtones. And of course *The Totem* was an out-and-out horror novel, although not based on a supernatural premise. There's even horror embedded in my espionage novels. This is not a general rule because I have done out-and-out supernatural stories, but for the most part my horror stories are studies of psychological breakdowns, more than anything else.

WIATER: Without patting myself on the back too loudly, you know that myself and horror critics like Douglas E. Winter were recognizing your special talents years ago, although you were never marketed as a horror writer per se.

MORRELL: That's probably why I associate with horror writers more than with any other type of writer. And the people I keep in the closest touch with are in the horror field. Because, as a group, these writers and readers seem to understand what I've been trying to do. Even though I'm presently writing what is called "international intrigue," it's with a strong dash of horror.

For example, in *The Brotherhood of the Rose*, after Saul's foster brother Chris has been killed, Saul goes on a very brutal mission of vengeance, having been worked up into what I call a "just rage." I'm hoping the reader will be cheering him on and saying, "Yeah, man! Go for it! Those bastards!" It's very *satisfying* to write a vengeance story [*laughs*]. It brings out all that venom in your soul, and you can just spew it out so you can finally get even. Better to do it on the page, than in real life. And throughout his mission of vengeance, Saul sees the ghost of his dead brother beside him.

WIATER: Have you ever written anything you later felt was too extreme, or perhaps too unsettling to publish?

MORRELL: There was a novel called *Intruder*, and I wrote it after *The Totem*. It's a book about spouse abuse. I wanted to do a book that dramatized the horror of what it was like for a wife to be stalked by an abusive husband. What began to occur to me was that most novelists dealt with this theme realistically, in sociological ways. But what I wanted to do was write it as a horror novel. The husband, whose name was Harry, just became an implacable force of evil. He had been in a fire, which had disfigured his face, and hence he took to wearing disguises.

So this poor woman, while she was on the run, never knew when this man was going to appear, or what he was going to look like! At one point in the narrative, he went to a plastic surgeon who gave him a "touch-up job," so to speak. But it didn't work, and as we near the climax, pieces of his face begin to fall off!

WIATER: Tremendous! So why was it never published? It sounds like a very strong premise to me.

MORRELL: The problem was, it may have been *too* strong. I went to my agent and a number of publishers, and they were just aghast that I had written this. They thought this guy was so grotesque he might as well have been from the moon. People *really* had trouble trying to understand what I was trying to do.

As a sidebar, someone who is in the publishing business—and I hasten to add it's nobody I was ever associated with—read the book in manuscript and actually said that the woman deserved to be beaten. I don't know what this guy did at home, but his reaction scared me a lot.

WIATER: Your career has had quite a few twists and turns. You've successfully explored several different genres, yet have never been trapped in any one "genre ghetto." Any advice for someone who wishes to write in a specific genre, yet doesn't want to be trapped while exploring it?

MORRELL: A good question. I was in a Waldenbooks store the other day, and I ran into an acquaintance of mine who used to be a doctor. She decided to quit the profession to pursue a full-time career as a science fiction writer. I said to her, "What are you working on these days?" She replied, "A science fiction novel, set in the future, which has to do with medicine." I said, "Well, let me make a suggestion. There are the best-sellers over there—do you find any science fiction among them?" (And I didn't mean an Asimov or a Clarke or a *Star Trek*, all of which are special cases.)

She didn't of course, because science fiction novels don't often appear on the list, and we notice it when they do because we aren't *expecting them to*. So what I said to her was, "For heaven's sake, don't tell your editor or your agent that you're writing a science fiction novel, set in the future, about medicine. Tell them you're working on a *futuristic medical thriller*." Her eyes lit up, and she began to understand the logic that I was using. We avoided the "science fiction" label. "Futuristic medical thriller" had such a good sound to it, hell, I was ready to try one!

My point is that often it's a question of marketing. There are writers in the horror field whom I have *immense* regard for. But they have never been able to break through, to get on the best-seller lists. They may be widely respected within the genre, but they don't have the broader base of readers outside their field. It may be that some people working within the horror form are doing their careers harm by thinking too "small," for lack of a better word. There was a panel of very experienced editors at a recent Horror Writers of America Conference talking about what makes for a break-through book. They were saying it's not so much the field that you're working in, it's the "canvas." (I hate using that overworked word, but it's one we all understand.) The scope and the breadth of the book.

Most horror novels tend to be short, they tend to be inbred—they rely on the ideas and concepts of others who have gone before them. Of course, a horror writer ought to be aware of the history of the genre. But to sell a lot of copies, a horror writer also has to find a large idea and head toward uncharted territory, announcing, in effect, that this book is *different* from other horror fiction. Easy to say. Very, very difficult to do.

Anne Rice

© Victoria Rouse

Not surprisingly, most novelists would be satisfied to find success in one genre, using a single identity. But Anne Rice, whose latest volume in her "Chronicles of the Vampires" series was 1988's *Queen of the Damned*, has in fact found varying degrees of success under three entirely different identities.

The first, of course, as the best-selling writer of such horror novels as 1974's *Interview with the Vampire* and *The Vampire Lestat*, a sequel published a decade later. *Interview with the Vampire*, her first published work, was written in what was reportedly a five-week, midnight-to-dawn marathon. In spite of her also having published two well-received historical works—*Cry to Heaven* and *The Feast of All Saints*—she is not at all displeased for being best known as a writer of elegantly written—and disturbingly sensual—horror novels. (The beginning of a new series, *The Mummy, or Ramses the Damned*, appeared in 1989.)

However, Rice is also no longer hesitant to admit that she has written mainstream novels using the pseudonym "Anne Rampling," which include *Belinda* and *Exit to Eden*. The Rampling books are more noticeably erotic in content than those published under her own name. Even so, the degree of contemporary explicitness in these works pales by comparison with her trilogy inspired by the Sleeping Beauty legend. Using the pseudonym "A. N. Roquelaure," Rice pens full-blown, S&M

pornographic fantasies—but skillfully realized in the tradition of *Story of O* or *Emmanuelle*. According to Rice, the situation was that she enjoyed reading erotica but could never find any that was well written. Her solution was to write her own: *The Claiming of Sleeping Beauty, Beauty's Punishment,* and *Beauty's Release*. No matter what the byline, an unmistakable erotic undercurrent courses through practically everything she writes—especially her horror.

A native of New Orleans, where she was born in 1941 and currently resides, Rice lives a very sedate life with her son Christopher, and husband, poet Stan Rice. She works in an office which she jokingly describes as "unbearable" because it is stuffed with books from floor to ceiling. The only visible office equipment is a word processer, printer, and a telephone. "It's a combination of high-tech and clutter," she explains with a smile. From fans of her vampire novels, a few bouquets of dead roses are visible from their precarious perches on the corners of bookshelves. Clearly, Anne Rice takes her readers just as seriously as she does the critics. Meanwhile, until a motion picture can be produced of her vampire Lestat, she has authorized a series of adult comic books to graphically tell the tale.

WIATER: To begin at the beginning, how did *Interview with the Vampire* originate?
RICE: It was very spontaneous. There was no plan at all. I was sitting at the typewriter and just thought I wanted to try it. I wrote very spontaneously in those days—with no plan as to even what word was going to come next. At first, *Interview* was a short story. I put it away, then took it out, rewrote it, put it away, took it out, rewrote it. Again and again. It was during one of these rewrites that I got ferociously involved with it, and it grew into this very weird novel. There were a number of false turns—at one point I threw out half of it and started over. But in general it was a great deal of experimenting and throwing stuff into the pot as if you were making soup.
WIATER: How did you come to make all of the main characters vampires?
RICE: You know, I was not a person who was obsessed with vampires, or who had pictures of them around the house. I hadn't seen any vampire movies in recent years, so it didn't grow out of any active obsession with them. It just happened that when I started to write through that

image, everything came together for me. I was suddenly able to talk about reality by using fantasy. So, it opened a door. In some ways, that's what it all is for me—just the opening of one door after another.

WIATER: So you've never claimed to be an expert on vampire movies or literature?

RICE: I wrote the vampire novel *I* wanted to read. That's what I did—I wrote the book that I had never been able to find. That really told me what the vampire did in his "off-hours." What he really felt. That's all I was doing. But obviously, if I wanted that, somebody else is going to want to be drawn into his living room at four o'clock in the morning and learn what he has to say in argument to his fellow vampires. And that's what the reader got, that kind of intimacy. And with all due modesty, the reader also got somebody who could *write* [*laughs*].

So they got descriptions and philosophical observations that were literate. I think that even people who don't like the books and criticize them would have to admit it's a tempting notion. Whether you think it succeeds or not, the attempt was sincere. I wanted to transcend the genre—but I also wanted to write the best damn vampire novel within the genre that has ever been written.

WIATER: So literary aspirations aside, you obviously were aware of the conventions of the classic vampire novel?

RICE: And I loved the conventions! It wasn't a matter of being faithful to them, I loved them! That was the whole idea, to take the cliches: the man in the cloak, the pale face, the flickering gaslights, the struggling victims. To take all the cliches and weave them into something completely different. That's really the key to all my work: to take those cliches and conventions—which I call classic—and then attempt to find a new depth.

WIATER: Considering the immense popularity of *Interview with the Vampire*, why did it take so long for a sequel?

RICE: Well, the main reason is I wrote other books! I just really deal with whatever obsesses me at the moment. As a writer, I feel like I'm about five different people, and only one of them writes the vampire novels. Also, frankly, in the beginning I was afraid of being typecast as a horror writer.

WIATER: Yet ten years ago was also the same time that such mainstream successes as King and Straub were beginning to appear.

RICE: I'm not in the least bit afraid now. That was before I understood that it didn't really matter; that the horror fans were easily the most intelligent and perceptive fans the books could have. I mean, you can do *anything* in that genre. You can write a great, great, great novel in the horror genre. There's nothing in it that forces you to write less well, or to create shallow characters. I'd be very happy now if I were to write nothing but occult novels under the name Anne Rice.

Before I wrote *The Vampire Lestat*, one of the things that made me return to the genre was reading Stephen King and Peter Straub and seeing what they were able to do. I wanted to get back in there and "outdo" them [*laughs*]! It's a wonderful desire! I also read a lot of the great English horror writers, like M. R. James, J. Sheridan Le Fanu, and Algernon Blackwood. Blackwood is a very erotic and wonderful horror writer.

WIATER: One of the strongest qualities of your novels is the degree of perverse eroticism, isn't it?

RICE: Oh, I feel horror fiction is *very* erotic. People have written really brilliant essays on that subject. It's absolutely inherent in vampire material: the drinking of the blood, the taking of the victim; all of that is highly erotic. It's an echo of the sex act itself. Since the Middle Ages, people have referred to the orgasm as the "little death." So the connections are there. But when I'm writing these novels, it's not thinking consciously about that: I'm just imagining I'm a vampire.

WIATER: You make it all sound so simple. Yet what do you say to those who would aspire to reach your phenomenal success?

RICE: What can I say? The only thing that's ever worked for me was to go where the passion was, to go where the pleasure is, to go where the pain is; to be very intense. Write like mad. Produce. Get the stuff out. I would be lying if I said I wasn't conscious of wanting to write a good story. I'm very conscious of wanting to write an exciting story, a gripping story. And I'm very aware of the fact that that is a commercial element.

WIATER: A strong story comes first, even before the characters?

RICE: With me, the storytelling has always come fairly naturally. Even my earliest work has this terrific narrative drive to it. It's always been a "and then this happened and then that happened" kind of thing. That gives a work a commercial edge. If I was giving advice, I would say don't ignore that. Remember what Aristotle said two thousand years ago about drama: You have to have plot, character, meaning, and spectacle. So remember that spectacle is important. You had that audience gathered into the arena and you had to show them something that was entertaining. There had to be an element of color, of pageantry, of sensuality. That's how I've always interpreted the term. And in my work, I love to elaborate and amplify the sensuous and dramatic elements. I try to make a very entertaining and spellbinding texture, if I can.

Even Shakespeare would not have written a play unless it was exciting and full of surprises. So don't think that the commercial and intellectual are at odds with one another. They're not. You can write a great novel and have it be really suspenseful and have a lot of spectacle to it. Yet it can still have all the philosophy and deep meaning that your soul needs to make your writing worthwhile.

WIATER: Although your first novel had its origins as a short story, what you've published to date has been solely novels. Do you recommend that someone try publishing short stories before taking on a novel-length work?

RICE: There are no rules; they should do absolutely what they feel like doing. But I would never advise a person to write short stories if they want to write a novel. There's just no point. *Interview with the Vampire* was a short story first, but I just didn't pursue short stories; they don't interest me now. The long form is what interests me. And frankly, I think you should go where the passion is. Many, many people start with novels. There is also a very practical concern: It's easier to sell a novel than it is a short story. There's almost no market for short stories in America; they don't reach the public or have the impact that a novel makes. And in terms of career, anyone who writes novels is going to have it easier than a short story writer.

But that shouldn't be the main concern either. The main concern is that you should do what you feel comfortable doing. I feel comfortable stretching it out. Going at it from all angles. I don't want to compress it into a short story. I really don't. Almost any idea that really grips me is worth a novel.

WIATER: I'm curious to know then just how the idea of *Queen of the Damned* originated. It does continue from where *The Vampire Lestat* ended, but deals with the "lives" of other vampire characters rather than just Lestat himself.

RICE: I was on a plane, and watching the second of the *Star Wars* movies, I believe, and suddenly the whole plot for the *Queen of the Damned* just came into my mind. It was inspired, I guess, by little things I kept seeing in the movie that I didn't really like all that much. I remember thinking what *I* wanted to do, as opposed to what I was seeing on the screen. And the whole plot just flashed into my brain. It happens all the time: You read or see something, and suddenly you realize what you want to do. So I decided to break off from working on my witchcraft novel, now that I saw the whole philosophical sweep and philosophical conclusion of *Queen of the Damned*.

A lot of this came into my head before I even wrote one word. Finally the time came when I couldn't afford to put it off any longer, and I sat down and wrote one word [*laughs*]. I became very determined to render exactly the book of my dreams. In other words, not to compromise in any way.

For me, it was the first book in which I really used the computer as the pure poetic tool it is capable of being. Because what the computer enables you to do is range back and forth across your work, and bring it up to your standards very easily. So even my smallest dissatisfactions, things I might have put up with if it had been typewritten, I was quickly able to boot up on the computer and change. So that's what I mean by pure and poetic: The computer really enables you to get *exactly* what you want to get. There's really no physical barrier anymore between you and your vision. If you can get it into words, you can really create what you see.

On the typewriter, I don't think that's true. You reach a point where you have this big, ponderous draft, and even to make minor changes in early chapters would mean making a mess, losing control of pages, having to retype.... You're dealing with the Industrial Revolution; you're dealing with a mechanism, with labor... and all of that's swept away by the computer—there's very little between your mind and what you're putting down there. There's really no excuse for not writing the perfect book. You're no longer making the mechanical compromises that move it away from poetry. I see poetry as meaning language at its very finest, and its most intense and most compressed. And you're able to get that essence with a computer.

WIATER: When you say *Queen of the Damned* was the "book of your dreams," do you mean in a technical sense due to the computer or more figuratively speaking?

RICE: No, frequently in the past I had imagined enormous books with many different things happening in them, and eventually that would not be the book I would ultimately produce. It would always be too big, too difficult to execute, too long, too complicated. So there was always a gulf between the books of my dreams and the books that were finally written. Like *The Feast of All Saints*, for example. That book takes place in the space of about a year or two. Originally I'd wanted it to go all the way from the 1840s to the Civil War into the twentieth century! But at that point as a writer, I couldn't write the book of my dreams. I didn't have enough skill, I didn't have enough craft to do what I envisioned. And when it came to the *Queen of the Damned*, I firmly resolved that I was going for the whole thing; to go for the enormous vision that had been born in my brain. I had finally reached a point where I could put all of that down; I was not going to compromise out of fear that I couldn't pull off a particular scene, character, or jump in time. That's really what I was talking about.

WIATER: As already noted, an aspect of your work which has practically become a trademark is your deft intertwining of the erotic with the horrific. But how do you actually set about creating the proper mood and tone to successfully evoke this complex set of emotions?

RICE: It is a difficult question to answer, because horror and sensuality have *always* been linked. Good horror writing is almost always sensuous writing because the threat posed in horror fiction is usually a veiled erotic threat. But if you go back to your earliest horror stories in English, there's always a tremendous emphasis on mood, and atmosphere, and the response of the physical body to the menace. Vampire fiction in particular is always sensuous, so there's no problem really [*laughs*]. I mean, horror writers are almost always dealing in atmosphere and suggestion . . . *suggestion*. Confusion of the senses, confusion of the mind to overwhelming physical responses. That's part and parcel of the genre.

With me, there's no method. Writing to me *is* sensuality. It is talking about the assault on the senses, and the effect on the individual. You either do that naturally, or you don't do it. You can't school yourself necessarily in doing that. The most you can do as a writer is stand back from your material and say, "What have I left out? What was I feeling physically? What textual details are missing?" But there can be some wonderful writing with no textual details. You just have to go with whatever way it goes. You can read just a few pages of Stephen King and can see that he's a very sensuous writer. It's the way he perceives the world, how a screen door closing sounds, or the flavor of a chocolate bar or a hamburger or whatever—it's all in there. But it's in there because that's what King notices. You may notice something else entirely from your own perspective. The main thing is to immerse yourself in the material, and reach for the intensity. Again, go where the intensity is, go where the pleasure is, go where the pain is. Go for the passion. Do that honestly, and the rest will fall into place.

WIATER: Passion is a word which comes to you so readily. What do you believe makes the pursuit of a writer's life so worthy of that passion—and the heartache?

RICE: Because it's the greatest creative profession. Anyone can do it any time. Unlike moviemaking, dancing, and classical music, painting—anything at all—writing requires a minimum of equipment, yet allows for a maximum expression of passion and creativity. You can do it at the kitchen table on paper you stole from the office with an old typewriter you got at a junk store. And you can make it from there to the best-seller lists. Somebody does that just about every year. Like Judith Guest, the housewife from Ohio who wrote *Ordinary People* and sent it in over the transom.

WIATER: But are you saying that if you just keep at it long enough, you're bound to succeed?

RICE: The important thing to remember is that it is an artistic realm—even if you're writing the most commercial fiction or nonfiction. That means there's no justice. It doesn't matter how hard you work, it doesn't matter who you know. What ultimately matters is what you put on that page—and whether somebody wants it at the moment. That's when anyone who wants to go into this profession has to (a) believe in themselves totally, (b) work like a demon, and (c) ignore the rejections. When you mail out a manuscript, you are not turning in a paper for a grade. You can mail out a perfectly wonderful and publishable novel and have it rejected ten times. And the reason it's rejected is because you hit ten different people who for various reasons don't want to work with this idea. You have to keep going. You have to never interpret rejection from New York publishers as a failing grade. They are not failing grades. They mean almost nothing.

WIATER: But your first novel wasn't accepted immediately. What kept you going until it did?

RICE: Some of the rejections I received for *Interview with the Vampire* were ludicrous. Fortunately I was confident enough to know that they were ludicrous. Somebody else might have been hurt and quit. But I kept writing, and kept mailing out. My attitude was "I'm going to become a writer." I *was* a writer. So my advice is to remember that you're dealing with people who make decisions on the basis of a whim, and just *keep going*. Keep going until you connect with a person who cares enough about what you've done to publish it. And don't be discouraged if you hit twenty people who aren't that one.

WIATER: Apparently you've had a few encounters with some less-than-kind editors over the years.

RICE: I really did get scathing rejections with *Interview*. And I paid not one whit of attention to them. So you've got to throw that switch in your head that says, "I'm going to succeed." And you've got to believe in yourself, and you've got to remember that the arts have always been tough. There's no point in whining about it. Say if you wanted to become an actor. The first people you would have met would have been sitting around in a cafe saying, "Go home, it's too tough, don't bother." But it's always been that way in the arts—a bunch of people sitting around telling you that you can't make it. Then others come out of nowhere and go right to the top.

What's important is what you've achieved at that moment and if somebody wants it. That's *it*. The arts have been basically the same for two thousand years. You just have to do your best, and make others want your work, and you have to keep looking for the people who want it. Above all, keep believing in yourself, because nobody can really tell you you're no good.

John Saul

In spite of the many talented writers working in the field, there are few so-called recognizable brand names, authors on whom the reading public can effectively depend to "deliver the goods" year after year, novel after novel. The first author who immediately comes to mind to most people is, of course, Stephen King. However, one can surely add to this short list native Californian John Saul, who had a bestseller in 1977 with his very first novel, *Suffer the Children*.

Born on February 25, 1942, Saul has since turned out a bestseller every year, with *Punish the Sinners, Cry for the Strangers, Comes the Blind Fury, When the Wind Blows, The God Project, Nathaniel, Brainchild, Hellfire, The Unwanted, The Unloved, Creature*, and his most recent, *Second Child*. Each of his novels has been on *The New York Times Book Review* list, and every one has sold in excess of a million copies. (Incidentally, with the exceptions of *The God Project, Creature* and *Second Child*, all his books have been published only as paperback originals). More important, as further validity of this author's popularity, all thirteen of his novels are still in print.

Shortly after the publication of *Creature*, I talked to Saul, who currently works on the seventh floor of a condominium building atop a hill in Seattle, Washington. There he works every day in a spacious office where he is surrounded by the latest in high-tech equipment, such as a word processor, laser printer, fax and photocopying machines. Except for the posters on the walls of the covers of several of his novels, one wouldn't readily believe that, among the stacks of books and clutter of papers and research material, a single person is responsible for transforming this chaos into an eagerly awaited thriller.

I found Saul to be one of the more atypical of the dark dreamers because he doesn't claim to be a lifelong fan of horror, nor does he involve himself with any of the conventions or organizations which support and promote the field. He also is one of the few writers I've encountered who doesn't seem to suffer any "withdrawal pains" if he's not at his word processor every morning. Although he has written some one-act plays, he is quite content to be recognized as a horror novelist. Then again, Saul is just as content to be sailing on Puget Sound in the Pacific Northwest as he is with coming up with the idea for his next, seemingly automatic, best-seller.

WIATER: Was *Suffer the Children* your first attempt at a novel?
SAUL: I've got my share of manuscripts on the shelf.
WIATER: May I ask how many?
SAUL: Oh, I'd say about ten.
WIATER: Wasn't that incredibly discouraging? Most people would have given up long before then.
SAUL: Well, my theory is that if you're easily discouraged, you'd better not try to be a writer! You just keep on going, no matter how bad everyone says your work is, and no matter how many people say, "You really have to face up to reality: You just can't do this."
WIATER: Was it always horror stories, these early attempts?
SAUL: No, I was doing comedy murder mysteries for a while. I found an agent who was interested in one of those, but she had no interest whatsoever from the publishers who told her, "Sorry—but there is absolutely no market for comedy murder mysteries!" And I kept hearing from my agent that my biggest problem was that I seemed to be writing things for which there was no market. Dell was looking for some kind of psychological or occult thriller. So I went down to the local supermarket and looked, and most of the books on the shelves were horror involving children. So I started working on ideas for horror novels, and came up with the idea for *Suffer the Children*.
WIATER: People were saying that you had talent, but you couldn't make a living from that genre? Peter Straub had a similar situation when publishers didn't bite for his first novels.

SAUL: You got it! In fact, for a while Peter Straub's agent in England, Carol Smith, was my agent. I remember her telling me that she loved what Peter was writing, but it was not earning him a living. So finally she said one day, "Look, we've got to do something about this!" They came up with *Julia*, I think.

WIATER: After being so commercially successful in this genre, have you since embraced horror, or just realized it's something you know how to do very well?

SAUL: Oh, I thoroughly enjoy writing them, and I think I have a knack for them, so it's worked out very happily. I guess it was very fortunate for me that when I decided to do my very small "market analysis" that something I had a a talent for happened to be popular. In fact, I was going through a box of old, old manuscripts—most of which have never been finished—and one of them I realized, as I began looking at it, was the beginnings of a horror novel!

WIATER: So it doesn't restrict you in any way that you're now universally recognized as a horror writer?

SAUL: No, that doesn't bother me at all. Because if I want to write other things, I feel perfectly comfortable about doing it. They may not be published under my own name—they may not be published at all—but the name is definitely associated with horror now, and I'm very comfortable with that. I happen to enjoy writing horror, and I suppose it will continue on in this way for as long as I can keep coming up with new ideas!

WIATER: You seem to suggest that you're publishing novels under a different name. As you know, both Stephen King and Dean R. Koontz have used pseudonyms in their careers—have you written horror novels under any other names?

SAUL: I've got a couple of things out under pseudonyms that are not horror—at all. That's as much as I'm allowed to say; the publishers have very strong clauses in the contracts. When I write under my own name, I write horror.

WIATER: But you also don't appear to follow the pattern of someone who grew up in the "classic" tradition of reading E. C. Comics or *Dracula*, or seeing hundreds of horror movies in your twisted youth.

SAUL: I was one of those who didn't read horror. I only saw one horror movie when I was a kid that I can recall, and that was the original *The Thing*. I remember it gave me nightmares for *days* afterward. The next horror movie I saw was as a teenager when *Psycho* came out, and I was eighteen. I wished I hadn't—it was a long time before I could use a tub-shower again.

WIATER: Maybe this is a major disappointment to you and maybe it's not—I'm referring to the lack of motion picture adaptations of your work. You would seem an obvious choice for Hollywood to go after, considering your large and faithful readership.
SAUL: Well, that's what *I* thought for a long time. But as I analyzed it, I came to realize that my books are not that easily filmable. There are usually pretty complex plots, and they are usually about four hundred pages in length—and not much can be taken out without the whole structure collapsing. When you try to take three hundred pages out of a four-hundred page novel to get it down to a one-hundred page shooting script, something has to go! And in my books, that invariably means plot and motivation. I think they're very visual, though, because I tend to write visually, and my novels tend to read as if you were watching a movie.
WIATER: Just one of your novels, *Cry for the Strangers*, was made as a movie for television in 1982, starring Patrick Duffy and Brian Keith, and directed by Peter Medak. What was your reaction to that production?
SAUL: I have very mixed feelings about it. I was a little bit amazed that it got made at all, because when it was under option, I talked to the producer one day when I happened to be in Los Angeles. And I asked him what the odds were that it was actually going to be made, and he said, "I figure we've got maybe a twenty-percent shot. Let's face it: We're planning to knock off six people in two hours, and the networks don't like that anymore!" And then, lo and behold, it came through.

I thought it was beautifully photographed, but I got tired of all those clouds rolling around. So I called the producer's office to find out what had happened, because I didn't think it hung together very well. It turned out it was the director's first shot at a made-for-television movie, and he'd mistimed everything, and when it came to editing it, they didn't have enough film for two hours. So they spliced in rolling clouds [*laughs*]! Over and over, to a point where I found it got a little giggly at the end: [*sings*] "Here come the clouds! Here come the clouds!"
WIATER: I understand you had some problems with the writing of *Brainchild*. This is surprising since once again a troubled teenager is the central focus of the plot, a young man with his brain damaged as the result of a car accident.
SAUL: The book had a *real* problem for a writer—it never occurred to me when I set out on the project—and that was it's next to impossible to have a lead character who has no emotional reactions whatsoever! It's not that easy to identify with someone who's a total "blank." I

found that I had to spend a lot of time building up a lot of sympathy and caring for this guy before I really had him start tearing up the town. Otherwise, my feeling would have been we should have killed him on the operating table! I will never again try to write a character who has no emotions.

WIATER: You've told me you try and do something different with every novel, yet in all your books there are at least three recurring themes: the setting in a small town, revenge against a wealthy or powerful family, and a child or adolescent as the protagonist.

SAUL: I really enjoy small towns. Because in a small town everybody knows everybody, and everybody's involved in everyone else's business. When something goes haywire, everybody immediately knows about it—and is immediately terrified about it. Whereas the same thing could happen in a major city, and ninety-nine percent of the population would never even know it was happening. It's much easier to build a great level of suspense in a small town. Also, the smaller and more isolated the town, the easier it is to have no one around to quickly figure out what's happening, or to put a stop to it.

As for children, usually in my books the villain is also the prime victim. And that works best with children, as there is an assumption that children are not necessarily responsible for their actions. If you have somebody who's an adult doing what my kids are doing, there's no sympathy for them.

WIATER: Your name rarely comes up when someone is asked to make a list of the best-selling horror writers working today. Perhaps the reason you're not always thought of in those discussions is because your audience is reportedly comprised mostly of adolescent females. Is this still the case?

SAUL: Well, actually it is slowly shifting because they are growing up, and they're sticking with me. The teenage audience is still very strong, and a lot of my fan mail is from teenagers, though that may be because teenagers tend to write fan letters more than adults do. But I get a lot of repeat fan mail from people I've been hearing from since *Suffer the Children*. They were in high school when it was published, and now they have children of their own. Every now and then one of them wants to know where they can get all my books in hardcover, because *their* kids are growing up and they're wondering if they'll be able to give these books to their kids at the age when *they* first started reading me. We'll see what happens.

WIATER: Considering your initial reputation in the field as a writer of quite "nasty" books, your later novels have become much less explicitly violent and, in turn, more intensely suspenseful.

SAUL: I never cared for the blood and gore, though *Suffer the Children* was my goriest. And I also think it's much more of a challenge to instill a sense of terror rather than simply to try to shock the reader.

WIATER: I take it then you're not a follower of the "gore is more" philosophy.

SAUL: [*angrily*] I think that is absolutely the cheapest thrill in the world! To me, if you can't think up a good plot, then you go about tearing people to shreds? I think it's revolting. If I pick up a book and see that's what the author is doing, I don't bother to buy it. If you can't think up a plot that's terrifying, if you can't dream up something that is truly frightening rather than just disgusting, you should go get an honest job. Basically, all it is is pornography.

WIATER: But just to keep on top of things, are you constantly sampling novels, or seeing nearly every new film that comes out?

SAUL: I tend to stay away from it all. I don't like horror movies because they scare me half to death! And I don't think you can be a successful horror writer unless you're easily frightened. I have a theory that if nothing frightens you, then you have no way of knowing what's going to frighten other people. Fortunately, I'm a card-carrying coward: *Everything* frightens me! I simply transfer all of my own fears on to the paper, and away we go! Consequently, I don't read horror novels, because they scare me. Actually, I love international spy thrillers; I'm one of the ones who is always waiting for the new Robert Ludlum to come out.

WIATER: But considering you're a brand name in the horror and dark suspense field, what do you think attracts readers to your books year after year, even though they have a lesser degree of sex and violence than the novels of many of your colleagues?

SAUL: I'm not sure the reader is expecting sex and violence—they're certainly not from me! They know when they pick up one of my books there's going to be essentially no sex in it, and although people might die, it's not going to be dwelled on in any kind of grisly detail. What I think the reader is looking for is the roller coaster ride. They want to be *scared out of their wits*—and I think there's a big difference between scaring someone and grossing them out.

I enjoy international spy thrillers, and what I enjoy is the thrill of the chase. I'm not interested in reading about how someone dies; I'm interested in the vicarious thrill of being in that dangerous situation and *just* squeaking out of it. What people are looking for in a thriller is *tension*. There are a lot of writers out there who seem incapable of coming up with genuine psychological tension, but they certainly can go rambling on describing sex and violence. Which I believe is the cheap or lazy way out.

I am also firmly convinced that you can get more mileage out of directing the reader's imagination than laying everything out for them in such detail that nothing is left to their imagination. I'm often given credit for incredibly realistic descriptions of people and places. The truth is, my descriptions are almost nonexistent. What I do is describe a house as a "Victorian pile." And *everybody* has seen dozens of Victorian piles, and everyone has one that stands out in their mind, whether they remember precisely it or not. And they think I've described it, when actually I didn't—I just cued an image in their mind.

WIATER: Robert Bloch wrote *Psycho II*, a sequel to his most famous novel. At the suggestions of your fans, have you ever given any thought to writing a sequel?

SAUL: Right. I'm *always* getting letters asking when is *The God Project II* coming out. Everyone wants to know what those two awful boys got into when they finally grew up [*laughs*]! And I've had a lot of interest in a sequel to *Suffer the Children*. I've never seriously entertained the idea of writing a sequel. I don't know if I ever will. Maybe, someday, if I come up with a really dynamite idea....

WIATER: What's the most pleasurable aspect of writing for you, and what's the least?

SAUL: Oh, that's easy! One of the Dorothys—it was either Parker or Thompson—said it, years ago: "It's not the writing I enjoy, it's having written." There's a point we all come to, halfway through every manuscript, when we know deep in our hearts that this time the publisher's going to ask for his money back! Every book has to stand on its own, and I still get nice comments from my editor, such as, "John, this is *not* the way we write a book." She used to be very polite!

WIATER: So how do you tackle a project?

SAUL: My most productive hours are from about two to six in the afternoon. I tend to spend my mornings thinking about what I'm going to do, and shaping it in my mind. I discovered that if I tried to put in eight hours, I got four hours of good writing and four hours of... rewritable stuff. I generally put it aside for the evening and try not to think about it until the next morning. Though when I'm in the middle of a book, it's hard to; I find then that I'm living in the town that it's set in, not Seattle.

I try to do the whole book in one fell swoop, as it were. I try to do a chapter a day. And I'll work weekends. Generally speaking, when

I'm in the throes of that first draft, it's written start to finish with no breaks.

WIATER: You're one of the few writers who will openly say that to sit down and write every day is a big pain in the butt. You told me once before that you spend as much time as possible cruising on your boat.

SAUL: Absolutely! I still believe that anyone who says they actually enjoy the process of writing is not working hard enough at it!

WIATER: Some authors begin their novel around a character. But, like Ira Levin, it would seem the strength of your work relies heavily on the "startling new idea" that makes up the basic plot.

SAUL: Absolutely. I always start with the idea, and then fill the book with characters who will serve that idea. There are characters who come alive suddenly—every now and then someone who was a minor character in the outline will blossom into a much larger role. But generally speaking, my books generate from the idea.

WIATER: Could you possibly cite an example of where you got the original idea? Let's try your most recent, *Creature*.

SAUL: I know *exactly* where I got the idea. I was watching the evening news about a year and a half ago, and there was a report on human growth hormones. The report got to talking in the future about "designer bodies." That there will come a time when you can pick your body style and there will be a combination of hormones that will allow you to have that body style. And I thought, "*That's* kind of creepy!" Two minutes later I thought, "There's the idea for the next book. How is this all going to work?" Immediately I saw one of those small towns where the major focus of everything is the high school football team, and what if one of these little towns figured out a way to make their team absolutely unbeatable? Bingo!

WIATER: Speaking of recurring themes, there was a distinct, almost singsong quality to the titles of your early novels: "suffer the children" and "cry for the strangers" and all the rest. Was that your idea?

SAUL: That *awful* rhythm which got to be the annual plague for us who were trying to come up with titles for the next one [*laughs*]! It began to sound like some kind of horrible litany.

Suffer the Children was my title. The second novel had no title at all, and my agent came up with *Punish the Sinners*, which I have always hated—but it had the same rhythm, which sort of begat the monster. The title for *When the Wind Blows* struck me very early on, but the book was scheduled to be published about the same time as Mary Higgins Clark's *The Cradle Will Fall*. I was concerned, but my editor thought it was wonderful: "Everybody will want to display them side by side!" And, by God, it happened. I came up with the title for *The God Project* at the same time I came up with the idea. And that one, thank God, broke the rhythm, and now I can call my books anything I want to [*laughs*]. Free at last! Free at last!

John Skipp & Craig Spector

Beth Gwinn

Publicly known as the "bad boys of horror," and even more infamous as the leading examples of that unspeakably bad attitude known as splatterpunk, John Skipp and Craig Spector are also recognized as being right on the cutting edge of the field. In only a few short years, this dedicated young writing team has blasted themselves into the forefront as masters of the genre with such acclaimed novels as *The Light at the End*, *The Cleanup*, *The Scream*, and 1989's *Dead Lines*. Besides composing as-yet-unpublished rock scores to their novels, they have also collaborated on a single novelization, *Fright Night*, and in 1989 edited one state-of-the-art anthology, the controversial *Book of the Dead*. (A sequel is threatened.)

The fact that *Book of the Dead* is a theme anthology dedicated to the brutal splatter films of director George A. Romero should give some indication that these two Pennsylvania-based writers do not want their horror restrained or subdued.

Owing to the graphic nature of their style, in which the reader is assaulted head-on with detailed descriptions of every shredded nerve and breaking bone, they have occasionally found themselves at odds with other writers who sincerely believe they have just gone too damn far in attempting to find their own particular heart of darkness.

But Skipp & Spector offer no apologies to anyone. They have already put the image of splatterpunks behind them (which was supposedly meant as a joke to begin with), since they believe they are moving too fast to risk looking behind. Although currently at work on their next novel, *The Bridge*, they have taken some time off from novel-length projects to start plotting their break into the motion picture industry. (Besides adapting their own novels into screenplays, they also cowrote the original story for *A Nightmare on Elm Street, Part 5*.) They will use any medium—prose, music, film—to get their message out.

In person, Skipp & Spector are two brash and highly charged personalities who confess they had first planned to conquer the world as rock musicians. On realizing they were not going to crack the music industry with their particular vision and sound, they turned their collaborative talents from one keyboard to another. In spite of their jovial and self-effacing attitude in public, these champions of what some critics have described as "rock 'n' roll horror" are deadly serious about what they do in print. Their stories, and their personal visions, are not for the faint of heart. Still in their early thirties, Skipp & Spector promise that the world has only heard the opening notes of what is to come: It's only rock 'n' roll, but they like it....

WIATER: I know both of you grew up on a steady diet of horror movies, and such wholesome magazines as *Creepy* and *Eerie*. Beyond that, were there any incidents in your childhood which further bent you in the direction of the macabre?

SKIPP: I can point directly to a fever I had when I was one and a half years old. I hallucinated like a sonofabitch: weird monsters running down the walls, crawling all over me. Aside from almost killing me, it left me afraid of the dark for years, and as I got older, left me determined to face down and conquer my fear.

SPECTOR: When I was about ten months old, I crawled into the kitchen and pulled on an electric cord leading to a skillet filled with frying chicken. It landed right on my head, and just fried the whole left side of my face; second- and third-degree burns, from forehead to chin. My parents, of course, were thrilled.

SKIPP: Colonel Spector's Kentucky Fried Toddler [*laughs*]. You want *fries* with that?

SPECTOR: [*laughs*] That precipitated some vividly symbolic nightmares that would plague me for years. It was always the same: There's a thin taut cable stretching into infinity, and the sound of murmuring voices in the background. Everything very quiet, *very* serene. A butterfly flits around the cable. It lands, and the *second* it does the cable snaps and I'm buried alive so badly I can barely hear my own screams. I'd always wake up in a state of complete berserk hysteria; once, I woke up on the front lawn.

My mother wrote a story about it, to sell to *Reader's Digest* or some such. It had a great title like "My Baby Pulled a Pan of Frying Chicken on His Head." Classic. Anyway, she gave it to me to read, and that was great because it allowed me as a child to see what had happened. I was able to connect it then with the imagery in the dream, and once I did that, the nightmares ended. The dialogue between the conscious and the unconscious is a real common thread in our stuff. Dreamscapes are very fertile soil.

SKIPP: So on the one hand, you've got Uncle Creepy and Frankenstein—the fun spooky stuff. On the other hand, you've got a personal relationship with pain and fear, a nodding acquaintance with death.

SPECTOR: And head wounds, lots of head wounds. We both had multiple concussions and shit [*laughs*].

SKIPP: It marks you; it defines your character. In my case, it led me to put the two together, turn those childhood monsters into the rat-things from *The Cleanup*. That's what we do: feed the mill with the grist of our lives.

WIATER: How do you two actually work together?

SKIPP: Having worked in bands together has helped a whole lot in terms of our flexibility and willingness to hear ideas restated. I'll think it sounds good like *this*, and he'll think it'll sound good like *that*, so we'll jam together and find out what works. To find that third voice.

SPECTOR: I think that's true, even for a solo act. There's you, the writer as a person, and then there's your *voice*. It's not the same thing. Your voice is a separate entity from your ego and your personality and your id. It demands autonomy. Whether you're working alone or in collaboration, you strive to find that, and be true to it. No matter what.

SKIPP: Right. With novels, we'll jam the story idea for a while, often over the course of years.

SPECTOR: We work with file cards a lot, and we'll just talk until we've got enough "bullets" or little bits to write on the cards. Any cogent image—a character, a scene, a gooshy bit—

SKIPP: —And then you start editing them out, until you start seeing some kind of order. It's storyboarding.

SPECTOR: Mix 'n' match. It's like jamming in the musical sense. You throw out an idea or a phrase and you kick it back and forth, and when it gels, you got it! Then you do another, and you just string 'em out.

Another way that being musicians trained us as writers is that the pacing of the prose develops a beat after a while, and you can almost hear the background music going on while it's happening. I have a recording studio in my office, and a lot of times if I want to get into the mood and nothing else is doing it, I'll write and record a piece of music. Then just turn it on and let it run.

WIATER: In other words, you play an original soundtrack for the imaginary movie in your mind so that you can then put the scene down on paper?

SPECTOR: Yes [*laughs*]. Music for the movies in your mind.

SKIPP: Absolutely.

WIATER: Your work has been interpreted by some as being too explicit, with too much emphasis on the blood and the gore. I'm sure you're both surprised and shocked by this charge.

SKIPP: Yeah, well. Some people just don't know how to have a good time [*laughs*]. Tell you what. Why don't you fire some specifics at us, and we'll tell you what we can.

WIATER: Fair enough. Your first novel, *The Light at the End*, introduced a punk vampire, Rudy Pasko, who in turn assaulted New York with a trail of psychic rapes, multiple decapitations, vampire sex—including undead sodomy in a torture chamber—and various other examples of what Anthony Burgess once termed "the old ultraviolence." Specific enough?

SKIPP: Those were the days [*laughs*]. We fired every megawatt of juice we had into that thing. It was sort of like the sessions at Termite Terrace must have been, where the great Warner Bros. cartoons of the thirties and forties were done. We just kept thinking of the wildest, most terrible things; and the worse it got, the more jazzed we got. I think it was that enthusiasm, and the fact that we *went for it*, that accounts for the book's appeal. They just hadn't seen a novel that was quite so unrelentingly, jubilantly *overt*.

SPECTOR: It certainly accounts for its appeal to *us*. We had a hell of a good time dreaming up that stuff, just going, "... and *then* what happens? Oooooooo-ooh. And *then* what happens?"

SKIPP: *The Light at the End* ended up being about the clash between the fantasy of violence versus the reality of violence. That's why the vampire motif worked out so well. A lot of people see vampires as these wonderfully romantic creatures.

SPECTOR: Vampires symbolize ruthless, icy exploitation of the living by those who are dead or might as well be, which as we all know is a mainstay of human civilization! The more we thought about it, the more we knew it was time to rip the too-cool skin off this beast, get a glimpse of the viscera beneath the veneer. And in doing so, give the reader what they're looking for, while compelling them to question why it's so damned appealing in the first place. *Plus* have a really good time doing it.

SKIPP: And that's what it's always been about, for us. Adding our two-cents' worth, in speaking our minds and having a wild time doing it. Only by the end of this one, we actually got *paid* for it.

SPECTOR: [*laughs*] Thus what was once a personality defect now became a lucrative career skill....

WIATER: Next from Skipp & Spector came *The Cleanup*, a supernatural vigilante story, also set in New York City. You may recall it contained one of the most controversial scenes in recent memory, or am I the very first to mention it?

SKIPP & SPECTOR: [*simultaneously*] The rape scene.

SPECTOR: Lord save us from the dreaded rape scene [*laughs*]. That one scene caused a furor that was alternately funny and appalling. One reviewer called it "the single most repellent" scene he'd ever read in a work of fiction, which I guess is some mark of distinction. How did we get into this mess? It was easy! We're trained professionals. It's our job!

SKIPP: Bottom line: *The Cleanup* is a story about urban violence—particularly sexual violence—and personal responsibility. When it came time to brutally rape one of our favorite characters, it was our responsibility to take the reader through it—to drag *ourselves* through it—in intimate, excruciating detail. Because too many rape scenes are played for racy thrills, cheap excuses for hard-ons at the women's expense. That kind of shit makes my teeth ache. We took the hard-line approach, by making the experience as horrible as it actually is. That upset a lot of people, which is good. It was never meant to be an "easy listening" experience.

WIATER: On to *The Scream*. Here you had a demonic rock band which murdered its groupies and turned them into worm-ridden zombie killers. A classic case of "rock 'n' roll horror," yes?

SKIPP: Yes. We took the documentary approach on that one.

SPECTOR: The demon "Momma" was Tipper Gore and Jerry Falwell's secret love child, with a little Age of Reagan thrown in for ballast. We decided to play the "What if . . . ?" game, like, "What if their rhetoric was taken literally? What if there really *was* a band sacrificing its groupies? And what if there was a malevolent force that fed on amoral brutality, that was an opportunistic fucker jockeying for a power base?

It got its last fix in Cambodia, but it was only enough to get a toehold on this world—to keep a talon in, working the rift. Now it's twenty years later, and it sees us heading for Central America, and it *likes* the kind of teenage robo-meat our society cranks out, 'cause they make a great army of believers.''

SKIPP: It was stylistically a cross of the first two books, in that it had a political agenda like *The Cleanup*—this time largely concerned with freedom of speech and creative expression—and *The Light at the End*'s freewheeling monster-movie approach. We had a lot of fun coming up with the gooshy bits for this one, and freely admit that with the worms is far and away our most disgusting work yet [*laughs*]. Kinda brings a tear to your eyes, don't it?

WIATER: And the suicide motif in *Dead Lines*? What was the attraction there?

SPECTOR: *Dead Lines* was a completely different direction, a much more interior story, and positively *demure* in comparison. The suicide sequence is pretty grim. But that's its job! Here's this tragic guy who just can't take it anymore, so he kills himself, just throws his life away. If you consider life to be the journey of the soul, then suicide is a real dead-end sort of move. Can't work out your problems in life? What, you think death is going to get *any easier*? He discovers that he's only trapped himself in a very private hell, and the book—the novel portion, at any rate—deals with his struggle to crawl back.

I try to imagine someone who's presuicidal reading this thing: [*mimes reader*] "Oh, I hate my life, I can't take it anymore, I'm gonna... I'm gonna... ooooh. Uh, maybe not." If *one* person reads that book and reconsiders, it's worth the price of admission.

WIATER: But you don't deny that your work physically upsets some readers? Is that a conscious goal you try to attain?

SPECTOR: To simply upset people is not a very hard thing to do. Throw a baby out a window and you've got everybody's attention. And some people have a low-tolerance threshold. They upset easily. Given our tastes, it sort of comes with the territory. But what we try to do is first our own personal interest in the story. Then build the reader's involvement in the story, build their sense of having a piece of themselves so personally at risk that they feel as if they lived it right along with the characters. Build to a crescendo, and then deliver them on the other side—

SKIPP: —with something—

SPECTOR: —with *something* they can hold on to, maybe even learned something from. We don't offer simple, "And let this be a lesson to you!" kind of morality plays—it's not our place, or our intention—but we like to genuinely touch people . . . even if it's only to scar them for life [*laughs*].

WIATER: Then why choose horror as the means for getting your message across at all?

SKIPP: In a lot of ways, I see horror as an intrinsically subversive medium. That has always been its appeal to me. You can talk about things that are not a part of polite conversation.

SPECTOR: You can literally talk about *anything*—

SKIPP: The taboo zones: of sex and death, birth and metaphysics. The extent to which you're allowed to explore your relationship with God, or what ever the hell you want to call it. And past that point, you're just supposed to leave it alone.

SPECTOR: There are reams of questions you are not supposed to ask, and things you are not supposed to look at. *And nobody ever tells you why*. Just throw it into the general catchall bin called "sin" and say, "Because . . . because God said *not* to!"

It's as if the act of *not* seeing something will protect you from it. It's the point at which ignorance becomes more than bliss, ignorance becomes salvation itself! To the best of my knowledge, not looking at something you fear is the best way in the world to give it even *more* power over you. It's like Room 101 in Orwell's *1984*—everybody's got the fear they cannot face. I'm in favor of training for a fearless imagination. I don't know if it's possible to face down every fear, but I think it's important to try.

SKIPP: And that's the danger in preserving the "unspeakable." When we talk about subversion, we're not just these little irresponsible pranksters, letting the air out of people's psychic tires for no reason at all. The fact is that, as a species, *we live in a state of active denial*, and all the backpedaling, flag-waving, what-about-the-children appeals to "morality" in the *world* won't spare us that one unwavering reality.

I mean, we've got Senator Jesse Helms leaning on the National Endowment for the Arts—to stop them from funding any art he labels "obscene"—while he harkens us back to "traditional family values." You know: "Only traditional family values can save America." But then you look at the national statistics on domestic violence, or you watch these poor fuckers on "Oprah" describe their own little real-life homespun horror stories, and suddenly "traditional family values" don't have quite the same Frank Capraesque cachet.

Suddenly you're looking at widespread wife beating and child abuse, a fine tradition of families raping their children and then forcing them not to tell anybody. And not to trust anybody. It's a fine family tradition of completely mutilating malleable young psyches, and then telling them that they can't read horror comics or see *A Nightmare on Elm Street* or listen to AC/DC because it might "warp their minds."

At which point, I get so mad that all I can think of is "*Fuck* you, Jesse. Crawl back under a manhole cover, you corrupt old puke!" But he won't, of course. And he won't leave it alone. Which is why we can't, either. Eternal vigilance is the price of freedom.

WIATER: Your detractors try to dismiss you as gorehounds or even pornographers. What do you say to those who can't deal with your work, and therefore summarily dismiss it?

SPECTOR: Grow up! Seriously, an interesting thing about criticism is that it just as often reveals as much about the critic as it does the critiqued. There's been a good bit of criticism of our work, from very enthusiastic to vehemently detractive. The range is so sweeping that we figure we must be doing *something* right. Of course, there'll always be those to whom our style or vision is too much. Fortunately for all concerned, it's still a free country, and let's keep it that way.

As for the gore... [*pauses*] It's interesting to note what people will *choose* to pay attention to. Sometimes gore is simply kinetic—a violent splash of red across the canvas to goose things along. But we spend a lot of time on the spiritual infrastructure of the books, make sure that it tracks accurately with itself; the juncture points between the physical and the metaphysical, the subtle linkage between the body and the soul. And the challenge I feel is to convey an intimate sense of a soul— which most of us will admit to having—residing in, and completely at the mercy of, a perilously frail physical form. Conveying a sense of being eternal spirits in a very transient material world. Denizens of the food chain.

SKIPP: That's why we amplify it as much as we do, because we want to be sure that when we put our thumb down, there's a pulse and a nerve twitching underneath it. And when the books go out there, we get the kind of feedback that lets us know we're hitting vital tissue.

SPECTOR: One thing people can trust about our work is that, whatever you get out of us, it's going to be the most we could give it. If we can't get behind something we've written, we can't expect anyone else to. Otherwise we're pandering to some oblique market demographic, supplying nothing more than commuter downtime fodder. That's the death of creativity. That's when it's time to find another job.

SKIPP: A-whooo! *Scary*, huh, kids?

SPECTOR: We want them to have to get up and walk around the room.

We want them to turn on every light in the house and *still* be scared. We want to scare them beyond the shadows in the corners, to scare them so bad that there's no safe place to hide. Then they'll *have* to face it.

WIATER: How do you go beyond the rules you've already broken? How far can the pendulum swing to the left?

SPECTOR: One thing I feel fairly confident of is that you never run out of rules to break, or things to be afraid of. God knows there's no shortage of fear in the world. We continue to do the things that are important to us. We write very much from the heart, and we feel that we're onto something. The freedom to change is essential. As we grow—and grow older—our interests change. As does our style. God knows what the future will bring... but rock 'n' roll is here to stay [*laughs*]! People have always been saying, "That's not music—that's just noise." And, "You'll grow out of it!" And, "This is just a phase, a fad."

SKIPP: But we're just getting *warmed up* here!

WIATER: So you intend to keep pushing the envelope, breaking more rules to try to discover what's on the other side?

SKIPP: When you set up a whole ring of taboos, what you're basically saying is "This is the end of the map."

SPECTOR: And beyond that, "Here there be dragons."

SKIPP: And you don't go past here—

SPECTOR: —or they'll eat you up [*laughs*]!

SKIPP: Yeah, here on the flat earth, our job—and the jobs of the creative people we most admire—is to map out those uncharted territories. To help us see those things we've been always told we are not supposed to see. Because that's where the wisdom is.

SPECTOR: That, and head wounds. Lots of head wounds.

Whitley Strieber

Whitley Strieber no longer has that *look*.
The look of someone who has dealt more with shadows than light, with fantasy more than reality. The look of a person previously haunted by vague yet myriad fears—fears which he attempted to purge through the writing of such well-received novels as *The Wolfen*, *The Hunger*, *Black Magic*, and *The Night Church*. Then as the coauthor (with James W. Kunetka) of the best-selling *Warday and the Journey Onward* and *Nature's End*. He has also written an award-winning juvenile, *Wolf of Shadows*, and a contemporary novel about witchcraft, *Catmagic*.

Two of his books, *The Wolfen* and *The Hunger*, have been made into major motion pictures. Of course, this success did not occur overnight: "It only took ten years, seven unpublished novels, and a lot of blood later before I sold *The Wolfen*."

But as most readers of his work are already aware, Whitley Strieber apparently has purged the greatest unknown fear from his life with the publication in 1987 of *Communion: A True Story*. On *The New York Times* best-seller list for more than seven months, it's the incredible story of his having been in contact with (to quote the dust-jacket copy) "intelligent non-human beings in his isolated cabin in upstate New York." Encounters with "visitors" which Strieber alleges have been occurring throughout his lifetime. In 1988, another best-selling book dealing with the subject, *Transformation*, appeared, though Strieber has since returned to writing novels with the publication last fall of *Majestic*.

Needless to say, his first person account in *Communion* was not greeted warmly by everyone in the literary community. Although a commercially successful and critically acclaimed author, Strieber was well aware that he took the greatest professional risk of his life by coming forth with such an undeniably fantastic document.

Born in San Antonio, Texas, in 1945, Strieber has lived in New York for the past twenty years. He invited me to his Manhattan apartment to spend the afternoon discussing his career and the events outlined in the two books dealing with the "visitors." Having interviewed him before, it was agreed to touch upon subjects which had been previously omitted from publication. At the time, those incidents seemed simply too strange to print—until the even more bizarre events described in *Communion* were made publicly known. As always, I found Strieber articulate, confident, and candid. Whatever has happened to him, it has apparently brought him out of the shadows he once seemed destined to live among.

WIATER: Following the publication of *Communion*, some of your colleagues in the horror and science fiction fields told me privately that: One, you have somehow gone "over the edge." Or two, you're doing this for the glory of "celebrity sainthood."

STRIEBER: A lot of writers are *very* supportive. I have some very dear friends who are writers. It depends on the individual. Some are jealous, openly so. I've pretty much closed off those writers who are in professional organizations because that seems to be where most of the jealousy lies. I probably won't go to conventions anymore, because I don't feel that's a healthy situation right now. Eventually I hope those people will realize it was an entirely legitimate and sincere effort on my part to write *Communion*. They have no more reason to be jealous of me than they do of any other writer. I couldn't have plotted this in advance—no one can! Especially when my own former publisher, Warner Books, turned me down. I had to write the whole book before I could even give it to another publisher! I wrote it without a contract, and then I submitted it to thirteen houses. And ten of them turned it down, flat. Many with contempt. I accepted the best offer of the three publishers interested.

WIATER: Others may suspect your sincere intentions due to the fact that you reportedly received a two-million-dollar advance.

STRIEBER: It was one million for the hard- and softcover rights. Which is not out of context with my previous work. I received seven hundred fifty thousand dollars for *Warday*, six hundred thousand dollars for *Nature's End*. So a million dollars is higher than those were, but it's not the first big advance I've gotten.

WIATER: Even so, there are those critics I've talked to who try to explain the situation by saying that for some unknown, twisted reason, you used your considerable talents as an author to make a fictional story sound quite true. In *Warday*, for example, you and coauthor James Kunetka appear as the main characters.

STRIEBER: [*angrily*] That's stupid! Anyone who reads *Communion* and draws that conclusion, draws it not from the facts but because that's what they would like to believe. I think that when people read *Transformation*, they are going to be forced to conclude that it *is* true on some level. Underlying the resistance is very real fear. Because our whole world view is threatened—very deeply threatened—by all this. We don't know what in the hell is here, but it's *something*. And it's not us!

I don't personally think that its primary origin is another planet. I think its primary origin is another aspect of reality. I think we're going to be forced to conclude from this that the soul exists, independent of the body. And that all of the consequences of that reality have to be faced by each one of us. That our lives are not lived in isolation. That we are not in a secret world between our ears. That what is going in us belongs to some larger reality. And that we are *not* alone, never have been.

WIATER: What about the situation in which *Catmagic* was originally published in hardcover as "Jonathan Barry with Whitley Strieber." The idea that you seemed compelled to create an imaginary collaborator for that novel has raised the hackles of some in the ranks.

STRIEBER: It's raising their hackles because they *want* a reason to be angry. It's as simple as that. What happened was perfectly straightforward: It turned out that *Catmagic* and *Nature's End* were going to be published at virtually the same time, and I couldn't have two books out at the same time under the same name. So I compromised, "Jonathan Barry with Whitley Strieber," so it would seem that I had done two collaborations. With the major collaboration in *Nature's End* first, and the lesser with *Catmagic* second, simply so I could publish both books. It was a perfectly reasonable thing to do. It was done for ethical reasons so as not to disadvantage the two publishers. It's assumed by people in this society that if you do things for ethical reasons, then you're weak. It's a big mistake to assume that I'm weak.

WIATER: In a previous interview, in an incident that was ultimately not published, you described how you could lie down on the couch in your office, and apparently feel as though you were traveling through time, both into the past and into the future. Would you care to elaborate on that now?

STRIEBER: I don't know what it means now, either. Except my relationship to time is something I'm very interested in. I don't think any of us understands the nature of time, and that to a degree the idea of temporal progression is an illusion. And that people are now trying to rattle the doors of that illusion, and that's what I was doing.

WIATER: The other mystifying incident left off the record dealt with your statement that you once stepped off a sidewalk outside your apartment here in New York, and believed you may have stepped out of this time frame, literally, into the past.

STRIEBER: That happened, yes. It was an extraordinary experience. I don't know what it was, except it was some sort of an act of mind. Of what though? It's certainly not similar to any act of mind I've experienced before or since. I had a vivid impression of stepping off the sidewalk, and for about fifteen seconds, I seemed to slip into the past, and ended up in a very, very vivid approximation of what seemed to be a period of anywhere between eighty and one hundred fifty years ago. Right on that corner. And it was so vivid that I saw a piece of paper with printing on it crumpled up in the granite gutter. And as I reached down to pick it up, I felt the most appalling loneliness I've ever felt in my life. Something told me that if touched that, I would never go home. I froze there and didn't touch the paper. Then our world just came up around me again. To this day, I don't know what that experience was. I view it as an example of what a really good imagination can do if it wants to. That's what I think it was. But I'm glad it happened because it's provided me with many hours of interesting speculation.

WIATER: Yet you've also stated previously that "the world I really live in is one of memory and imagination. Where imagination may be, in fact, a form of memory." It's difficult for some of us to grasp the concept that your imagination and memories are more closely interwoven to reality than most of us would like to contemplate.

STRIEBER: At that time, I think I was coming toward a realization that there was something more real than dreams in my life, and less real than this physical world. What I think I'm dealing with is something that's more substantial than thought, and less substantial than a physical object. There is a life—and an intelligence, at that level of reality. In the past we've called what lives there "the gods." It's responsible for religious experiences, it's responsible for the fairy lore, it's responsible for probably such things as Sasquatch, UFOs, for "Nessie" at Loch Ness, and so forth and so on. It's probably responsible for most of those manifestations that have a quasi-real quality to them. Things that can never be pinned down but have a sort of undertone of evidence that they really exist.

WIATER: Are you saying you believe a single theory can explain all the unknown or mysterious phenomena reported on this planet?

STRIEBER: I suspect that, not only is there a theory, but a technology somewhere available to learn to manipulate this level of reality in ways that are productive to humankind. Thought has a very indeterminate relationship to the "real." And that, to a degree, the way we think, the way we perceive the universe, may be able to profoundly alter the way in which it manifests in our reality. In other words, we may be able to make choices which make the universe more accessible to us on a certain level. I hope I'm making myself clear—I'm not at all sure that I am. I don't think the universe is as it seems. I don't think time is what it seems. I don't think *we* are what we seem. . . . This is not the world as it is; this is the world *as it seems*.

WIATER: Another aspect of *Communion* that bothers the skeptics is the fact that you are far from the first person to have claimed to have met with extraterrestrials. Others have claimed contact with space beings for decades, from George Adamski in the 1950s to Betty and Barney Hill in the 1960s.

STRIEBER: When people talk about *Communion*, they inevitably talk about "extraterrestrials." However, right in the front of the book, there is this statement: "This book is about forming a new relationship with the unknown." Not with extraterrestrials, but with the *unknown*. "Instead of shunning the darkness, we can face straight into it with an open mind. When we do that, the unknown changes. Fearful things become understandable, and a truth is suggested: The enigmatic presence of the human"—not extraterrestrial—"mind winks back from the dark."

People amuse themselves with fears of extraterrestrials, and fear of flying saucers. In the case of a lot of intellectuals, that fear is expressed as contempt. But what they really fear is what is true. And what is true is the real unknown is *in our mind*. Not out there. The inner man is in a great darkness, and we don't know what's moving around in the shadows. When we look up at the skies, we're in the same position! People don't like to be in that position, dangling between two unknowns. They like everything to be safe, and secure, and sure. But there is no way to get out of the mystery in the end; every one of us is going to die. And the barrier has never been crossed—we don't know what's on the other side. So every one of those pompous, vicious people has the same problem I have: and that is that we live in the unknown.

WIATER: You've stated that both your wife and young son also went through similar experiences with the "visitors." Following the events described in the two books—and since you released this information publicly—how has it affected you and your family?

STRIEBER: All three of us were shocked at first by what happened, what *began* happening with the visitors. But we got used to it. I don't fear it so much anymore; I'm fascinated. And so is my wife. For my son, it's a small part of his reality. It's not central to him at all. It's something he will gladly talk about, and something he thinks about sometimes. But he's never lost a night's sleep over it and has had only one bad dream about the experience. It's a strong family. We were strong before this happened, and we're stronger now. As far as my personal life is concerned, my real friends got closer, and stood really close, and the others went to hell. Our experience was not negative. Anyone who turned away from me who used to be a friend, and isn't now, was just an acquaintance. I have received only two or three pieces of hate mail from the public, and I've made many, many new friends.

WIATER: But there are those who say that your lifelong interest with the occult and science fiction may have biased you to more readily believe that UFOs and alien beings exist.

STRIEBER: Belief simply isn't an issue in my case. I'm not a "believer." I don't "believe" anything! My book never asserts any beliefs at all. What it does is try to open up a lot of questions—and good questions, I think. Very valuable questions. I don't think I was necessarily abducted aboard a "space craft" by "extraterrestrials." Nor do I think that I had a real bad dream! Something else may have happened—*I'm not sure what*. It could be any number of possibilities. Maybe some we haven't even conceived of yet.

WIATER: I know you were not overly satisfied with the film versions of *The Wolfen* and *The Hunger*. Is that why you decided to produce *Communion* independently as a motion picture?

STRIEBER: Yes... with director Philippe Mora and I owning the production company. It'll be distributed by New Line. I wrote the screenplay for it, and I will write the screenplay for all my movies in the future. I will never again sell another book to be written by somebody else. We will be doing my new book, *Majestic*, as well.

WIATER: Obviously this experience, whatever its true origin may ultimately turn out to be, has changed your life forever. Yet, wouldn't you have rather waited until you could have come forth with some hard, physical evidence to better substantiate your claims?

STRIEBER: I'm indifferent to that issue. I'm not interested in "proving" things to people. That's not what my work is about—somebody else has to do that. I'm going to communicate what has happened to me, and what that means to me. *That's it*. And I will be glad to work with people who have had similar experiences. I'm not much interested in the source of the experiences—only in their effects. And as far as whether other people believe me or not, it's a matter of indifference, too. Because if they haven't had the experience, it doesn't matter very much if they believe me or not, and if they have had the experience, then they'll already believe me.

WIATER: Before your books on the "visitors," you wrote several horror and speculative novels—or as you preferred to term them, *novels of fear*. You told me that your childhood was one which inevitably led you to writing that kind of fiction. In what way?

STRIEBER: My early life was filled with arbitrary tragedies. From the age of ten to the age of twenty, it's just a litany of one catastrophe after another in my family. Beginning with my grandfather's sudden and early death, which really threw the family into a very bad situation. One of my uncles was murdered about a year later. Six months after that, his wife was nearly burned to death and ended up in the hospital for two years—and she had five kids. My father lost his voice to cancer, and we nearly went bankrupt. Our house burned down. This all happened at about the same time, and it was like some dark force coming in just striking us, again and again and again.

WIATER: Your earlier novels were primarily marketed as horror; what value do you think the genre has as popular literature?

STRIEBER: What horror writing is about, in my opinion, is the archetypical journey through the netherworld. We all come from somewhere, and we're all going somewhere—and we don't know where. And we're all frightened. Every one of us, in nightmares, has lived through this fear. Now someone with a uniquely terrible series of experiences like I've had, maybe has a special relationship with fear. But most people walking the street have experienced the Ultimate Fear. I certainly don't know anyone who can't look back on a nightmare, and even if it didn't make much sense, it still drew them to a level of ultimate terror. So we all know what it's about, we all know what the terror *is*.

Horror novels are important because they help us deal with this. Mainstream novels are generally a type of moral fiction that concerns the consciousness of everyday life. Horror novels are about the *inner* consciousness; about extending consciousness into the dark places of the soul. The novelist is a guide through the netherworld, and in a good horror novel, the *reader* is the hero of the journey. Not the main characters who are acted upon by the disasters. Stephen King, for example: His best characters are always his victims. When you read his books, you find yourself literally the hero of the story in the sense that he is guiding you from event to event, deeper and deeper into this netherworld.

And guiding you out again, too. There are some sonsofbitches who leave you dangling in the darkness [*laughs*]; people who really don't know what they're doing or just out for a kick. The old "hack 'em up and scare 'em" deal. I'm not interested in that. I'm interested in horror as a serious fictional form.

WIATER: In that sense, *Warday* deals very effectively with the Ultimate Fear facing all of mankind—annihilation by nuclear warfare.

STRIEBER: It takes the movement the farthest it's ever gone—I don't think there's ever been a horror novel as vitally connected to the issues and the reality of terror in our time. Horror fiction is uniquely capable of dealing with the *real* nightmares of this period; there isn't another form of literature that is capable of doing it. If we're going to learn to be able to grapple consciously with these terrors, it's going to be through the medium of horror fiction.

WIATER: No matter what others may believe, you seem to have gone through this entire experience in going public with the "visitors" remarkably well. May I also say that you no longer have that look of someone who had previously spent his life "haunted" by fear.

STRIEBER: I know what effect the visitor experience has had on me. A lifetime of hiding from it, turning away from it, of being terribly frightened—has ended. I've become incredibly empowered by facing it. I'm happy. I have a very happy family. I'm living the life I want to live, which is life as a creative person, and I have also, I think, managed to preserve my respect in the common community. These are things that are just absolutely priceless. It certainly hasn't hurt me at all! I've gotten a lot of money because of it as well, which for a writer is always a wonderful and surprising experience.

Chet Williamson

From a traditional (or stereotypical, if you like) viewpoint, Chet Williamson is a perfect example of what a dark dreamer should be. To begin with, in appearance he acts like a very innocent, very rational sort of person. He is quiet, polite, and has a lovely wife, family, and home in Pennsylvania. He discovered horror in the classic tradition of those growing up in the fifties: He read his parents' standard library volume of Edgar Allan Poe, then discovered H. P. Lovecraft (in the Lancer paperback editions) in the early 1960s, along with the Ballantine horror series. He also credits as a major influence in his youth the discovery of the "monster movie" magazine *Famous Monsters of Filmland* (issue number 5) and the equally important *Castle of Frankenstein*.

Williamson is also among the long list of writers who claims to have been influenced by the now legendary E. C. Comics of the 1950s, though he will confess that he didn't actually read them until they were reprinted as "underground comix" in the 1970s. Just as important, he paid his dues by building the now classic Aurora monster model kits, surely an unmistakable sign of someone destined to work professionally in the genre. ("I've still got the Mummy, Wolfman, and Dracula down in the basement.")

Born in Lancaster, Pennsylvania, in 1948, Williamson appeared on the scene in 1981, with the second short story sale of his career to *Rod Serling's Twilight Zone Magazine*. He has the distinction of being the only person I know of who has sold short stories to *Playboy, The New Yorker,* and *The Magazine of Fantasy & Science Fiction*—perhaps the three top magazines in the country. His stories continue to be published, not only in the major periodicals, but in a growing number of original anthologies as well. In 1989, I was fortunate to engage him as one of three contributors (along with Gary Brandner and Richard Laymon) to *Night Visions 7,* which I edited. His delightfully black novella, *The Confession of St. James,* stands as one of the most unforgettable portraits of a flesh-eating Methodist minister as you might ever hope to meet.

Beyond his growing body of short stories, Williamson has also begun to make his mark as a novelist. Since 1986, six have been published: *Soulstorm, Ash Wednesday, Lowland Rider, McKain's Dilemma, Dreamthorp,* and *Reign.*

His work has been well received from the start and indicates a talent of which readers have so far only seen the tip of the iceberg. So don't let the pleasant smile and boyish charm fool you: Chet Williamson is going to get you, sooner or later.

WIATER: I must say it seems clear you were destined to write in this field, after hearing about your formative years.
WILLIAMSON: I've *always* loved this stuff. I mean, it does sort of follow a pattern. First there were the monster magazines and the horror movies when I was a teenager. Then, when I got into college, I read a lot of fantasy: J.R.R. Tolkien, and Howard's *Conan,* and a lot of the William Morris-type of story. I even read *Thongor* novels, God help me [*laughs*]. I read so much of it I overdosed, and I find I can't read fantasy anymore. But I didn't read the real masters of horror—M. R. James, Algernon Blackwood—until after I was out of college. Again, only if it was reprinted in paperback, though I started buying the Arkham House books when I was in college, and kept that up. In fact, I was looking at them the other day, and found I only need about twenty-five more to complete my collection. But they're all the most expensive ones [*chuckles*]!
WIATER: So you feel that rather than by any subconscious compulsion which demanded you write horror, it was more out of a lifelong interest that drew you to it when you decided to become a professional writer?
WILLIAMSON: It was the latter. I didn't feel I had to express myself or anything because of a compulsion. I should explain that I started out not as a writer, but as an actor. And through acting I got into writing

and producing these industrial shows for conventions. You'd write a full-length musical for a business convention. When I realized I was writing book-length material with characters and a plot, I just thought, "Why not do this in fiction and try a few short stories?" Naturally, I gravitated toward horror, because that was what I always enjoyed reading most.

WIATER: You once told me that another reason you enjoyed horror so much was because you felt, of all the genres, it offered the most freedom. What exactly did you mean by that?

WILLIAMSON: Horror is not a genre of time and place, such as the Western. Or the private eye novel, which is a restriction of character and situation; there's a mystery, and you have to solve it. Horror is more a genre of emotion, and the emotion of fear or terror can be expressed in an infinite number of ways, with an infinite number of characters, times, places, situations, and plots. So you're very free with what you want to do with it because you're dealing with an emotion—or set of emotions—and not just a situation or a character.

WIATER: I've noticed in reviews of your novels that some critics intimate that you're a splatterpunk, while others note that your work is sometimes better categorized as quiet horror. What's your opinion on this literary name-calling?

WILLIAMSON: I don't know—I think the whole idea of bringing up these two schools of writing is kind of silly. I don't feel I fit in particularly either of them. There may be some writers who like being in a group, and I like being in a group, too. But I like being in that group of people who call themselves horror writers. Boiling it down into separate categories like that is self-defeating. It may make for some interesting panels at conventions, but I don't think it has much overall value.

WIATER: But you have no thoughts about those who choose to write in a very explicit mode?

WILLIAMSON: You can write about *anything* if you write well. There's no problem with subject matter; it's just if the writer is skillful enough to carry it off without merely making it an exercise in gut throwing. I don't really worry about it in my own work, though *Dreamthorp* is probably my most explicit in terms of describing violent acts, more than anything else I've written.

WIATER: So you don't see the "new wave" of horror as an exercise as to who can be the most terrifying in their style?

WILLIAMSON: Everybody talks about horror as if it always *has* to be scary. I'm always amused when I read reviews which say, "This provides the required amount of chills." Or, "There aren't quite enough scares here." What the hell? [*angrily*] Are we writing just to make the reader wet his pants? That's a pretty dumb reason for writing a story! There's got to be more to it than that. What I'm concerned with is the other human emotions. There *are* emotions other than fear. Fear is a very easy emotion to evoke. All you do is pull a knife on somebody and hold it to their throat, and they're going to be scared. And you can do the literary equivalent of that a half a dozen ways per page. It's easy to scare a reader. It's easy to gross out a reader.

What isn't easy is to reach down inside the reader and hold the mirror up and get to the more serious subjects that horror writing can reach, such as self-recognition. And by that I mean the monster being ourselves. My goal is to make the reader take a second look at himself. The way he thinks, the way he lives. I'm not crusading, by any means. I'm just saying that there's more to my stories than just providing thrills. Or there should be.

WIATER: Critics of the movement in horror toward the ultraexplicit charge that it's really no different from having a sex scene every five pages in a story. That this style of horror is simply a pornography of violence and clinical medical detail. Do you go along with that charge?

WILLIAMSON: It depends on the individual work. But there's very little difference in giving the reader an erection—and giving him an erection of the spine. There's *got* to be more to it than that.

WIATER: Without making you sound like a neophyte, you haven't been in the field as a novelist that long, regardless of the early critical acclaim. How pleased are you then with what you've produced so far?

WILLIAMSON: I like to believe I'm getting better. But the book that I'm working on now is the one I always think is the worst. It's awful! Then, once it's done, I can sit back and say, "Well, that wasn't as nearly as bad as I thought it was." But I like them all—or I wouldn't have written them. There are some passages that when I look back I would like to change, but those mistakes come with the territory.

WIATER: In many ways, your most interesting novel is *McKain's Dilemma* (1988), which is full of the emotions of life and death which you say you're striving to explore. It's actually a suspense novel, with the hero literally dying from a disease while trying to solve a case. What inspired you to write it?

WILLIAMSON: I write a lot about the way one approaches death, and confronts his own mortality. The clearest example of that theme is *McKain's Dilemma*. It's also my shortest novel, and my tightest. For those who haven't read me before, that might be a good place to start, even though it's not a horror novel.

WIATER: Your most traditional horror novel was your first, *Soulstorm* (1986), where you had the setting of a haunted house. Again, considering your past influences, it seems highly appropriate you should choose such a classic theme.

WILLIAMSON: *Soulstorm* is the one I would recommend least to start with. It's the most derivative of my novels, just because the situation has been handled before: an isolated group of people in a haunted house. I mean, you can think of a dozen people who have done it before me. But people keep telling me how much they like it. It's almost as if people want to read what they've read before, you know? And I don't want to write what I've written before. I think *Soulstorm* is the only time I've ever written what somebody else has written about before, though I had my own twist on it. It was really a variation on a theme. I prefer to write original themes.

WIATER: What kind of daily work pace do you set for yourself?

WILLIAMSON: I try to get to my office before nine o'clock. When I'm "in" a book, I try to do six pages a day. Hopefully, I can do a little more. When I'm ending a book, the last few days I tend to do ten to fifteen pages. It's when I'm planning a book that I'm lazy. Research takes such a *long* time, doesn't it [*laughs*]? But I like to do a full outline before I start, so that always makes it a lot easier for the ideas to flow.

WIATER: Any special trick to start or end your day with?

WILLIAMSON: I use that old trick of ending the day in the middle of a sentence. It works.

WIATER: Seriously, what about research? You told me an interesting anecdote at Necon about your preparations to write the novella *The Confession of St. James*.

WILLIAMSON: I always go to the library first. I went to my town library, and I got out books on careers in the clergy, another book on the preserving and drying of meats, and another book on cremation and funeral practices. I took them to the librarian, and she looked at them and said, "My—this is going to be a *weird* book, isn't it?"

WIATER: You use a word processor. Do you find it helps or hinders the creative flow in any way?

WILLIAMSON: I used to write my first drafts in longhand on legal pads, just because when I started writing, I did it during my lunch hour when I worked a real job. When I bought a word processor, I thought, "Oh, wow, I'm really prostituting myself now, because when I wrote before it was like every word was slow and thought out and came from my innermost soul" [*laughs*]. When I first sat down, I thought, "Will I be able to do this?" But it was wonderful! The first day I had the damn thing I wrote a short-short story that was the second story I ever sold to *Playboy*. I mean, I sent it in, and it sold! So I said to myself, "This is a good sign! Good ju-ju, bwana" [*pats word processor affectionately*].

A weird thing happened to me once. I had written a short story, and I was printing it out, and instead of stopping after the last page, the printer went on and printed a page from somewhere in the middle of my novel *Dreamthorp*! And I stopped it, and I thought it must have jumped on to another file on the hard disk. But when I punched up the list of files, I discovered that I had taken that file off months before. It didn't exist in the directory. Whoaaaaaaaa [*laughs*]! So I called the manufacturer, and the response I got was, "Oh, that was probably just a ghost file in there."

WIATER: Though I think I already know the answer, how important is it for you to be literally scared while you're writing? Or reading?

WILLIAMSON: Books don't scare me. When I read horror, I don't read it really to be scared. I read it to be *moved*. So I don't write to scare. If that comes along with it, that's fine. But I write primarily to express emotions, or an idea, or a concept in a certain way. What I try to do primarily is to take the reader into the characters. And if they feel fear, that's fine. If they feel other emotions, that's fine too. But my purpose is not to write a book that is going to "keep you up at night." That's a bonus if that happens.

I would prefer that you be moved emotionally the way I try to be moved emotionally when I'm writing it. What excites me is when *I* can really get into a character, and try to feel what he or she is feeling. Then there's the hard part: to get that down on paper. But it's like every day is a new scene, when you're working on a book. Something is going to happen, and your characters are going to do things. It's fun to go along with them.

WIATER: You're obviously very concerned with presenting characters with real emotions. To what extent do you involve your own emotions or personal experiences in your work?

WILLIAMSON: There's a piece of me in all my characters. It's like the old line, "We are multitudes." I've always felt we hold many, many people within us, and many, many emotions. And that when you write, you just peel off layers until you reach certain people. Sometimes that can get kind of fun and scary and very dark. My favorite example of that is Thomas Harris's *Red Dragon*. I think there is a potential in all of us for doing evil, horrible things. But because of our upbringing, society, and nice little things like that, we are able to cover those over. But they still exist way deep down inside us, and we as writers can delve down into those places. I think that's why I named my villain in *McKain's Dilemma* Carlton Runnells, because Carlton is my middle name. So there are all sorts of people inside all of us, and they pop out now and again.

WIATER: Although we've established that you're not a "gut thrower" in terms of style, are there any taboo areas you feel uncomfortable about investigating?

WILLIAMSON: Well, I will NOT write about telepathic lesbian vampire dolphins [*laughs*]. No, I don't really think there is any subject matter that I would consider taboo. You can write about *anything* if you do it "tastefully." I've even done slasher material—in *Dreamthorp* there's a very nasty, sociopathic, sexual killer, and it's some of the toughest stuff I've written. It wasn't easy to write.

WIATER: You've investigated both supernatural and psychological themes in your work. Any direction that you're leaning toward, regarding one over the other? That is, the "inner monsters" of the mind rather than the "outer monsters" of the supernatural and the occult?

WILLIAMSON: I think I'm tending toward the inner monsters, only because they're more real. Although I don't personally believe this, I like the idea that the mind is strong enough to create something nasty and external. But it all comes from the mind. And we live in pretty damn horrible times. I mean, some nasty things are happening out there. Horror, just like every other popular art, is a reflection of the times. We don't create these monsters; society creates them, and we just reflect them in our work.

WIATER: But by bringing these monsters into sharp focus, are we enlightening society, or only further numbing them to the most unpleasant aspects of life?

WILLIAMSON: You've got to go through the darkness before you can come out into the light. I would use the term *shadows to illuminate*. There are exceptions, but most of what I've written—in the books anyway—ends on a note of triumph or hope. At least hope. If there's not hope . . . if a novel is absolutely full of despair and nothing else, I really wouldn't want to read it. "We go through hell to get to heaven." But there is the question: What if some readers can't see *that*?

WIATER: You mean, those who are reading only for titillation?

WILLIAMSON: [*angrily*] "I read it for the *good* parts." But you can't let that stop you from doing what you want to do.

WIATER: Does it ever start to get under your skin, to deal with the dark side of reality on a daily basis?

WILLIAMSON: No. For me, it's sort of a cleansing agent.

WIATER: Have you ever felt that your publishers or editors were ever trying to steer your career in one direction or another?

WILLIAMSON: No. I've always written my books on speculation, and I feel a lot freer that way to do what I want to do. If there's any direction that I'm moving in, it's away from a straight horror novel into something that's more mainstream. It's a balancing act. What I would like to do is to keep appealing to the readers I already have; that is, to appeal to the horror reader as well as to a larger audience.

It's kind of tough to survive when your books are placed in that—dare I say—horror ghetto, where there are fifty of those books out on the shelves, and they all look the same, and your last name starts with W. The novel that's in the planning stages now has a horror element, but I really wouldn't call it a horror novel at all.

WIATER: So you feel that the packaging of a novel for a specific category can put off as many potential readers as it can attract?

WILLIAMSON: When I read, *I don't care* if it's a horror novel or whatever. If it's a good book, with well-developed characters that I can become involved with, that's fine. I read *writers*, as opposed to a genre. If I find a writer I like, I'll read his books and I don't care if he writes horror, mystery, Westerns, or all three. When we get into discussing genres, we sometimes tend to get so limited that we forget that there are other kinds of writing out there, including the mainstream. There's *wonderful* writing in the mainstream. You just have to look for it.

WIATER: So are you satisfied with yourself as a writer?

WILLIAMSON: [*sighs*] It's hard work. The more you do, the more you push yourself. A couple of years ago I came to the realization that I am never going to be content in life because I am always going to be trying to do something a little better than I did before. This is not the kind of thing where you can build your career by going up through sales and marketing, and then you're vice president, and if you're a good boy and the company doesn't fold, you can retire with a great pension.

In this line of work, you're only as good as your last book.

And your next book.

J. N. Williamson

Although he has been a novelist for little more than a decade, J. N. Williamson has become a force to be reckoned with in the field. Not only has he published more than thirty novels since his very first, *The Ritual*, he was also an instructor (specializing in horror) for the Writer's Digest School, and the editor of the very first-commissioned book on the subject: *How To Write Tales of Horror, Fantasy, and Science Fiction*. He is the editor of the award-winning *Masques* series, with volume four now in progress. Williamson is also the author of the gruesomely hilarious *The New Devil's Dictionary: Creepy Cliches and Sinister Synonyms*, required reading for anyone who believes they're breaking new ground in horror and supernatural fiction. Along the way he has produced more than one hundred short stories, and has, I believe, been published in every possible magazine which would consider exploring the macabre.

Born in Indianapolis, Indiana, in 1932, Williamson is recognized not only for his own work, but for his ability to discover new talent, and to help young writers move forward in their own careers. His *Masques* series has increasingly become a showcase for that new talent, as well as publishing such brand names as King, Matheson, and Bradbury. His kindness toward other writers is quickly becoming legendary. (For example, Graham Masterton in his interview made mention of Williamson by name for his assistance in the contacting of authors for *Scare Care*.)

But it is for his novels that J. N. Williamson is readily recognized as a dark dreamer. I can't think of anyone who has appeared so suddenly, and published so many books in such a relatively short span of time. They include *The Houngan, The Tulpa, Death-Coach, Death-Angel, The Evil One, Noonspell, The Offspring, Ghost, The Longest Night, Babel's Children, The Black School, Shadows of Death*, and *Monastery*. Amazingly enough, he writes everything on a manual typewriter.

In person, Williamson naturally presents himself in the role of a white-haired professor who has spent a lifetime studying and writing in the genre. He is always ready to lend a sympathetic ear, or suggest a possible market or editor for a story or novel. He is perhaps the most important connection between the small-press writers of horror and the professionals working in the genre, always trying to make the dreams of unknown writers come true. Always smiling, he makes it hard to believe that such a genial disposition should be accepted by the public, when one considers how boldly he writes of the supernatural and the unknown forces lurking around us... even now.

WIATER: Your first novel was published in 1979. Why did you wait until you were in your forties to begin writing horror?
WILLIAMSON: Actually, I began writing professionally as early as the age of nineteen, when I wrote the most ridiculously titled thing you ever heard of: *A Critical History and Analysis of the Whodunit*. This was sixty-eight pages long, so it wasn't very critical, and it wasn't very analytical [*laughs*]! But I wrote it and self-published it, and it was reviewed in *The New York Times*, and I made some money out of it. But, over the years, I sold a lot of stories to *Ellery Queen's Mystery Magazine*, and each of them had a kind of "gray area" that was the seed for horror all along.

Yet I was *completely* unaware that there were any markets for horror short stories when, at the age of twenty-seven, my first story of any consequence was published. For that reason I didn't really get into horror until I was forty-three, when I finally wrote a horror novel. That came to me in a nightmare, and I actually dreamed the entire story of *The Offspring*. (Which was not the first book that I sold, but it was what got me into writing novels.) It had always been short stories before that, which were either mysteries or poor imitations of F. Scott Fitzgerald. Who was, and probably still is, my favorite writer.

WIATER: I've heard that, like John Saul, you took an informal "market survey" after you wrote your first horror novel to see if anyone might be interested in reading another?

WILLIAMSON: Yes, I had the usual discovery that everyone had in the mid-to-late seventies, that there were paperback horror novels all over the place. So I said, "All right, what's wrong with that—I'll write another one!" [*laughs*] And I went on from there.

WIATER: As the publicists might say—"with a vengeance!" You no doubt hold some kind of unofficial record for the greatest number of novels published in the same genre, under your own name, in the shortest amount of time. *The Longest Night, Horror House, Queen of Hell, Ghost Mansion, Horror Mansion, Playmates, Premonition* . . . to name only a few.

WILLIAMSON: My basic plan, being forty-three when I wrote my first novel, was what I really should do was establish a reputation with publishers as fast as I possibly could. So the first bunch of novels were very quickly written, and written too fast for much of any judgment to be rendered on them other than "the guy's prolific!" Many of those I would like to disavow—except most of them are being reprinted like crazy!

WIATER: Not to make too obvious a pun, but aren't those early novels coming back to haunt you?

WILLIAMSON: Exactly! They haunt me in the sense that some can hurt my reputation. But at the same time I'm finally making some decent money, so it's craziness. Hopefully, my work will be increasingly known for the books I've written over the last few years. And a few others.

WIATER: But it's no exaggeration to say that, for a time, you appeared to have a novel out virtually at the rate of one a month.

WILLIAMSON: It reached such a height of productivity that in 1982 and 1983, in a period of ten months, I believe something like eleven novels of mine came out. Now there obviously can't be a great deal of quality in *much* of the writing of those books. But I'm not ashamed of all that earnest creative effort, except now I have this difficulty with people taking me a little bit more seriously, when I'm taking much longer to write a novel.

WIATER: It's true that you've diminished to the point where you're "only" publishing a few books a year, and to much better reviews. May I ask just how swiftly were some of those early books written?

WILLIAMSON: My own "world record" was for one I wrote in fifteen days. I was talking to Dean Koontz earlier about that, who said, in effect, "Bravo!" And he told me about a couple of his books—that he probably wouldn't want me to identify—that he wrote in a comparable period. It's fun to test yourself like that in many challenging ways. But on *The Longest Night*, I'd guess it was about a year and a half that it took to write it. The same with *Monastery*.

Some of my books I'll point to and say, "Well, that's a good read, if you don't mind all the typos, or that I made six or seven errors in fact." Or that "this is a *fast* read" or "the ideas in this one are fresh and clever." If you were to make a list separately of which are the good ones and which are the bad ones, I'd probably agree with yours!

WIATER: Don't you think that was taking a love for writing a little over the limit? I mean, what was driving you so hard to produce so much?

WILLIAMSON: A combination of things. I'm not ashamed to say that I've wanted to be a novelist, and a writer of some importance, since I was about fourteen years old and wrote my first story. When I was fifteen, nineteen, and twenty-one, I edited three Sherlockian [Sherlock Holmes] collections that today are extremely rare and valuable. I was given the idea to write by people like August Derleth, Vincent Starrett, Christopher Morley, Anthony Boucher, Rex Stout, "Ellery Queen"— who were two-or-three-times-a-month correspondents of mine when I was fifteen. After they found out how old I was, there was no decline in the amount of correspondence. I thought, "What *great* guys—what fine people; they'll mess around with a little kid like me. That's marvelous!" From that point on, I wanted to be a writer, too.

When I was twenty-seven, I married a woman with four children, we added two, and instead of doing what I should have done when I made a concerted effort at age forty-three to write, I played it society's way. I tried instead to turn myself into a businessman. Now I will tell any creative person that if they're bitten by the creative bug then they should do that *now*—because it won't go away. And why should it? I'm often happier now than I've ever been before in my life, and I think I'm mentally twenty years younger than when I wrote my first book!

WIATER: The work pace you set for yourself must be tremendous, correct?

WILLIAMSON: I never "just" edit an anthology, or "just" write a novel, or "just" create short fiction. I find it wonderfully healthy to be able to go to various parts of your mind and probe. And that's what I'm doing. I've written at every hour of the day of the twenty-four, and I've begun projects as late as three or four o'clock in the morning. Sometimes successfully; other times I've looked at the material and said, "What the hell is *this*?" [*laughs*] But there are so many subjects to explore—UFOs and astrology, philosophy and psychology, sports, cosmology and sociology, music—it's endlessly absorbing, and I want to write about *all* of it!

WIATER: Do you still carry on with your correspondence? I must say your letters to me remind me of those epics H. P. Lovecraft did for the amusement of his wide circle of colleagues.

WILLIAMSON: I have a *huge* correspondence which I would somehow like to reduce, but I have no idea how to do it. It just keeps growing. I think I probably will write, in an average week, somewhere between twenty and thirty letters. And I mean, *letters*. My days are exceedingly full; they'll probably always remain that way. I take very few days off. When I go away to a convention, it seems almost abnormal not to be writing and reading. I'm more at home, more comfortable, and more myself—perhaps a better *version* of myself—when I'm working.

WIATER: Of all your novels, which is your favorite, and which do you believe is your most frightening?

WILLIAMSON: While I respect my work on *The Longest Night* more, my own favorite novel surely must be *Ghost* or *Ghost Mansion*. Or maybe the new *Monastery* [*laughs*]. I'm not sure if I could choose between them. In terms of my most frightening novel—gee whiz, that's a marvelous question, I've never thought about it—I think the one that frightens me the most is between *Playmates* and *The Evil One*. But for overall originality of idea, and the numerous fresh effects that were used—and I think it's truly horrifying from start to finish—I would have to say *The Evil One*. Or maybe *Monastery* [*chuckles*].

WIATER: What kind of advice would you give to aspiring writers? It seems most appropriate to be asking since you were an instructor at the Writer's Digest School.

WILLIAMSON: I agree with Ray Bradbury who says, "Idea is damn near everything." Unfortunately, I found that a lot of my students believed that too literally! The idea grabs them, and they simply dash through it, and I had to kind of yell at them and say, "Back up, let's have some characters with flesh on their bones—and remember to put a comma in occasionally." Nonetheless, I think you have to gear yourself to making internal connections, no matter where it is that you are. In the sense that a doctor is always a doctor, no matter where he goes; a lawyer is always a lawyer. I think a writer should always consider him- or herself a writer.

Beyond the great importance of original idea and the concept of always thinking like a writer and living and working like a writer, is the fact that writers *read*. People who say they want to write, I believe, don't really read enough. And don't always read enough in categories beyond which they want to write.

You can't go on writing forever about, say, vampires. Be aware of what's going on in the world; be more aware of *many* topics to bring authenticity and verisimilitude to your work. And if you don't have that, you may have to depend solely on your idea—and that may not be enough. The other thing is of course to write, write, write—then write some more. Whether you send it out or not. You should also try to be more self-critical. And if you're more self-critical of yourself now than I was when I started my full-time career, you won't be submitting material which is consistently, indubitably unpublishable. Some of it will finally be good, then.

WIATER: But the question remains: Can horror be taught, or are good horror writers somehow simply born to write it?

WILLIAMSON: I don't want to tell you how many of them are trying to write horror or think they can write it because they're fans of horror *movies*! I'm afraid a lot of new writing in the field is terrible dreck. But I succeeded in teaching a couple of students to write horror well and, in each case, they didn't particularly have an interest in horror to begin with. Others found their fears locked deep inside and could not, or would not, communicate them. Even so, I believe you must first be badly frightened, even if only at an unconscious level, to write believable horror.

WIATER: Your anthologies have attracted some great talents, while at the same time you're actively seeking new writers who in many ways could be potentially just as gifted.

WILLIAMSON: I think the greatest joy that I'm deriving from the *Masques* series is that it has kind of put a question mark over everybody's head about this guy Williamson. Because how can he have the taste to discover these people, and to find such good stories, if he's really just a fast, "prolific" writer?! So I'm indebted to the initial *Masques* publisher, John Maclay, because mostly I was trying to please him and the readers in editing the first anthology. I'm delighted that I—we—succeeded. And the way I do it stems from the fact that I was a reader and a fan for a long time before I was a writer and an anthologist.

WIATER: With the exception of the limited edition *Anomalies* and *Nevermore!* you've yet to have a short story collection. Why not?

WILLIAMSON: That's a whole other ball game. I sold some twenty to twenty-five short stories before I wrote my first novel, and they composed about a quarter of what I had written in that period. But it's only in the past three years that I've really gotten to the point where I know how to craft a good, solid short story. The ones that were successes were sheer serendipitous accidents. I found myself in a position where my novels sold far easier than my short stories until about 1985.

I take some pride in saying that I've written only one novel this year, yet I have written about thirty-five short stories in the same period. And I've sold *all* of them. But that's an example of my idiosyncratic craziness—you're supposed to master the short story form *first*, and after twenty novels, I'm writing really decent short stories.

WIATER: How do you feel regarding the difference between having a reputation as "only" a paperback writer versus being published in hardcover?

WILLIAMSON: Well, in defense of the paperback novelist—for the benefit of your readers who want to become writers—the truth of the matter is, that with the exception of a handful of writers at the very top, the average author's hardcover novel will probably have no more than ten to twelve thousand readers if it's minimally successful. The fewest number of readers I ever had for any of my books was, I believe, twenty-five thousand. That's not all bad. And when a paperback writer reaches the point of best-sellerdom, you're talking one hundred thousand readers and up—way up! So you're beginning to acquire quite a lot of readers! And it's important to me that people read my books; I'm not writing in a vacuum. It's also not *that* important to me that my books be made into movies or hardcover novels. But, on the other hand, I wouldn't fight film deals either.

WIATER: You mentioned Ray Bradbury earlier, and, of course, he has contributed twice to your *Masques* series. Considering how enormously busy Bradbury is, how did you entice him to contribute to your *How to Write Stories of Horror, Fantasy, and Science Fiction* volume?

WILLIAMSON: I doubt if the *How to...* book or at least two of the first three *Masques* books would exist except for Ray Bradbury. What Ray does when he agrees to be in a book is to give it the Good Housekeeping Seal of Approval. So when you approach other writers and say, "Oh, by the way, Ray is contributing," you don't have to say much more! I simply contacted him by phone and asked him if he would like to write a chapter, and he replied, "What topic would you like me to approach?" Well, the question we get asked most as writers is the one that is ultimately boring—to me—of "Where do you get your ideas?" So with a rueful attitude I posed that suggestion to him, and he said, "I would love to answer that question, once and for all!" Now he can refer people to *How to...* and his chapter in it.

WIATER: Do you feel it's the job—or one of the jobs—of the horror writer to do more than just try to "scare the hell out of the reader"? That they should be "socially relevant" as well, when the occasion demands?

WILLIAMSON: Yeah, I think so. Particularly in my own short fiction, I've been increasingly able to deal with social issues without necessarily overstressing my own opinions and values. My opinions are always kept secondary to the plot and to the story, even though my major views are how I define Jerry Williamson to Jerry Williamson. So I've managed to say some things in unpopular areas, such as the topics of abortion and child neglect, without anybody getting violent with me. But if they're reading the story intelligently, it surely must be clear that I'm taking certain stances that may, amongst some people, be highly unpopular. If they understand my ideals and values only subliminally, so much the better. They'll stick, then.

WIATER: But do you think the public sees beyond the "scary parts" in most contemporary horror fiction?

WILLIAMSON: I wish I could honestly say I believe that. I think that's where horror someday is going to go, where it will have that kind of broader acceptance and significance. The only concern I have about the so-called *new wave* or *splatterpunk* or whatever term is currently popular, is that the reader may not pick up any beneficial messages that the writers working in that style are saying. By the same token, *any* of us can get so stuffy and pretentious it will mar the impact of our work. I think that for any of the styles we're talking about, we need to remember that *story* is first. And should always come first. There's nothing wrong with "shocking the hell" out of your readers. But in terms of my own personal growth, I always put down the idea and the story first, then, hopefully, find the suitable, distinctive format and voice for that work.

WIATER: With all the writers working today, what would you say to someone standing before a crowded bookrack and considering purchasing a J. N. Williamson novel for the first time? Why should they choose you amongst all the other dark dreamers?

WILLIAMSON: That's a marvelous question! [*long pause*] Several years ago I read a review of an Ira Levin novel. The review was complimentary until it got to the last few lines, where the critic said, "But of course Ira Levin is only a storyteller." And I thought...!!! Stanley, I think I'm a very good, sound storyteller. I was talking with Douglas Winter the other day about other writers who are derivative of Stephen King. I don't think I've ever "borrowed" from another writer—to say I'm not *influenced* is a major difference—and I know I've never consciously imitated another writer or worked off his material.

So I think what that new reader of mine will get is fresh idea and content, a tight story line, suspense, and some fresh horrific devices. And they will get one other thing, Stan: At the end of the story they'll have a very clear-cut impression of what they just read. It will *not* be vague, it will *not* be an obscure, "lost" feeling of "*What* did he say?" I, for one, will not play mind-games with the people who are good enough to read my work. Why be so pretentious; why try consistently and consciously to create great, subtle art? Great art is accidental. Any writer is lucky when it occurs. Entertain and inform and scare them into a few moments of real, reflective thought, and you've done more than most of the writers in any field have achieved.

Gahan Wilson

Courtesy "Gahan Wilson"

Take a look at any recent edition of *Who's Who*, and you'll find the basic biographical data: "Wilson, Gahan, cartoonist, author; born Evanstan, Ill., Feb. 18, 1930; son of Allen Barnum and Marian (Gahan) Wilson; student Art Institute of Chicago, 1948–1952; married Nancy Dee Midyette (Nancy Winters), Dec. 30, 1966." Although a list of his published works is included, what is omitted is the obvious: Gahan Wilson is the greatest cartoonist of the macabre in the world.

And a major influence on the horror genre as well. Anyone who is a longtime reader of *The New Yorker, Esquire, The Magazine of Fantasy & Science Fiction, Punch, Audubon, Paris Match, National Lampoon*, and of course *Playboy* will remember now where that quirky idea for a short story or a movie may have first originated. (I'll confess that the inspiration for my short story "The Man Who Would Not Be King" was the result of studying the back cover of one of his collections.)

His work has been reprinted in a number of collections, beginning in 1965 with the Ace paperback of *Gahan Wilson's Graveside Manner*. They include *The Man in the Cannibal Pot, I Paint What I See, "... And Then We'll Get Him!" Nuts, "Is Nothing Sacred?"* and *Gahan Wilson's America*. He has also written several children's books and edited two anthologies, one of them most appropriately titled *Gahan Wilson's Fa-*

vorite Tales of Horror. He has illustrated numerous children's books for other authors. Beyond that, he was one of the originators of the annual World Fantasy Convention, and even designed its award, the Howard. (In name *and* appearance after H. P. Lovecraft.)

In spite of the international acclaim he has received as an artist and cartoonist, much less known to the general public are his horrific short stories, which have yet to be collected in a single volume. He has, however, increased his visibility lately as an author, with two well-received novels, *Eddy Deco's Last Caper* and *Everybody's Favorite Duck.* And followers of the regrettably defunct *Rod Serling's Twilight Zone Magazine* had the opportunity to enjoy Wilson's skills as a movie reviewer for the entire run of the publication. In 1988, he even coauthored a screenplay with his stepson for the low-budget thriller *Freeway Maniac.* Whatever the medium, his name continues to be universally associated with the odd, the bizarre—the hilarious.

With his wife Nancy, who is also a novelist and journalist, Wilson lives and works primarily in a brownstone in New York. He is always gracious with his time, and is one of those people who truly deserves to be called "a gentleman." Even if his smile usually reminds you of the cat who's just swallowed a mouse....

WIATER: Going back quite literally to the very beginning, could you relate the tale of having been "born dead"?
WILSON: That's the truth. I came out blue and unbreathing. The doctors were going to forget it, to console my parents and tell them, "Better luck next time." And the family doctor did happen by, and looked in and saw the event. He came in and ducked me into hot and cold water ... that literally saved my life! What interests me is that it probably *did* have an effect—I think the whole birth process is pretty fierce, anyway. The French have a marvelous method where they're born in darkened rooms, then immediately slid into tepid water, and it's all very peaceful—which makes complete sense to me! The result is that they all have this marvelous sort of Buddha expression on their faces, but I don't think any of them will become macabre cartoonists!
WIATER: A "chicken or the egg" question: Which came first, the macabre drawings or the macabre sense of humor?
WILSON: I don't know. I was apparently always very much into drawing, and also drawing *odd* things. We came across a fascinating trove several

years ago. My mother was always saving stuff—which I did not know about—and they are cartoons I did when I was a teeny little kid! Monsters, skeletons, all sorts of stuff like that. So I was into that sort of thing way back then.

I don't know when the humor got started, quite honestly. But it's always been there. By and large, I think, people are set at a terrifyingly early age, so far as their conceptual equipment is concerned. I remember, just the other day, Nancy and I saw this worried little baby, and he *was* a businessman, with that sort of preoccupied little frown. But that's *it*. You're programed very, very early on, genetically.

WIATER: Since you've been a film critic in your multifaceted career, I'd like to know what you think of horror movies—especially the much maligned splatter films.

WILSON: I think it's a perfectly acceptable art form. One of the most accepted literary forms is the Elizabethan drama, and God knows that's just *full* of gore! In Marlowe, and Shakespeare, and so forth, you've got people squeezing other people's eyeballs out, and inflicting ghastly tortures on one another—just total Grand Guignol. And Grand Guignol has always been an accepted art form. And visually, in the history of art, the church adored paintings of the saints being hideously mutilated. Paintings done by absolutely marvelous painters—practically every classical painter has done the crucifixion of Christ, which is one of the most ghastly torture scenes there is.

WIATER: Yet horror movies never seem to receive any respect from the critics, unless they are "classics" such as your favorites, the original *Phantom of the Opera* and *Frankenstein*. Why do you think that is?

WILSON: Horror movies have never been the Main Tent—they've always been the sideshow. And serious critical attention has come to very few of them. Usually when they're long gone, and they've become relics, and their historical importance has become obvious. It's the same as in literature: H. G. Wells is still read. He's there; he's a fixture. And Edgar Allan Poe . . . and Nathaniel Hawthorne. No matter how many times somebody might try to second-rate them, they're now accepted. But with very rare exceptions, horror movies and spooky stuff in the theater have never been accepted as respectable. But that's very much part of their appeal.

WIATER: What I always appreciated about your work, especially in your earlier cartoons, is how you often paid homage to one of the greatest horror writers of all time, H. P. Lovecraft.

WILSON: Oh, Lovecraft has been an *enormous* influence. I really admire very much what he did—he actually blasted the division between fantasy and science fiction. He really messed it up, and he did it by means of writing horror his own particular way.

WIATER: Has any contemporary writer come to you and admitted that something he wrote was inspired by one of your cartoons?

WILSON: It's happened a couple of times. Steve King told me that one whole section of *'Salem's Lot* is based on one of my cartoons, and he brings me up in some other parts of the book, too. But if you just hang around long enough, you sort of become part of these people's psyches. And they grew up with you. So just as various people bent me in different directions—and I'm very grateful for them having done so—I've apparently "bent" a few of them in turn [*laughs*].

WIATER: Not to brashly ask, "Where do you get your ideas?" but could you cite an example of where a cartoon was inspired by something you witnessed in real life?

WILSON: At Bloomingdale's, on the escalator, there was a couple of nuns in their habits. And one of the nun's habits actually got caught in the thing. In real life, what happens is that there's a little dohickey that halts the apparatus. But I quickly whipped out my little notebook and jotted the incident down. It later appeared in *Playboy*—the one where the people are being *ground* into the escalator. It was something that was simply too good not to use. But usually what happens is that ideas perk through, and eventually what emerges has gone through some change.

WIATER: Fabulous. But how about the other side of the coin—did you ever do a cartoon that later was mirrored almost exactly in reality?

WILSON: Oh, sure! The reality outstripping the fiction? That's *constantly* happening! The cute little touches that life provides are *way* better than anything any little artist could ever come up with [*chuckles*]! I guess the most humiliating one was when I did a cover for the graphic section of, I think, the *Miami Herald*, and they had me do a Gahan Wilson drawing of people dying in their cars from the gas and the fumes. So I made it as ghastly as I could, and I was quite proud of it, and I sent it off to them. And on that very *day*—that precise day—*The New York Times* on the front page had a picture of a freeway with fumes that were so much worse than what I had done that I was just shamed by it. Crushed! I never really got over that [*laughs*].

WIATER: One series I always thought was perhaps your most powerful was the splatter cartoons you did for *Playboy* in the late sixties. For the first time, you had psychos and snipers taking the place of vampires and werewolves as the true monsters in our society.

WILSON: They were definitely splatter cartoons. That was tied in with an absolutely ghastly period of our history when they just started killing everybody. Bang!—goes Kennedy. Bang!—goes King! Bang!—goes another Kennedy. It seemed that whenever someone of any real interest came along, some moron would blow him apart! And there was Vietnam ... it was a very splatter point of history in our time. It was infuriating. So I reacted in rage, really, to a degree. I think I was going through some of the same process that Lovecraft went through, when he first thought of his work as fantasy, and then realized, "Shit! This is the way it really is." He was playing around with contemporary American themes.

But it's the same business; I realized that Frankenstein's monster was small pickin's next to the atom bomb. You know, there's an endless range of quite horrible things going on. And I drafted them into the cartoons because they were so horrific. One of the aspects of this business is that humor allows you to examine topics that ordinarily you just blink and don't look at—*can't* look at. But humor kind of holds you steady and says, "There, there, you can look at it." So you *do* look at it. And in that way, it's helpful. So I was saying, "Look at it. *Look at it*." And I still am, in various ways.

WIATER: Your work has become steadily "darker" over the years, more openly political in tone.

WILSON: I did get more political. Charles Addams always stayed in the style of the 1930s' black-and-white movies, and he worked that theme marvelously. But the world became more violent and nastier, and I just got madder. There was a long period in there—in fact I still am!—pissed off because of the outrageous things that still go on. I mean, the dreadful things that people are doing to each other and to the planet, and they don't seem to be slowing down.

Oil spills. The hole in the ozone. The murders—when you consider that in 1888 how Jack the Ripper was one of the few people who had ever done anything that extreme, and nowadays nobody knows how many serial killers there are wandering around, doing these obscene acts. And these serial murderers aren't even in the running if we're tearing holes in the ozone, possibly killing us all and perhaps destroying irrevocably the planet. It may have already happened, God forbid! So this situation is grim in the extreme, and I'm furious, and that shows in the cartoons.

I like to think that what I do is of some use, but frankly I'm dubious. As I've said on previous occasions, one of the greatest flourishings of humor and satire of all time in the arts was in Germany during the rise of Hitler and that whole period. A lot of that satire was directed at

Adolf himself. But it didn't do a damn thing to stop him. When push came to shove, he just said, "Kill them." And that was that. It didn't even slow him down. But I figure what the hell—full speed ahead. Sometimes it works. Humor is great at saying the emperor has no clothes. So maybe.

WIATER: How long does it take you to produce a small black-and-white cartoon versus one of your larger color cartoons?

WILSON: A black-and-white usually takes a day, or the better part of a day. A color cartoon is at least a couple of days, because I like to fool around with it a bit, to get it right. In the last bunch I did for *Playboy*, there was one that was technically a swell drawing, but it didn't work—I didn't get the gag right. I goofed. So I had to tear that one up and start fresh with another one. And if I have the luxury of time, I'll let it sit for a couple of days and study it. You do the best job you can on whatever the hell it is you're doing, but you should *always* let it rest, and then go back and do it better than before. "Let's improve the damn thing one more time before we throw it out there!" And sometimes you improve it quite dramatically.

WIATER: Is your day anything like a typical nine-to-five day, or is it something geared specifically to your own particular needs as a cartoonist, illustrator, and writer?

WILSON: Oh, it has to be like a nine-to-five day! A free-lancer has *got* to be enormously disciplined. I work very hard. Oh God, I start sometimes at seven-thirty or eight in the morning, and almost always put in a full day, with a little dinky lunch break. But I always have the option—which is very nice!—of saying, "Screw it! Today I'm not going to work." Or I'll take an afternoon off. But I have a little calendar, with notes and due dates and so on. But you've got to do it; you've got to be sure to accomplish what is owed, or it's just not going to work. And it gets complicated, because there's always other projects going on—movies, writing. It's a terrific balancing act because you have to make sure you don't shortchange any particular project. Because if you do, it shows. But I find it extremely stimulating to work in a variety of areas.

WIATER: Does anyone still come up to you with the assumption that you're as strange as your cartoons? It's long been the bane of horror writers and filmmakers that they're supposed to be warped in some way.

WILSON: Oh, yes, yes. It's kind of touching—they'd like you to be a lot weirder. Of course, you *are* weird. But then, so aren't *they* [*chuckles*]! Boris Karloff was once asked about this sort of thing, and he said, [*imitates Karloff*] "Well, one thing that always cheers me, is

that even on the brightest, sunniest day, there's always a dark corner
... a strange shadow." And he's right; it's always there. It's just part
of life, and that's all there is to it.

WIATER: But isn't it unusual that only you and the late Charles Addams
made successful careers as cartoonists by blending the macabre with
the humorous?

WILSON: I think what happened is that you kind of corner the field, and
Charlie and I did. But it's like in the movies, there was only Boris
Karloff and Bela Lugosi—there were some other people, but they were
the stars. Karloff was a very intelligent, very sweet man. I remember
one time an interviewer who really meant well asked him, "Gee, Mr.
Karloff, isn't it a shame you've been so typecast and forced to play
these kinds of roles. And the public always knows what to expect from
them, and they only think of you in a certain way." And Karloff raised
one blue-veined hand and said, [*imitates Karloff*] "My dear boy, I'm
ever so grateful for them to have done this." And he's right! It's a
boon. I mean, Karloff was still working even when they had to wheel
him around the set. Lugosi could have done it too, except the poor guy
got all tied in with dope and other junk.

That's just the way it worked out for me and Charlie. It's been great,
and I'm delighted. But there's another thing to consider—Addams *was*
scary. It's not easy being scary and funny at the same time. *It's just
not easy.* That also may have something to do with it.

WIATER: Which gives you the greater satisfaction—making people laugh
or making them shudder?

WILSON: The primary task is to make them laugh, making a joke. But
making them shudder is fun, too. I remember being on a panel back at
the very first World Fantasy Convention. And among the very illustrious
people on the panel was dear old Manly Wade Wellman. And somebody
asked all of us, "Why do you like to do these things that frighten
people?" So we all sort of stalled around one way or another, and some
tried to answer profoundly, but Manly had the best answer. He said
when he was a kid, he remembered they'd be out there in the woods,
and sitting around a fire. And he'd start to tell a story, and he'd make
it scarier, and scarier, and scarier. And he said, "Their eyes would
pop. I loved to make their eyes ... pop!" Then he paused and said, "I
still do—I love to make their eyes ... pop!" [*laughs*]

And that's true for me. But the first duty of the cartoonist is to make
them laugh, and after they laugh, then they can shudder. And if you
can make them shudder and laugh at the same time, so much the better!

WIATER: You mentioned earlier that you are "weird" quote-unquote, and quite happily so. Yet I have to confess I grew up with parents who thought that reading *Famous Monsters of Filmland* and seeing Vincent Price movies at the Saturday matinee were somehow going to "warp my mind." More likely than not, there are still parents out there who'd be more upset at finding a *Fangoria* or *Fear* in their youngster's room than they would an issue of *Playboy*.

WILSON: Oh, I'm sure! But I can see how parents are nervous about it. But the basic situation is that the parents have this little savage—which they love dearly—but it's a little animal! It starts out as this very primitive little baby, and it's their responsibility to try to have it later function properly in society. A society that the parents dimly understand themselves. And they're just afraid that the kid is going to go off on the wrong tack. And when they come across an issue of *Fangoria*, it must very much strike them that their kid *is* going off on the wrong tack, you know? I can sympathize with them; it can be alarming. But actually, all the kid's doing is seeing what's out there, and experimenting. Some will experiment more this way than the other. It's very problematical; I have no righteous feelings about parents. I think they're wrong, and that reading these publications is perfectly okay. But it's understandable why they fret.

WIATER: But you have no regrets over your lot in life to be "professionally strange"?

WILSON: Oh, God, no! I'm extremely, absolutely delighted, that everybody's accepted it. I adore all this sort of stuff. I always have, and I suppose I always will. I have the greatest affection for monsters. And I think it speaks to the idea that we are all "monstrous," that we aren't perfect, and that we have to accept that with grace and amusement.

It's an absolutely *horrifying* world, and dreadful things are always happening. And you've got to be able to deal with it. And if you can deal with it with gentleness, with a lack of hatred, that's all to the good. *But you've got to learn how to handle it*. The news is a lot worse than anything that's in *Fangoria*. Monsters and horror are really a kind of primer on how to handle these things. You might go nuts if you really didn't have these aids.

WIATER: The traditional last question: What advice do you have for the fledgling artist or author?

WILSON: Basically, to persist. And if anybody asked me, I would do my best to discourage them, because if I *could* discourage them, then they've got no business doing it because they're going against incredible odds. And they have to be half mad to think they can succeed. I was. I am! Anybody in the arts is. It's impossible to succeed. It's like winning the lottery. Forget it—out of the question. And it's a heartbreaker. Artists always make a big deal out of that—but so is life [*laughs*]!

Selling insurance is a heartbreaker, you know? Working at a counter is a heartbreaker, too. And because of all these sacrifices and absurd risks you take, if you are dishonest and do sleazy junk, God help you, because then you're just a hack. You may make some money, but you'll rot inside. I've seen it happen. So just do it as well as you can—and then do it better.

You'll always find that you can do it better.

Iris D. Wiater

STANLEY WIATER is a widely published journalist, cineteratologist, and short story writer. He has interviewed more horror authors, filmmakers, and artists than any other writer for such magazines as *Rod Serling's Twilight Zone Magazine, Prevue,* and *Writer's Digest.* He is a contributing editor to *Fangoria* and *New Blood* and England's *Fear.* His first published short story was the winner of a competition judged by Stephen King. Several of his interviews with King were reprinted in *Bare Bones* and its sequel, *Feast of Fear.* He has also contributed to the anthologies *Reign of Fear, Clive Barker's Shadows in Eden, Stephen King and Clive Barker: The Masters of the Macabre, Fly in My Eye, James Herbert: By Horror Haunted,* and *The Shape Under the Sheet: The Complete Stephen King Encyclopedia.*

His short stories have appeared in *Rod Serling's Twilight Zone Magazine, Castle Rock, Cavalier, Mike Shayne,* anthologies such as J. N. Williamson's *Masques* series, Gary Raisor's *Obsessions,* and have also been adapted for horror comic books. In 1989 he edited the anthology *Night Visions 7* and is currently compiling another entitled *After the Darkness.* He is also completing the companion volume to *Dark Dreamers,* entitled *Dark Visions: Conversations with the Masters of the Horror Film.* He lives with his wife and daughter in western Massachusetts.